HISTORY

— OF —

MISSOURI

THE GENERAL HISTORY

ILLUSTRATED

CHICAGO:
THE GOODSPEED PUBLISHING CO.
1888

New Material Copyright 1992 by:
Southern Historical Press, Inc.

All rights reserved. No part of this publication may be
reproduced, stored in a retrieval system or transmitted
in any form or by any means without the
prior permission of the publisher.

SOUTHERN HISTORICAL PRESS, INC.
PO BOX 1267
Greenville, SC   29601

ISBN #978-0-89308-477-8

Printed in the United States of America

PUBLISHER'S PREFACE

When the Goodspeed brothers originally published their respective state histories during the 1880-1890's the format they followed was as follows: 1. A General History of the State itself, consisting of from 120, 196 to 796 pages depending upon the state being written about. 2. The counties of the particular state were then divided into geographical regions, such as Central, Southeast, Western, Southern, etc., and persons were assigned to write Business, Civic, Religious and Educational histories of each respective county with all pertinent statistical information about the county. 3. This was then followed by Bibliographical sketches of various individuals living in each county arranged alphabetically by the county and also alphabetically by the surname of the biographee. There is no known reason as to why certain persons were included in the biographical sketches and others were omitted, as undoubtedly there were many persons in each of the counties who should have been listed and were not and visa versa.

When Southern Historical Press, Inc. began reprinting these Goodspeed Histories of Tennessee, Arkansas, Missouri and other states, we first printed the General History of each state as a separate volume with its own index and then reprinted the regional county histories and biographical sketches in combined volumes. Therefore, if you have ordered a particular volume containing certain geographical areas and it begins on, for instance, page 198, 797, etc., please know that you have received the correct book, as only the General History has been omitted from your volume.

The Publisher

CONCERNING THE PAGINATION OF THIS BOOK

The reader will notice that the text of this *General History* begins on page 13 with numerous blank and un-numbered pages from the Title Page to page 13. The reason that there are omissions in some page numbers is that in the original edition, each page prior to page 13 contained a detailed Table of Contents for each of the counties for which history and biographical sketches were given.

In this reprint edition of the *General History*, we have purposely omitted these pages prior to page 13 which do not contain specific data pertaining to this *General History*, and all prefatory pages pertaining to this particular edition are included, even though the pagination does not add up to 12 pages for these pages.

The Publisher

PREFACE.

This volume has been prepared in response to the prevailing and popular demand for the preservation of local history and biography. The method of preparation followed is the most successful and the most satisfactory yet devised—the most successful in the enormous number of volumes circulated, and the most satisfactory in the general preservation of personal biography and family record conjointly with local history. The number of volumes now being distributed seems fabulous. Careful estimates place the number circulated in Ohio at 50,000 volumes; Pennsylvania, 60,000; New York, 75,000; Indiana, 40,000; Illinois, 40,000; Iowa, 35,000; Missouri, 25,000; Minnesota, 15,000; Nebraska, 15,000, and all the other States at the same proportionate rate. The southern half of Missouri has as yet scarcely been touched by the historian, but is now being rapidly written.

The design of the present extensive historical and biographical research is more to gather and preserve in attractive form, while fresh with the evidence of truth, the enormous fund of perishing occurrence, than to abstract from insufficient contemporaneous data remote, doubtful or incorrect conclusions. The true perspective of the landscape of life can only be seen from the distance that lends enchantment to the view. It is asserted that no person is competent to write a philosophical history of his own time; that, owing to imperfect and conflicting circumstantial evidence, that yet conceals, instead of reveals, the truth, he cannot take that correct, unprejudiced, logical, luminous and comprehensive view of passing events that will enable him to draw accurate and enduring conclusions. The duty, then, of an historian of his own time is to collect, classify and preserve the material for the final historian, of the future. The present historian deals in fact; the future historian, in conclusion. The work of the former is statistical; of the latter, philosophical.

To him who has not attempted the collection of historical data, the obstacles to be surmounted are unknown. Doubtful traditions, conflicting statements, imperfect records, inaccurate public and private correspondence, the bias or untruthfulness of informers, and the general obscurity which, more or less, envelops all passing events, combine to bewilder and mislead. The publishers of this volume, fully aware of their inability to furnish a perfect history, an accomplishment vouchsafed to the imagination only of the dreamer or the theorist, make no pretension of having prepared a work devoid of blemish. They feel assured that all thoughtful people, at present and in future, will recognize and appreciate the importance of their undertaking, and the great public benefit that has been accomplished.

In the preparation of this volume the publishers have met with nothing but courtesy and assistance from the public. The subscription list was smaller than the publishers hoped and expected to receive; and although the margin of profit was thus cut down to the lowest limit, no curtailment or omission of matter was made from the original extensive design of the work. No subject promised is omitted, and many not promised are given. The number of pages given (1,215) exceeds the number promised (700) by over 500—a volume alone. The extreme difficulty of securing the correct spelling of French and German proper names, must be the excuse of the publishers for the few mistakes of that character to be found in this volume. In all cases the personal sketches have been submitted by mail, and in most cases have been corrected and approved by the subjects themselves. The publishers disclaim responsibility for the substance of the matter contained in the Biographical Appendix, as the material was wholly furnished by the subjects of the sketches. This volume is one of the most important and valuable of many ever issued by the publishers. The history proper possesses unusual literary merit. The student of local history will find therein an account of many important events connected with the early French settlement of Southeast Missouri never before published and not known to exist. This matter has been collated at great labor and expense, and has already attracted the attention of historical societies throughout the United States and Canada. The historians of the publishers have been materially assisted by the leading citizens of every county, scores of whom deserve special mention for interest shown and assistance rendered. Particular acknowledgments are due Louis Houck and Judge Wilson, of Cape Girardeau, Linus Sanford of Jackson, and Gen. Rozier and Mrs. Menard of Ste. Genevieve. With many thanks to our friends for the success of our difficult enterprise, we respectfully tender this fine volume to our patrons.

August, 1888. THE PUBLISHERS.

CONTENTS.

	PAGE.
Attitude of Missouri before the War	83
Article XV	140
Amendments to the State Constitution	142
Attorney Generals	156
Auditors of Public Accounts	156
Boone's Lick Country	50
Black Hawk War	62
Beginning of Civil War	83
Boonville	107
Belmont	120
Battle of Pea Ridge	121
Battle of Kirksville	123
Battle of Independence	125
Battles of Lone Jack and Newtonia	125
Battle of Cane Hill	126
Battles of Springfield, Hartsville and Cape Girardeau	127
Battles in Missouri, List of	135
Baptist Church	150
Clay Compromise, The	59
Constitutional Convention of 1845	73
Campaign of 1861	107
Carthage	108
Capture of Lexington	117
Campaign of 1862	120
Compton's Ferry	124
Campaign of 1863	127
Campaign of 1864	130
Centralia Massacre	133
Churches	150
Christian Church	151
Congregational Church	151
Dred Scott Decision, The	82
Death of Bill Anderson	135
Drake Constitution, The	137
Divisions in the Republican Party	140
Dates of Organization of Counties, with Origin of Names, etc.	172
Early Wars	61
Early Discoveries and Explorers	38
Early Settlements	38 and 43
Earthquakes at New Madrid	53
Events Preceding the Civil War	74
Efforts toward Conciliation	98
Emancipation Proclamation and XIIIth Amendment	105
Execution of Rebel Prisoners	126
Election of 1884, The	144
Early Courts, The	145
Education	146
Episcopal Church	151
Floods	49
French and Indian War	44
Founding of St. Louis, The	45
From 1785 to 1800	50
First General Assembly	60
Fremont in the Field	118
Friends' Church	151
Fire at St. Louis, The Great	189
Geology	12
Gov. Jackson and the Missouri Legislature	91
Gov. Crittenden's Administration	143
Governors	154
Growth	56
Hannibal & St. Joseph Railroad Controversies	190
Indian and Other Races	38

	PAGE.
Israelite Church	151
Jackson Resolutions, The	74
Judges of Supreme Court	156
La Salle	42
Louisiana, District and Territory of	52
Louisiana Purchased by the United States	51
Lewis and Clark's Expedition	53
Lutheran Church	152
Lieutenant-Governors	155
Minerals and Mineral Springs	87
Manufacturing	194
Marquette	41
Missouri a Territory	55
Mormons and Mormon War, The	66
Mexican War, The	69
Military History	92
Martial Law Declared	117
Murders at Gun City	189
Methodist Episcopal Church	152
Methodist Episcopal Church South	153
Miscellaneous Items	189
Missouri's Delegation in the Confederate Congress	159
Official	153
Organization of Kansas and Nebraska	76
Operations against Guerrillas	122
Order No. 11	127
Officers Previous to State Organization	153
Officers of State Government	154
Political Review since 1865	136
Pontiac, Death of	46
Public and Private Schools	146
Presidential Elections	160
Population	186
Proclamation by Gov. Jackson	99
Resources	11
Rock Formation	12
Railroads	195
Revision of State Constitution	142
Representatives to Congress	157
Rebel Governors	160
Religion	150
Soils, Clays, etc	13
State Organization	57
State Convention	58
Seminole War	63
Secession	84
Surrender of Camp Jackson	92
State Convention, The	103
Springfield	119
Shelby's Raid	130
State Constitutional Convention	136
Secretaries of State	155
State Treasurers	155
Salaries of State Officers	172
Territorial and State Organization	55
United States Senators	157
Various War Measures	121
Votes by Counties at Presidential Elections from 1836 to 1884	162–172
Wealth	196
War of the Revolution, The	48
War with Great Britain in 1812	61
Western Department, The	111
Wilson's Creek	112
Year of the Great Waters	49
Yellow Creek	125

HISTORY OF MISSOURI.

INTRODUCTORY.

MISSOURI, the eighth State of the Union in size, the seventh in wealth, and the fifth in population and political power, lies in the very heart of the Mississippi Valley. Extending from the thirty-sixth nearly to the forty-first degree of north latitude, it has considerable diversity both of soil and climate.

Its eastern limit is marked from north to south by the great "Father of Waters," and the Missouri washes its western boundary, from the northwest corner southward about 250 miles to the mouth of the Kansas, and thence flows south of east through the heart of the State, and joins its muddy torrent with the waters of the Mississippi. These two mighty rivers have many tributaries which are, to a greater or less extent, navigable for steamboats, keelboats and barges.

The extreme length of the State is 328 miles; the extreme breadth, in the southern part, is 280 miles; and the average breadth 250 miles. Missouri has an area of 65,350 square miles, or 41,824,000 acres. It has 18,350 more square miles than the State of New York, is nearly nine times the size of Massachusetts, and exceeds in extent all of the New England States combined.

There is no State in the Union which surpasses Missouri in respect to geographical situation and natural resources. Other

NOTE.—In the compilation of the State History the authors consulted, among others, the following authorities: "State Geological Reports;" "Charlevoix's Journal of a Voyage to North America in 1721;" Stoddard's "Historical Sketches of Louisiana;" Schoolcraft's "Narrative Journal;" H. M. Brackenridge's "Views of Louisiana;" Pike's "Expedition;" Switzler's "History of Missouri;" Bradbury's "Travels;" "Silliman's Journal;" "American Cyclopedia;" Beck's "Gazetteer of Indiana and Missouri," 1823; Wetmore's "Gazetteer of Missouri," 1837; Shebard's "Early History of St. Louis and Missouri;" Parker's "Missouri As It Is in 1867;" Davis & Durrie's "History of Missouri," 1876.

regions may boast of delightful climate, rich and productive soil, abundant timber, or inexhaustible mineral deposits, but Missouri has all of these. She has more and better iron than England and quite as much coal, while her lead deposits are rivaled by that of no other country of equal area upon the globe.

The population of the State, according to the census of 1880, was 2,168,380, showing an increase of 25.9 per cent within the preceding decade.

GEOLOGY, PHYSICAL FEATURES, ETC.

The stratified rocks of Missouri may be classified as follows, enumerating them from the surface downward:

I. Quaternary or Post Tertiary.—Alluvium, 30 feet thick. Soils—Pebbles and sand, clays, vegetable mold or *humus*, bog iron ore, calcareous tufa, stalactites and stalagmites, marls; bottom prairie, 35 feet thick; bluff, 200 feet thick; drift, 155 feet thick.

II. Tertiary.—Clays, shales, iron ores, sandstone, fine and coarse sands.

III. Cretaceous.—No. 1, 13 feet, argillaceous variegated sandstone; No. 2, 20 feet, soft bluish brown sandy slate, containing quantities of iron pyrites; No. 3, 25 feet, whitish brown impure sandstone, banded with purple and pink; No. 4, 45 feet, slate, like No. 2; No. 5, 45 feet, fine white siliceous clay, interstratified with white flint, more or less spotted and banded with pink and purple; No. 6, 10 feet, purple, red and blue clays. Entire thickness, 158 feet.

IV. Carboniferous.—Upper carboniferous or coal measures, sandstone, limestone, shales, clays, marls, spathic iron ores, coals. Lower carboniferous or mountain limestone, upper Archimedes limestone, 200 feet; ferruginous sandstone, 195 feet; middle Archimedes limestone, 50 feet; St. Louis limestone, 250 feet; oölitic limestone, 25 feet; lower Archimedes limestone, 350 feet; encrinital limestone, 500 feet.

V. Devonian.—Chemung group: Chouteau limestone, 85 feet; vermicular sandstone, 75 feet; lithographic limestone, 12.5 feet. Hamilton group: Blue shales, 40 feet; semi-crystalline limestone, 107 feet; Onondaga limestone, Oriskany sandstone.

VI. Silurian.—Upper silurian: Lower Helderberg, 350 feet; Niagara group, 200 feet; Cape Girardeau limestone, 60 feet. Lower silurian: Hudson River group, 220 feet; Trenton limestone, 350 feet; Black River and Birdseye limestone, 75 feet; first magnesian limestone, 200 feet; saccharoidal sandstone, 125 feet; second magnesian limestone, 230 feet; second sandstone, 115 feet; third magnesian limestone, 350 feet; third sandstone, 60 feet; fourth magnesian limestone, 300 feet.

VII. Azoic Rocks.

The Quaternary rocks, the most recent of all the formations, contain the entire geological record of all the cycles from the end of the Tertiary period to the present time; and their economical value is also greater than that of all the other formations combined. This system comprises the drift and all the deposits above it. There are, within the system, four distinct and strongly defined formations in the State, namely: Alluvium, bottom prairie, bluff and drift.

Soils.—Soils are a compound of pulverized and decomposed mineral substances, mingled with decayed vegetable and animal remains, and containing all the ingredients necessary to the sustenance of the vegetable kingdom. The soils of Missouri have been produced by the mixing of organic matter with the pulverized marls, clays and sands of the Quaternary deposits which are found in great abundance in nearly all parts of the State, and are of material best designed for their rapid formation. For this cause the soils of the State are marvelously deep and productive, except in a few localities where the materials of the Quaternary strata are very coarse, or entirely wanting.

Clays.—Clays are dark, bluish-gray strata, more or less mixed with particles of flint, limestone and decomposed organic matter. When the floods of the Mississippi and the Missouri subside, lagoons, sloughs and lakes are left full of turbid water. The coarser substances soon subside into a stratum of sand, but the finer particles settle more slowly and form the silico-calcareous clays of the alluvial bottom. Thus, after each flood, strata of sand and clay are deposited, until the lakes and lagoons are filled up.

Then a stratum of *humus*, or decayed vegetable matter, is

formed by the decomposition of the annual growth and of the foreign matter which falls into the water, and every succeeding crop of vegetation adds another such stratum. Thus are rapidly formed thick beds of vegetable mold, yielding support to the magnificent forest trees which grow upon the sites of those ancient lakes and morasses. In this manner have been formed the vast, alluvial plains bordering upon the Missouri and Mississippi Rivers, which comprise about 4,000,000 acres of land, based upon these strata of sand, clays, marls and *humus*. The soil formed upon these alluvial beds is deep, rich and light almost beyond comparison, and is constantly increasing by the filling up of lake and sloughs as above described.

The Bluff or Loess occurs in the Missouri bluffs forming a belt several miles wide, extending from the mouth of the Missouri to the northwest corner of the State, where it is found beneath the soil, and also in the bluffs of the Mississippi from Dubuque to the mouth of the Ohio. Thus while the bottom prairie occupies a higher geological horizon, the bluff is usually several hundred feet above it topographically. The latter is generally a finely comminuted, siliceous marl, of a light brown color, and often weathers into perpendicular escarpments. Concretions of limestone are often found, and to the marly character of these clays may be ascribed the richness of the overlying soil. It is to this formation that the Central Mississippi and Southern Missouri valleys owe their superiority in agriculture. Where it is best developed in Western Missouri the soil is equal to any in the country.

Drift formation exists throughout Northern Missouri. The upper members consist of stiff, tenaceous, brown, drab and blue clays, often mottled and sometimes containing rounded pebbles, chiefly of granite rocks. The lower division includes beds of dark blue clay, often hardening on exposure, frequently overlaid and sometimes interstratified with beds and pockets of sand, sometimes inclosing leaves and remains of trees. Good springs originate in these sand beds, and when they are ferruginous the springs are chalybeate.

Tertiary System.—A formation made up of clays, shales, iron ores, sandstone, and a variety of fine and coarse sand, extends along the bluffs, skirting the bottoms, from Commerce, in Scott County, westward to Stoddard, and thence south to the Chalk Bluffs in Arkansas.

The iron ore of these beds is very abundant and exceedingly valuable. The spathic ore has been found in no other locality in Southeastern Missouri, so that the large quantity and excellent quality of these beds will render them very valuable for the various purposes to which this ore is peculiarly adapted.

The white sand of these beds is available for glass making, and for the composition of mortars and cements. The clays are well adapted to the manufacture of pottery and stoneware.

Cretaceous Rocks.—These strata are very much disturbed, fractured, upheaved and tilted, so as to form various faults and axes, anticlinal and synclinal; while the strata, above described as tertiary, are in their natural position, and rest nonconformably upon these beds. In these so-called cretaceous rocks no fossils have been observed.

Carboniferous Rocks.—This system presents two important divisions: The upper carboniferous, or coal measures; and the lower carboniferous, or mountain limestone.

The coal measures, as seen by the table, are composed of numerous strata of sandstone, limestone, shales, clays, marls, spathic iron ores and coals. About 2,000 feet of these coal measures have been found to contain numerous beds of iron ore, and at least eight or ten beds of good, workable coal. Investigation shows a greater downward thickness of the coal formation in Southwest Missouri, including beds whose position is probably below those of the northern part of the State. These rocks, with the accompanying beds of coal and iron, cover an area of more than 27,000 square miles in Missouri alone.

The geological map of the State shows that if a line were roughly drawn from Clark County on the northeast to Jasper County in the southwest, most of the counties northwest of this line, together with Audrain, Howard and Boone, would be included in the coal measure. There are also extensive coal beds in Cole, Moniteau, St. Charles, St. Louis and Callaway Counties.

The Missouri coal basin is one of the largest in the world, including besides the 27,000 square miles in Missouri, 10,000 in

Nebraska; 12,000 in Kansas; 20,000 in Iowa, and 30,000 in Illinois; making a total of about 100,000 square miles.

The fossils of the coal measure are numerous, and distinct from those of any other formation. This latter fact has led to the discovery of the existence of coal measures and the coal beds contained in them, over an area of many thousand miles, where it had been supposed that no coal measures and no coal existed.

Of the lower carboniferous rocks, the upper Archimedes limestone is developed in Ste. Genevieve County.

The ferruginous sandstone is generally found along the eastern and southern limit of the coal fields, passing beneath the coal formation on the west. It varies from a few feet to 100 feet in thickness. In Callaway it occurs both as a pure white sandstone, a ferruginous sandstone, and a conglomerate. In Pettis and Howard Counties it is found a coarse, whitish sandstone; in Cedar, Dade and Lawrence, a very ferruginous sandstone, often containing valuable deposits of iron ore. In Newton County it occurs in useful flaglike layers.

The St. Louis limestone, next in descending order, forms the entire group of limestone at St. Louis, where it is well marked and of greater thickness than seen elsewhere in this State. It is more often fine grained, compact or sub-crystalline, sometimes inclosing numerous chert concretions, and the beds are often separated by thin, green shale beds.

Its stratigraphical position is between the ferruginous sandstone and the Archimedes limestone, as seen near the Des Moines, and near the first tunnel on the Pacific Railroad. It is found in Clark and Lewis Counties, but, as has been said, attains its greatest development at St. Louis—hence its name.

The most characteristic fossils yet described are *Palæchinus multipora, Lithostrotion canadense, Echinocrinus nerei, Poteriocrinus longidactylus* and *Atrypa lingulata*.

The lower Archimedes limestone includes the "arenaceous bed," the "Warsaw, or second Archimedes limestone," the magnesian limestone, the "Geode bed," the "Keokuk, or lower Archimedes limestone" of Prof. Hall's section, and the lead-bearing rocks of Southwestern Missouri; which last, though different from any of the above beds, are more nearly allied to them than to the encrinital limestone below. All of the above beds are easily recognized in Missouri, except, perhaps, the Warsaw limestone, which is but imperfectly represented in our northeastern counties, where the "Keokuk limestone," the "Geode beds," and the magnesian limestone are well developed.

This formation extends from the northeastern part of the State to the southwest, in an irregular belt, skirting the eastern border of the ferruginous sandstone. The extensive and rich lead deposits of Southwestern Missouri are partly in this formation, these mines occupying an area of more than 100 square miles, in Jasper, Newton, and the adjoining counties.

The upper beds of encrinital limestone are gray and cherty. The top beds in St. Charles County include seventeen feet of thin chert beds with alternate layers of red clay. The middle beds are generally gray and coarse, the lower ones gray and brown, with some buff beds.

Crinoid stems are common in nearly all the beds, hence it has been appropriately termed encrinital limestone.

The lower beds often abound in well preserved *crinoidea*. This rock occurs at Burlington, Iowa, Quincy, Ill., Hannibal and Louisiana, Mo., and is well exposed in most of the counties on the Mississippi River, north of St. Louis, and from the western part of St. Charles to Howard County. South of the Missouri River and along its southwest outcrop it is not generally well developed.

In Greene County it is quite cavernous. It has not been recognized east of Illinois, and is not separated from other carboniferous stones of Tennessee.

The Devonian Rocks occupy a small area in Marion, Ralls, Pike, Callaway, Saline and Ste. Genevieve Counties; also narrow belts along the carboniferous strata to the south and west.

In the Chemung group, the Chouteau limestone, when fully developed, is in two divisions.

Immediately under the encrinital limestone, at the top of the formation, there are forty or fifty feet of brownish gray, earthy, silico-magnesian limestone in thick beds, which contain scattered masses of white or transparent calcareous spar.

The upper division of the Chouteau limestone passes down

into a fine, compact, blue or drab, thin-bedded limestone, whose strata are considerably irregular and broken. In the northeastern part of the State the Chouteau limestone is represented only by a few feet of coarse, earthy, crystalline, calcareous rock, like the lower division of the encrinital limestone.

Vermicular Sandstone and Shales.—The sandstones of this division are generally soft and calcareous. They are easily recognized, being ramified by irregular windings throughout, resembling the borings of worms. This formation attains a thickness of seventy-five feet near Louisiana, in Pike County. It is seen in Ralls, Pike, Lincoln, Cedar and Greene.

The lithographic limestone is a fine grained, compact limestone, breaking with a free conchoidal fracture into sharp, angular fragments. Its color varies from a light drab to the lighter shades of buff and blue. It gives out, when struck with the hammer, a sharp, ringing sound, and is therefore called "pot metal" in some parts of the State. It is regularly stratified in beds varying from two to sixteen inches in thickness, and often presents, as in the mural bluffs at Louisiana, on the Mississippi, all the regularity of masonry.

Where elsewhere seen, it somewhat resembles the upper beds of the group. At Taborville, St. Clair County, it is of a salmon drab color, occurring in thick beds having an open texture, and contains a characteristic fossil—*Pentremites Rœmeri.* This limestone is found in Pike, Ralls, St. Clair, Cedar and Greene Counties.

The Hamilton Group.—This is made up of some forty feet of blue shales, and 107 feet of semi-crystalline limestone, containing *Dalmania, Calliteles, Phacops bufo, Spirifer mucronatus, S. Sculptilis, S. Congesta, Chonetes carinata* and *Favosites basaltica.* The Hamilton group is found in Ralls, Pike, Lincoln, Warren, Montgomery, Callaway, Boone, Cole and probably Moniteau; also in Perry and Ste. Genevieve.

Onondaga Limestone is usually a coarse gray or buff, crystalline, thick bedded and cherty limestone, abounding in *Terebratula, Reticularis, Orthis resupinata, Chonetes nana, Productus subaculeatus, Spirifer euruteines, Phacops bufo, Cyathophyllum rugosum, Emmonsia hemispherica,* and a *Pentemerus* like *galeatus.* Generally it is course, gray and crystalline; often somewhat compact, bluish and concretionary, having cavities filled with green matter or calspar; occasionally it is a white saccharoidal sandstone; in a few localities a soft, brown sandstone, and at Louisiana a pure white oölite.

Oriskany Sandstone.—In spite of its name, this is a light gray limestone, containing the *Spirifer arenosa, Leptoma depressa,* and several new species of *Spirifer, Chonetes Illœnus* and *Lichas.*

Silurian Rocks are divided into upper and lower silurian. Of the former are the following: The lower Helderberg group, which is made up of buff, gray, and reddish cherty, and argillaceous limestones, blue shales, and dark graptolite slates. The Cape Girardeau limestone, found on the Mississippi River, about a mile above Cape Girardeau, is a compact, bluish gray, frangible limestone, with a smooth fracture, in layers from two to six inches in thickness, with thin argillaceous partings.

There are at least ten formations belonging to the lower silurian series. There are three distinct formations of the Hudson River group, as follows: First—Immediately below the oölite of the Onondaga limestone, in the bluffs both above and below St. Louis, there are forty feet of blue, gray and brown argillaceous, magnesian limestone. Above, these shales are in thick beds, showing a dull, conchoidal fracture. Below, the division becomes more argillaceous, and has thin beds of bluish gray crystalline limestone. Second—Three and one half miles northwest of Louisiana, on the Grassy River, some sixty feet of blue and purple shales are exposed below the beds above described. Third—Under the last named division are, perhaps, twenty feet of argillo-magnesian limestone resembling that in the first division, and interstratified with blue shales. These rocks crop out in Ralls, Pike, Cape Girardeau and Ste. Genevieve Counties. On the Grassy, a thickness of 120 feet is exposed, and they extend to an unknown depth.

Trenton Limestone.—The upper portion of this formation comprises thick beds of compact, bluish gray and drab limestone, abounding in irregular cavities, filled with a greenish substance. The lower beds abound in irregular cylindrical pieces, which quickly decompose upon exposure to the air, and leave the rocks perforated with irregular holes, resembling those made in timber by the *Toredo navalis*. These beds are exposed between Hannibal and New London, north of Salt River, and near Glencoe, St. Louis County. They are about seventy-five feet thick. Below them are thick strata of impure, coarse, gray and buff crystalline magnesian limestone, containing brown, earthy portions, which quickly crumble on exposure to the elements. The bluffs on Salt River are an example of these strata. The lowest part of the Trenton limestone is composed of hard, blue and bluish-gray, semi-compact, silico-magnesian limestone, interstratified with soft, earthy, magnesian beds of a light buff and drab color. Fifty feet of these strata crop out at the quarries south of the plank road bridge over Salt River, and on Spencer's Creek in Ralls County. The middle beds sometimes develop a beautiful white crystalline marble, as at Cape Girardeau and near Glencoe.

The Black River and Birdseye limestones are often in even layers; the lower beds have sometimes mottled drab and reddish shades, often affording a pretty marble. Near the base this rock is often traversed by vermicular cavities and cells. These may be seen from Cape Girardeau to Lincoln, and in St. Charles, Warren and Montgomery Counties, thinning out in the latter.

The First Magnesian Limestone is generally a buff, open-textured, thick and even-bedded limestone, breaking readily under the hammer, and affording a useful building rock. Shumard estimated its thickness in Ste. Genevieve County to be about 150 feet. In Warren County, in North Missouri, it is seventy feet thick. It is found in Ralls, Pike, Lincoln, St. Charles, Warren, Callaway and Boone. Southwesterly, it is not well marked—indeed it seems to be absent in some counties where, in regular sequence, it should be found. It occurs in Franklin, St. Louis, and southwardly to Cape Girardeau County.

Saccharoidal Sandstone is usually a bed of white friable sandstone, sometimes slightly tinged with red and brown, which is made up of globular concretions and angular fragments of limpid quartz. The formation is well developed in Lincoln, St. Charles, Warren, Montgomery, Gasconade, Franklin, St. Louis, Jefferson, Ste. Genevieve, Perry and Cape Giradeau Counties. Besides the above, it is also developed in a more attenuated form in Callaway, Osage, Cole, Moniteau and Boone. This sandstone is probably destined to be one of the most useful rocks found in Missouri. It is generally of a very white color, and the purest sandstone found in the State, and is suitable for making the finest glassware. Its great thickness makes it inexhaustible. In St. Charles and Warren Counties it is 133 feet thick, and in Southeast Missouri over 100 feet thick.

The Second Magnesian Limestone occurs in all the river counties south of Pike as far as the swamps of Southeast Missouri, and is more often the surface rock in all the counties south of the Missouri and Osage Rivers, to within fifty miles of the western line of the State. It is generally composed of beds of earthy magnesian limestone, interstratified with shale beds and layers of white chert, with occasionally thin strata of white sandstone, and, near the lower part, thick cellular silico-magnesian limestone beds. The layers are more often of irregular thickness, and not very useful for building purposes. It is often a lead-bearing rock, and most of the lead of Cole County occurs in it. It is from 175 to 200 feet thick.

The second sandstone is usually a brown or yellowish-brown, fine-grained sandstone, distinctly stratified in regular beds, varying from two to eighteen inches in thickness. The surfaces are often ripple-marked and micaceous. It is sometimes quite friable, though generally sufficiently indurated for building purposes. The upper part is often composed of thin strata of light, soft and porous, semi-pulverulent, sandy chert or hornstone, whose cavities are usually lined with limpid crystals of quartz.

The Third Magnesian Limestone.—This also is an important member, occurring in nearly all the counties of Southern Missouri. It is generally a thick-bedded, coarsely crystalline bluish gray, or flesh-colored magnesian limestone, with occasional thick chert beds. It is the chief lead-bearing rock of Southeast and Southern Missouri. In some counties it is as much as 300 feet thick.

The third sandstone is a white, saccharoidal sandstone, made up of slightly-cohering, transparent, globular and angular particles of silex. It shows but little appearance of stratification.

The Fourth Magnesian Limestone.—This formation presents more permanent and uniform lithological characters than any other of the magnesian limestones. It is ordinarily a coarse-grained, crystalline, magnesian limestone, grayish-buff in color, containing a few crevices filled with less indurated, siliceous matter. Its thick, uniform beds contain but little chert. The best exposures of this formation are on the Niangua and Osage Rivers.

This magnesian limestone series is very interesting, both from a scientific and an economical standpoint. It covers a large part of Southern and Southeastern Missouri, is remarkable for its numerous and important caves and springs, and comprises nearly all the vast deposits of lead, zinc, copper, cobalt, the liminite ores of iron, and nearly all the marble beds of the State. The lower part of the first magnesian limestone, the saccharoidal sandstone, the second magnesian limestone, the second sandstone, and the upper part of the third magnesian limestone belong, without doubt, to the age of the calciferous sand rock; but the remainder of the series to the Potsdam sandstone.

Azoic Rocks.—Below the rocks of the silurian system is a series of siliceous and other slates, which present no remains of organic life; we therefore refer them to the Azoic age of the geologist. They contain some of the beds of specular iron. In Pilot Knob appears a good exposition of these Azoic strata. The lower fossiliferous rocks rest non-conformably on these strata.

Igneous and Metamorphic Rocks.—Aside from the stratified rocks of Missouri, there is a series of rounded knobs and hills in St. Francois, Iron, Dent and the neighboring counties, which are composed of granite, porphyry, diorite and greenstone. These igneous and metamorphic rocks contain some of those remarkable beds of specular iron of which Iron and Shepherd Mountains are samples. This iron ore often occurs in regular veins in the porphyry.

Historical Geology.—When North America began to emerge from the primeval ocean, Pilot Knob, Shepherd Mountain and the neighboring heights were among the first bodies of land that reared themselves above the surrounding waters. When Pilot Knob thus grew into an island, it stood alone in the ocean waste, except that to the northwest the Black Hills, to the northeast a part of the Alleghany system, and to the southwest a small cluster of rocks lifted their heads out of the flood. These islands were formed in the Azoic seas by mighty internal convulsions that forced up the porphyry and granite, the slates and iron beds of the great ore mountains of Missouri.

Coal.—Missouri's coal fields underlie an area of nearly 25,000 square miles, including about 160 square miles in St. Louis County, eight square miles in St. Charles, and some important outliers and pockets, which are mainly cannel coal, in Lincoln, Warren and Callaway Counties. This area includes some 8,400 square miles of upper coal measures, 2,000 square miles of exposed middle, and about 14,600 square miles of exposed lower measures.

The upper coal measures contain about four feet of coal, including two seams of one foot each in thickness, the others being thin seams or streaks.

The middle coal measures contain about seven feet of coal, including two workable seams of twenty-one and twenty-four inches, one other of one foot, that is worked under favorable circumstances, and six thin seams.

The lower measures contain about five workable seams of coal, varying in thickness from eighteen inches to four and one-half feet, thin seams varying from six to eleven inches, and several minor seams and streaks, in all, thirteen feet six inches of coal. We therefore have in Missouri a total aggregate of twenty-four feet six inches of coal. The thinner seams are not often mined, except in localities distant from railroad transportation.

All beds over eighteen inches thick are workable coals. The area where such may be reached within 200 feet from the surface is about 7,000 square miles. Most of the State underlaid by the coal measure is rich farming land. That underlaid by the upper measure includes the richest, which is equal to any upon the globe. The southeastern boundary of the coal measure has been traced from the mouth of the Des Moines through Clark, Louis, Scotland, Adair, Macon, Shelby, Monroe, Audrain, Callaway, Boone, Cooper, Pettis, Benton, Henry, St. Clair, Bates, Vernon, Cedar, Dade, Barton, and Jasper Counties into the Indian Territory, and every county on the northwest of this line is known to contain more or less coal. Great quantities exist in Johnson, Pettis, Lafayette, Cass, Chariton, Howard, Putnam and Audrain. Outside the coal fields, as given above, the regular coal rocks also exist in Ralls, Montgomery, Warren, St. Charles, Callaway and St. Louis, and local deposits of cannel and bituminous coal in Moniteau, Cole, Morgan, Crawford, Lincoln and Callaway. In 1865 Prof. Swallow estimated the amount of good available coal in the State at 134,000,000,000 tons. Since then numerous other developments have been made, and that estimate is found to be far too small.

Lead.—This mineral occurs in lodes, veins and disseminations, which are, as yet, only partially determined. Enough, however, is known of the number, extent, dip and thickness of these deposits to show that their range and richness exceed those of any other lead-bearing region in the world.

Galena occurs in this State in ferruginous clay, that becomes jointed, or separates into distinct masses, quite regular in form when taken out and partially dried; also in regular cubes, in gravel beds, or with cherty masses in the clays associated with the same. These cubes in some localities show the action of attrition, while in others they are entirely unworn. Lead is found in the carboniferous rocks, but perhaps the greater portion is obtained from the magnesian rocks of the lower silurian, and in one or two localities galena has been discovered in the rocks of the Azoic period. At Dugals, Reynolds County, lead is found in a disseminated condition in the porphyry.

The Southeast Lead District.—The Mine La Motte region was discovered about 1720 by La Motte and Renault. Not until this territory was ceded to Spain was considerable mining for lead done in this part of Missouri. Moses Austin, of Virginia, secured from the Spanish Government a large grant of land near Potosi, and sunk the first regular shaft, and, after taking out large quantities of lead, erected, in 1879, the first reverberatory furnace for the reduction of lead ever built in America.

In all this region are found crystallized cubes of galena in the tallow clay, occurring as float. In Franklin, Washington and Jefferson Counties galena is found in ferruginous clay and coarse gravel, often associated with small masses of brown hematite iron and the sulphuret of iron, sometimes lying in small cavities or pockets.

The Virginia mine in Franklin County has produced by far the greater portion of lead from this section.

At the Webster mines the silicate and carbonate of zinc are found always accompanying the lead. At the Valle mines silicate of zinc and baryta occur, as well as hematite iron ore. The Mammoth mine was a succession of caves, in which millions of pounds of lead were found adhering to the sides and roof, and on the bottom was mixed with clay and baryta.

The Frumet or Einstein mines are the most productive ever opened in Jefferson County, and yield also large quantities of zinc ore. There are other valuable mines, in some of which silver has been found.

In Washington County lead mining has been carried on, uninterruptedly, for a greater length of time, and more acres of land have been dug over that have produced lead than in any other county in the State.

In St. Francois County lead deposits are found in the ferruginous clay and gravel. These mines formerly produced many millions of pounds, but have not been extensively worked for many years.

Over portions of Madison County considerable lead is found in the clay. There is lead in several locations in Iron County. In Wayne, Carter, Reynolds and Crawford Counties lead has been found.

Ste. Genevieve has a deposit of lead known as the Avon mines on Mineral Fork, where mining and smelting have been prosecuted for many years. In this vicinity lead has also been found as "float" in several places.

Lead exists in the small streams in several places in the western part of Cape Girardeau County.

In the region above described at least 2,000 square miles are underlaid with lead, upon which territory galena can be found almost anywhere, either in the clay, gravel openings, or in a disseminated condition.

The Central Lead District comprises the counties of Cole, Cooper, Moniteau, Morgan, Miller, Benton, Maries, Camden and Osage. During later years the lead development of Cole County has been more to the northwestern corner, passing into Moniteau and Cooper Counties. In the former several valuable mines have been opened.

The West diggings have been extensively developed and proved rich. The mineral is found in connected cubes in limestone rock, and lies in lodes and pockets. Lead has been found in several places in Cooper and Osage Counties. The later discoveries in that vicinity, although not yet fully developed, give promise of great richness.

Camden County possesses considerable deposits of lead; a number of mines having been successfully worked, and, as the entire northern portion of the county is underlaid with the magnesian limestone formation, it may be discovered in many places where its existence has never been suspected. Miller County is particularly rich in galeniferous ore.

Paying lead has been found north of the Osage River, on the Gravois, Big Saline, Little Saline and Bush Creeks; and the Fox, Walker, Mount Pleasant and Saline diggings have yielded millions of pounds of lead.

Benton County contains a number of lead deposits, the most important being the Cole Cany mines. Lead has been found as a "float" in many localities.

Morgan County, like Washington, can boast of having lead in every township, either as clay, mineral, "float," or in veins, lodes, pockets and caves. The magnesian limestone series of Morgan, in which the lead ores now are, or have all existed, are the most complete and well defined of any in Missouri.

The most extensive deposits of lead in Morgan County have been found south of the center of the county, yet in the northwestern part are several well-known lodes. We can not even name the hundreds of places in the county where lead is found in paying quantities. There seems to be a region, covering 200 square miles, entirely underlaid by lead. These wonderful deposits are as yet but partially worked.

The Southern Lead Region of the State comprises the counties of Pulaski, Laclede, Texas, Wright, Webster, Douglas, Ozark and Christian. The mineral deposits of this region are only partially developed. In Pulaski County lead has been discovered in several localities. Laclede County has a number of lead deposits; one about eleven miles from Lebanon, where the ore is found in a disseminated condition in the soft magnesian limestone. In the southwestern part of Texas County, along the headwaters of the Gasconade River, there are considerable deposits of lead ore. Wright County has a number of lead mines almost unworked, which are situated in the southeastern part of the county, and are a continuation of the deposits in Texas County. In Douglas County, near the eastern line, and near Swan Creek, are considerable deposits of galena. Ozark and Christian Counties have a number of lead deposits, zinc being invariably found in connection.

The Western Lead District comprises Hickory, Dallas, Polk, St. Clair, Cedar and Dade Counties. In Hickory County quite extensive mining has been carried on, the larger deposits having been found near Hermitage. In the northern part of the county and along the Pomme de Terre River, lead occurs as "float," and in the rock formation. The more prominent lodes are found in the second magnesian limestone, with a deposit occurring in the third. The lead deposits of Hickory County are richer and more fully developed than any other in this district. Dallas County has a few deposits of lead, and float lead has been found in various localities in Polk. In St. Clair County the galeniferous deposits are in the second sandstone, and in the ferruginous clay, with chert, conglomerate and gravel. Cedar County presents a deposit of lead, copper and antimony. Galena is found in the clay and gravel. In Dade County a considerable quantity of galena has been found in the southeastern corner of the county.

The Southwest Lead District of Missouri comprises the counties of Jasper, Newton, Lawrence, Stone, Barry, and McDonald. The two counties first named produce more than one-half of the pig lead of Missouri, and may well boast their immense deposits of galeniferous wealth. The lead mining resources of Jasper and Newton Counties are simply inexhaustible, and new and rich deposits are continually being found. Lead ore seems to have been obtained here from the earliest recollection, and furnished supplies to the Indians during their occupation. Formerly smelted lead, merchandise and liquor were the principal return to the miner for his labor; as the distance from market and the general condition of the county precluded enlarged capital and enterprise. Since the war capital has developed the hidden wealth, and systematized labor, and rendered it remunerative. This, with the additional railroad facilities, has brought the county prominently and rapidly before the public as one of the most wonderful mining districts of the world. The total production of lead in Jasper County for the centennial year was, according to the estimates of the best authorities, over half the entire lead production of the State, and more than the entire lead production of any other State in the Union. Later statistics show a steady and rapid increase in the yield of these mines.

One fact, worthy of notice, is, that Jasper County, the greatest lead producing county of the greatest lead producing State, raises every year, upon her farms, products of more value than the lead dug in one year from her mines.

Iron.—In the mining, shipping, smelting and manufacturing of the ores of iron, there is, perhaps, more capital invested and more labor employed than in all the other metal industries of the State combined.

There are three principal and important iron regions in Missouri: The Eastern Region, composed of the southeastern limonite district, and the Iron Mountain specular ore district, the Central Region, containing principally specular ores, and the Western or Osage Region, with its limonites and red hematites.

These three principal regions combined form a broad ore belt running across the State from the Mississippi to the Osage, in a direction about parallel to the course of the Mississippi River from southeast to northwest, between the thirtieth and fortieth township lines. The specular ores occupy the middle portion of this belt, the limonites both ends of it. The latter are, besides, spread over the whole southern half of the State, while these sub-carboniferous hematites occur only along the southern border of the North Missouri coal field, having thus an independent distribution, and being principally represented in Callaway, St. Clair and Henry Counties.

Iron Mountain is the greatest exposure of specular iron yet discovered. It is the result of igneous action, and is the purest mass or body of ore known. The work of years has only just uncovered the massive columns of specular ore that seems to pass down through the porphyry and granite to the source of their existence. The region about is covered with the ore debris. The broken masses have the same general color and quality as the vein ore of Iron Mountain. The fresh fracture presents a light gray, tinged distinctly with blue. The crystallization is often coarse, presenting an irregular fracture. All the ore is more or less magnetic. The streak is a bright cherry red, and possesses considerable hardness. Analysis shows it to contain from 65 to 69 per cent of metallic iron.

The ore of Shepherd Mountain is called a magnetite. In some portions of the veins it shows itself to be granular, brown in color, and to have a clear black streak. Other portions present all the qualities of a specular ore. In portions of the specular, as well as magnetite, beautiful crystals of micaceous ore are found. The streak of this specular and micaceous is a dark red; upon analysis it is found to contain from 64 to 67 per cent of metallic iron. The magnetic qualities of this ore are quite variable, usually the strongest at or near the surface, but this is not the case in all the veins. The ore of Shepherd Mountain is superior to any yet developed in Missouri, not quite as rich as that of Iron Mountain, but so uniform in character, and devoid of sulphur and phosphoric acid, that it may be classed as superior to that, or any other ore in the State.

The ore of Pilot Knob is fine grained, very light bluish gray in color, in hardness not unlike that in Iron Mountain, with a luster sub-metallic. There is a most undoubted stratification to the deposition, occurring as before indicated. The ore of Pilot Knob gives from 53 to 60 per cent metallic iron, and is almost free from deleterious substances. The ore below the slate seam is much the best, containing only about from 5 to 12 per cent of silica, while the poorer ores show sometimes as high as 40 per cent. There have been more than 200,000 surface feet of ore determined to exist here.

The Scotia Iron Banks, located on the Meramec River, in Crawford County, are most remarkable formations. Here the specular ore is a deep, steel-gray color, with a metallic luster.

The crystals are fine, and quite regular in uniformity. This ore is found in the shape of boulders, sometimes small and sometimes of immense size, resting in soft red hematites, that have been produced by the disintegration of the specular ores. These boulders contain a great number of small cavities in which the ore has assumed botryoidal forms; and upon these, peroxide iron crystallizations are so formed that a most gorgeous show of prismatic colors is presented.

In these banks there are some carbonates and ochraceous ores, but not in any quantity to deteriorate or materially change the character of the other ores. Many of the boulders present a soft red mass with a blue specular kernel in the center. This ore is found to be slightly magnetic, and gives from 58 to 69 per cent metallic iron.

Simmons Mountain, one-half mile south of Salem, Dent County, is about 100 feet high, and covers nearly forty acres. The second sandstone is the country rock, and at the summit is uncovered, and mixed with specular and brown ores. Down the elevation larger masses of ore are met with that have the appearance of being drifts from the main deposit, higher up. Shafts have been sunk in this elevation determining more than thirty feet of solid ore. The ore is a splendid, close, compact, brilliant specular, very hard and free from deleterious substances. The ores of this mountain do not show nearly as much metamorphism as many of the other banks in the second sandstone of this region. The ore is quite strongly magnetic, and gives a bright red streak. This is the largest specular iron deposit, with the exception of Iron Mountain, that is known in the State.

Some of the most extensive red hematite banks in Missouri are located in Franklin County. Along the Bourbeuse there are thirteen exposures of fine red hematite iron ore. Near Dry Branch Station is an elevation, capped at the summit with saccharoidal sandstone, beneath which there is a large body of red and specular ore. The red hematite, however, predominates, and is remarkably pure and free from sulphur or other deleterious substances. The sinking of a number of shafts upon this hill reaches the deposits in several places, in all of which the red hematite shows itself to be the prevailing ore. This ore will be found to work well with the hard specular and ores of the siliceous character, like Pilot Knob.

In Miller, Maries, Cole and Camden Counties, also in Bollinger, Stoddard and Butler Counties, along the line of the St. Louis, Iron Mountain & Southern Railroad, there are a number of red hematite banks of considerable promise. There are similar banks in the northern part of Texas and Wright Counties, and in Morgan, Benton, Cedar and Laclede.

In Wayne County there are over seventy different limonite ore banks. In Miller, Maries, Camden, Cole, Moniteau and Callaway Counties there are very extensive banks of the same kind. In Morgan, Benton, St. Clair, Cedar, Hickory and Vernon Counties, considerable brown hematite has been found.

In Franklin, Gasconade, Phelps, Crawford, Laclede, Christian, Webster and Greene Counties large limonite beds have been found. In the Moselle region very large deposits have been opened and worked for many years. In Osage County there are a number of promising brown ore banks, as well as fine specular and red hematite.

It is impossible, in the brief space granted, to describe the number of banks, rich in iron ore, which are situated in the above and other counties of this State; but a glance at the tables found in the works of prominent geologists of the State, will give some idea of the resources of Missouri as an iron producing region.

Zinc.—The ores of zinc in Missouri, almost as numerous as those of lead, are distributed throughout mostly all the geological strata, and scattered through nearly every mineral district; but the principal supply of the metal for commercial purposes is obtained from a very few ores, the more important of which are zinc blende (sulphuret of zinc), the silicate of zinc and the carbonate of zinc, and these are furnished by a comparatively few localities.

In reference to their geological position, the ores are in two classes: The first class includes all zinc ores which occur in the regular veins of the older rocks, and hence are associated with other metalliferous ores. The second mode of occurrence, and the ore by far of paramount importance in Missouri, is that of the third magnesian limestone of the lower silurian series, where it usually occurs in association with galena in the cave formation.

Zinc blende abounds at Granby and Joplin, and is found at many other mines of the Southwest. It also occurs at the lead mines of Franklin and Washington Counties, and at some other points in Southeast Missouri.

The pockets of coal in Central Missouri nearly all contain zinc blende. The lead mines of the same section also sometimes carry it.

There are quantities of silicate of zinc at Granby and Joplin, and the ore is found at most of the lead mines of the Southwest, and occasionally in Central and Southeast Missouri. Carbonate of zinc occurs at Granby, Joplin, Minersville and Valle's mines. It is in the Granby, Joplin and Valle mining districts that zinc ore is principally worked.

Copper, in several varieties, exists in the Missouri mines. The copper mines of Shannon, Madison and Franklin Counties have been known for a long time. Some of those in Shannon and Franklin were once worked with bright prospects of success, and some in Madison have yielded good results for many years.

Deposits of copper have been discovered in Dent, Crawford, Benton, Maries, Green, Lawrence, Dade, Taney, Dallas, Phelps, Reynolds and Wright Counties, but the mines in Franklin, Shannon, Madison, Crawford, Dent and Washington give greater promise of yielding profitable results than any other yet discovered.

Nickel and Cobalt.—These ores abound at Mine La Motte and the old copper mines in Madison County, and are also found at the St. Joseph mines.

Sulphuret of nickel, in beautiful hair-like crystals, is found in the limestone at St. Louis, occupying drusy cavities, resting on calcite or fluor spar.

Manganese.—The peroxide of manganese has been found in several localities in Ste. Genevieve and other counties.

Silver and Gold.—Silver occurs to a limited extent in nearly all the lead mines in the State. Gold, though found in small quantities, has never been profitably worked in any part of Missouri.

Marble.—Missouri has numerous and extensive beds of marble of various shades and qualities. Some of them are very valuable, and are an important item in the resources of the State.

Fort Scott marble is a hard, black, fine-grained marble, with veins of yellow, buff and brown. It receives a fine polish, and is very beautiful. It belongs to the coal measures, and is common in the western part of Vernon County.

There are several beds of fine marble in the St. Louis limestone, of St. Louis County.

The fourth division of encrinital limestone is a white, coarse-grained crystalline marble of great durability. It crops out in several places in Marion County.

The lithographic limestone furnishes a fine, hard-grained, bluish-drab marble, that contrasts finely with white varieties in tessellated pavements.

The Cooper marble of the Devonian limestone has numerous pellucid crystals of calcareous spar disseminated through a drab or bluish-drab, fine compact base. It exists in great quantities in some localities of Cooper and Marion Counties, and is admirably adapted to many ornamental uses. There are extensive beds of fine, variegated marbles in the upper silurian limestones of Cape Girardeau County. Cape Girardeau marble is also a part of the Trenton limestone, located near Cape Girardeau. It is nearly white, strong and durable. This bed is also found near Glencoe, St. Louis County.

In the magnesian limestone series there are several beds of very excellent marble. Near Ironton there are beds of semi-crystalline, light-colored marbles, beautifully clouded with buff and flesh colors. In the third magnesian limestone, on the Niangua, is a fine-grained, crystalline, silico-magnesian limestone, light drab, slightly tinged with peach blossom, and beautifully clouded with deep flesh-colored shades. It is twenty feet thick, and crops out in the bluffs of the Niangua for a long distance.

There are numerous other beds in the magnesian limestones, some of which are white and others so clouded as to present the appearance of breccias.

The Ozark marbles are well known, some of them having been used to ornament the Capitol at Washington. Wherever the magnesian limestones come near the igneous rocks, we may expect to find them so changed as to present beds of the beautiful variegated marbles.

Sulphate of Baryta, in its pure white form, is very abundant in Missouri. It occurs in large beds in the mining regions, as the gangue of our lead veins, and as large masses, especially in the magnesian limestone of the lower silurian rocks. It is utilized as a pigment in connection with lead, and may be made valuable for the same purpose in connection with some of our ferruginous and argillaceous paints.

Clays.—Fire clays, possessing refractory qualities, suitable for making fire brick, occur beneath most of the thicker coal seams.

Potter's clay is abundant, especially among the coal measure clays. It is also sometimes found associated with the lower carboniferous rocks.

Kaolin is only found in Southeast Missouri, where porphyries or granites prevail.

Brick clays have been found and worked in nearly all the counties where there has been a demand for them. The argillaceous portions of the bluff formation make good brick, as shown in the brick yards all along the large rivers. Some of the tertiary clays will make the very best brick.

Caves, etc.—There are several very interesting and quite remarkable caves in the State. Hannibal Cave, one mile below the city of Hannibal, and about a quarter of a mile from the Mississippi River, is approached through a broad ravine, hemmed in by lofty ridges, which are at right angles with the river. The antechamber is about eight feet high and fifteen feet long. This descends into the Narrows, thence through Grand Avenue to Washington Avenue, and through the latter to Altar Chamber. This is a ferruginous limestone formation, and crystal quartz, carbonate of lime and sulphate of magnesia abound. Stalactites and stalagmites are continually forming by limestone percolations. In Bat Avenue Chamber the bats may be seen hanging from the ceiling in clusters, like swarms of bees, some of them fifteen inches from tip to tip. Washington Avenue, over sixteen feet high, with long corridors of stalactites and stalagmites, is the largest division of the cave. It contains a spring, and a deep pool, in which are found the wonderful eyeless fish. The Devil's Hall, Alligator Rock, Elephant's Head, two natural wells filled with limpid water, Table Rock, and numbers of other curiosities, will amply repay the tourist for his exploration.

Cliff Cave, thirteen miles below St. Louis, has been utilized by the Cliff Cave Wine Company as a wine cellar.

There are several caves in Miller County, the largest of which is on Big Tavern Creek, in the bluff near its confluence with the Osage River. The entrance is about twenty-five feet square, and is situated thirty or forty feet above the river, in a solid limestone bluff. During the Civil War it was used as a retreat by the bandit, Crabtree. The stalactite formations are of strange and fantastic appearance, some of them looking like colossal images of marble, and the whole effect by torchlight is wierd and solemn.

Phelps County contains several interesting caves, the most accessible of which is Freide's Cave, about nine miles northwest of Rolla. Its mouth is 60 feet in width and 35 feet in height. It has been penetrated to a distance of three miles without finding any outlet. The Stalactite Chamber is a beautiful apartment 200 yards in length, varying from 15 to 30 feet in width, and from 5 to 30 feet in height. The Bat Chamber contains thousands of wagon loads of guano, which is extensively used by the farmers of the neighborhood. The cave also contains quantities of saltpetre, and during the war large amounts of powder were manufactured there.

There are also caves in Christian County. The principal one is two and a half miles northeast of Ozark. Its entrance is through a rock arch 50 feet across and 80 feet high. About 400 feet from the entrance, the passage is so contracted that the explorer must crawl through on his hands and knees. A fine stream of water, clear and cold, gurgles down through the cave.

About twelve miles south of Ozark, near the Forsyth road, on the top of a very high hill, is a small opening, which, about 100 feet from the surface, expands into a hall 30 feet wide and about 400 feet long, the sides and top of which are of rock lined with beautiful stalactites.

In Stone County at least twenty-five caves have been explored and many more discovered. One mile from Galena is an extensive cave from which the early settlers procured saltpetre in large quantities. About two and a half miles above this is a smaller one of great beauty. From the ceiling depend glittering stalactites, while the floor sparkles with fragments of gem-like luster. A pearly wall, of about half an inch in thickness and 15 inches high, encloses a miniature lake, through whose pellucid waters the wavy stalagmite bottom of this natural basin can be plainly seen. The sacred stillness of the vaulted chamber renders its name, "The Baptismal Font," a peculiarly fitting one.

A cave about twelve miles from Galena is well known among curiosity seekers in the adjacent country. The entrance chamber is a large, dome-shaped room, whose ceiling is very high; a glittering mound of stalagmites rises in the center of the room, nearly one-third the height of the ceiling. Stretching out at right angles from this are long shining halls leading to other grand arched chambers, gorgeous enough for the revels of the gnome king and all the genii of the subterranean world. One can not but think of the Inferno, as, wandering down a labyrinthian passage, he reaches the verge of an abyss, striking perpendicularly to unknown and echoless depths. The name, "Bottomless Pit," is well bestowed on this yawning gulf.

Knox Cave, in Greene County, about seven miles northwest of Springfield, is of large dimensions, and hung in some parts with the most beautiful stalactites.

Fisher's Cave, six miles southeast of Springfield, is of similar dimensions, and has a beautiful stream of water flowing out of it.

There are a number of saltpetre caves along the banks of the Gasconade, which were once profitably worked. Some of these caves are large and interesting, consisting frequently of a succession of rooms joined to each other by arched halls of a considerable height, with walls of white limestone, upon which, as well as upon the floors, the saltpetre is deposited, and is generally so pure as to need but one washing to prepare it for use or export. When these caves were first discovered, it was not unusual to find in them stone axes and hammers, which led to the belief that they had formerly been worked for some unknown purpose by the savages. It is doubtful whether these tools were left there by the Indians or by another and more civilized race which preceded them.

There are numerous caves in Perry County, two of which penetrate beneath Perryville.

Connor's Cave, seven miles southeast of Columbia, has an entrance twenty feet wide and eight feet high, and has been explored for several miles.

There are extensive and beautiful caves in Texas, Webster, Lawrence, Laclede, Oregon and several other counties.

Mineral Springs.—Salt springs are exceedingly abundant in the central part of the State, discharging vast quantities of brine in Cooper, Saline, Howard and the adjoining counties. These brines are near the navigable waters of the Missouri, in the midst of an abundance of wood and coal, and might furnish salt enough to supply all the markets of the continent.

Sulphur springs are also numerous throughout the State. The Chouteau Springs, in Cooper, the Monagaw Springs, in St. Clair, the Elk Springs, in Pike, and the Cheltenham Springs, in St. Louis County, have acquired considerable reputation as medicinal waters, and have become popular places of resort. There are similar sulphur springs in other parts of the State.

Chalybeate Springs.—There are a great many springs in the State which are impregnated with some of the salts of iron. Those containing carbonates and sulphates are most common, and several of these are quite celebrated for their medicinal properties. Sweet Springs, on the Blackwater, and the Chalybeate Spring, in the University campus, are perhaps the most noted of the kind in the State. The Sweet Springs flow from cavities in the upper beds of the Burlington limestone. The hill is here forty-seven feet high above water in the Blackwater, spreading out at the back in a flat table-land. The spring itself is about twenty-feet above the river, and has a sweetish alkaline taste. It is useful as a promoter of general good health, and is much resorted to at the proper season. The water is used for ordinary cooking and drinking purposes, except for making tea.

Petroleum Springs.—These are found in Carroll, Ray, Randolph, Cass, Lafayette, Bates, Vernon and other counties. Many of these springs discharge considerable quantities of oil. The variety called lubricating oil is the most common. It is impossible to tell whether petroleum will be found in paying quantities in these localities, but there is scarcely a doubt that there are reservoirs of considerable quantities.

EVENTS CONNECTED WITH THE EARLY DISCOVERIES, SETTLEMENTS, ETC.

The Indians.—When Christopher Columbus set sail from Palos, it was with no expectation of finding a new continent, but with the hope of discovering a direct western route to those far-famed Indies, whose fabulous riches were the unfailing theme of travelers and geographers. Even to the day of his death the illustrious explorer had no suspicion of having discovered other than the remote islands and shores of the old world, and, accordingly, he called all the inhabitants of the mysterious country "Indians" —a name which has not only outlasted the error of early navigators, but is destined to cling to this unhappy race as long as a vestige of it remains. Whence they came, and to what other family of the earth they are allied, or whether they were originally created a distinct people in the forest wilds of America, have been questions much mooted among the learned and unlearned of modern times, but thus far have elicited only hypotheses in reply. The most common supposition is, however, that the Indians are a derivative race, sprung from one of the more ancient people of Asia, and that they came to this continent by way of Behring's Strait, and this, doubtless, is the true theory.

The tribes with whom the first settlers of Missouri came principally in contact were the Pottawattomies, the Iowas, the Kickapoos, the Sacs and the Foxes.

Other Races.—The ancient cities of Central America, judging from their magnificent ruins of broken columns, fallen arches and the crumbling walls of temples, palaces and pyramids, which, in some places, bestrew the ground for miles, must have been of great extent, magnificent and very populous. When the vast period of time necessary to erect such colossal structures, and the time required to reduce them to their present ruined state are considered, something can be conceived of their antiquity. These edifices must have been old before many of the ancient cities of the Orient were built, and they point, without doubt, to a civilization at once considerably advanced and very far removed from the present.

The Mound-Builders, of a much less degree of culture, but reaching back into an antiquity so remote as to have left behind no vestige of tradition, present themselves to the archæologist as a half-civilized people who once occupied Missouri and various other parts of the country now included in the United States. This pre-historic race has acquired its name from the numerous large mounds of earth left by them. Remains of what were apparently villages, altars, temples, idols, burial places, monuments, camps, fortifications and pleasure grounds have been found, but nothing showing that any material save earth was used in the construction of their habitations. At first these works were supposed to be of Indian origin, but careful examination has revealed the fact that—despite several adverse theories—they must have been reared by a people as distinct from the North American Indian as were those later people of Central America. Upon making excavations in these mounds, human skeletons were found with skulls differing from those of the Indians, together with pottery and various ornaments and utensils, showing considerable mechanical skill. From the comparatively nude state of the arts among them, however, it has been inferred that the time of their migration to this country, if indeed they did migrate, was very remote. Their axes were of stone, their raiment, judging from fragments which have been discovered, consisted of the bark of trees interwoven with feathers, and their military works were such as a people would erect who had just passed to the pastoral state of society from that dependent alone upon hunting and fishing. They were, no doubt, idolaters, and it has been conjectured that the sun was the object of their adoration. The mounds were generally built in a situation affording a view of the rising sun; when enclosed in walls their gateways were toward the east; the caves in which their dead were occasionally buried always opened in the same direction; when bodies were buried in graves, as was frequently the case, they were laid in a direction east and west, and, finally, medals have been found representing the sun and his rays of light.

The mounds and other ancient earth-works constructed by this people are far more abundant than is generally supposed, from the fact that while some are quite large, the greater part of them are small and inconspicuous. Along nearly all the water courses, that are large enough to be navigated by a canoe, the mounds are almost invariably found, so that when one places himself in such positions as to command the grandest river scenery he is almost sure to discover that he is standing upon one of these ancient *tumuli*, or in close proximity thereto.

St. Louis was originally known as the "Mound City," from the extent and variety of the curious monuments found there, and although these, as well as numbers of others scattered over various parts of the State, have been defaced or entirely obliterated, Missouri still presents an unusually fruitful field of investigation to the archæologist. This is particularly true of the southeastern counties, especially in the region of New Madrid.

Mr. Brackenridge, who examined the antiquities of the West in 1817, speaking of the mounds in the Mississippi Valley, says: "I have sometimes been induced to think, that, at the period when they were constructed, there was a population here as numerous as that which once animated the borders of the Nile or Euphrates, or of Mexico. I am perfectly satisfied that cities similar to those of ancient Mexico, of several hundred thousand souls, have existed in this country."

Early Discoveries and Explorers.—Ferdinand De Soto, an adventurer recognized as a Spanish cavalier, who had been associated with Pizarro in the conquest of Peru, but whose ambition and cupidity were only increased by his success in that country, determined to possess himself also of the boundless wealth reputed to lie hidden in the mines of Florida. Undismayed by the fate of other adventurers, he equipped at his own expense a band of 700 men, or more, and landed in Tampa Bay, in the spring of 1539. Thence, in spite of hostile Indians, he forced his way to the Northwest, and, although not finding gold or precious stones, he made himself immortal as the discoverer, in 1541, of the Mississippi River. The point at which De Soto first saw the Mississippi was at the lower Chickasaw Bluffs, a few miles below Memphis. There he constructed boats, and, after crossing the stream, proceeded up its west bank, and made his way into the region now known as New Madrid, in Missouri. At this point, therefore, and at this time, the first European set foot on the soil of Missouri. In 1542, overcome by disease, privation and discouragement, De Soto died, and those of his followers who remained, having secretly sunk his body in the Mississippi, lest the Indians should discover his death, floated down the river to the Gulf of Mexico, and returned to their homes. The design of the expedition had been conquest as a means of acquiring gold, and it left behind no traces of civilization.

Marquette.—While Spain had attended to the conquest of Mexico, South America, the West Indies and Florida, and English colonists had made feeble beginnings in Virginia and New England, the French, advancing still farther north, had possessed themselves of the St. Lawrence River, and were fast pushing their way into the interior by way of the great lakes. Jacques Marquette, a Jesuit missionary, belonging to an ancient family of France, arrived in Canada at a time when the public mind was much exercised upon the subject of exploring the Mississippi River. A plan of operations was accordingly arranged, and Louis Joliet, a native of Canada, joined Father Marquette at the Jesuit mission on the Straits of Mackinaw, and with five other Frenchmen and a simple outfit, the daring explorers, on the 17th of May, 1673, set out on their perilous voyage to re-discover the great river. Coasting along the northern shore of Lake Michigan they entered Green Bay, and passed thence up Fox River and Lake Winnebago to a village of the Muscatines ("Mascoutens") and Miamis, where great interest was taken in the expedition by the natives. Procuring guides they proceeded up the river. Arriving at a portage between the Fox and Wisconsin, they soon carried their light canoes and scanty baggage to the latter stream, about three miles distant. Their guides now refused to accompany them further, and endeavored, by reciting the dangers incident to the voyage, to induce them to return. They stated that huge demons dwelt in the great river, whose voices could be heard a long distance, and who engulfed in the raging waters all who came within their reach. They also represented that if any of them should escape the dangers of the river, fierce tribes of Indians dwelt upon its banks ready to complete the work of destruction. The explorers proceeded on their journey, however, and on the 17th of June, with joy inexpressible, pushed their frail barks out on the bosom of the stately Mississippi, 132 years after its first discovery by De Soto. Journeying down the mysterious stream, which Marquette named the "Conception," they passed the mouth of the Illinois, Missouri and Ohio, landing at various places, and, after proceeding up the Arkansas a short distance, at the advice of the natives, they turned their faces northward. After several weeks of hard toil they reached the Illinois, up which stream they proceeded to Lake Michigan, and entered Green Bay in September of the same year, having traveled a distance of 2,500 miles in a little more than four months.

La Salle.—About the time of Marquette's return, Robert de La Salle, of Normandy, set about discovering a northwest passage to China and Japan, the scientific men of that time generally coinciding in the belief that such a passage existed in the direction of the Great Lakes. He was accompanied from France by an Italian named Tonti, and was joined in his enterprise by Louis Hennepin, a Franciscan friar of a bold and ambitious disposition. After various hindrances and perils, they arrived at the present site of Peoria on the Illinois River, where they built a fort, which, on account of their many vicissitudes, they named Creve Coeur, or Broken Heart. There they separated, Hennepin turning northward to discover, if possible, the source of the Mississippi; La Salle, after visiting Canada, to perfect his arrangements, descending that river in search of its mouth, and Tonti remaining at Creve Coeur in command of men and supplies left at that point. La Salle reached the junction of the Illinois and Mississippi Rivers, in February, 1682, and on the 5th of April following, passed safely through one of the three channels by which the latter stream discharges its waters into the Gulf of Mexico. Three days afterward, with the most imposing ceremonies, La Salle took formal possession of the country in the name of Louis XIV, the reigning king of France, in whose honor he named it Louisiana. The region thus acquired by the French embraced territory on both sides of the Mississippi, and, comprising rather indefinite limits, included the present States of Louisiana, Mississippi, Tennessee, Arkansas and Missouri.

La Salle subsequently returned to Canada, thence to France, and led an expedition to the Gulf of Mexico for the purpose of entering the Mississippi at its mouth, and establishing settlements in Louisiana. Being unable to find the mouth of the river, he landed upon the coast of Texas, and after some fruitless wanderings, was shot by one of his own disaffected followers. However, he had effectually opened the way for the French occupancy of the Mississippi Valley.

Early Settlements.—A few years after La Salle's death, forts and colonies were located at Biloxi Bay, Mobile, Natchez, New Orleans and other points farther north. It is a fact worthy of notice that the first French settlements, all of which were projected in the interest of gold and silver mining, were confined entirely to the eastern bank of the river. It was not until 1705 that the Missouri River was explored as far as the mouth of the Kansas.

In 1720 Renault, the son of a French iron founder, came to Louisiana for the purpose of engaging in gold and silver mining. He brought with him from France 200 miners and artificers, and purchased 500 slaves at the island of San Domingo. Proceeding up the Mississippi River, he established himself at Fort Chartres, about ten or fifteen miles above the present site of Ste. Genevieve, on the opposite bank of the stream. From this point he dispatched miners to "prospect" for the precious metals, and they crossed the river to the west bank, and explored what is now Ste. Genevieve County. Although Renault failed to discover either gold or silver, he found lead ore in great abundance, and having built rude furnaces for smelting it, conveyed it on pack-horses to Fort Chartres, and thence by boat to New Orleans and France.

The date of the actual settlement of Ste. Genevieve is disputed by historians, though all agree that it was the first in the State of Missouri. There is some evidence to support the theory that there might have been inhabitants at this place as early as 1735. The cultivation of tobacco, indigo, rice and silk had already been introduced into the southern part of the province of Louisiana, the lead mines of Missouri were opened, and the culture of wheat was commenced in Illinois. In the meantime the French were firmly establishing their power in the Northwest. By the middle of the eighteenth century (1750) they had control of all the water routes leading from the Great Lakes to the valley of the Mississippi. They had more than sixty military stations from

Lake Ontario by way of Green Bay and the Illinois River, the Wabash and Maumee Rivers, down the Mississippi to New Orleans.

French and Indian War.—The French had formed the design of establishing a magnificent empire in the interior of the continent, having abundant and uninterrupted intercourse with the outside world by means of the Great Lakes and the St. Lawrence and Mississippi Rivers. The English, whose colonies were scattered up and down on the Atlantic coast, claimed the right to extend their possessions as far westward as they chose. As long as the latter nation confined itself to the eastern part of the country there was little reason for controversy. As soon, however, as the English became acquainted with the beautiful and fertile Mississippi Valley, they not only learned the value of the vast territory, but also resolved to set up a counter-claim to the soil. The French, besides establishing numerous military and trading posts from the frontiers of Canada to New Orleans, in order to confirm their claims to jurisdiction over the country, had carved the lilies of France on the forest trees, or sunk plates of metal in the ground. These measures did not, however, deter the English from going on with their explorations; and though neither party resorted to arms, yet the conflict was gathering, and it was only a question of time when the storm should burst upon the frontier settlement. The French based their claims upon discoveries, the English on grants of territory extending from ocean to ocean, but neither party paid the least attention to the prior claims of the Indians. From this position of affairs, it was evident that actual collision between the contending parties would not much longer be deferred. The English Government, in anticipation of a war, urged the governor of Missouri to lose no time in building two forts, which were equipped with arms from England. The French anticipated the English, and gathered a considerable force to defend their possessions. The governor determined to send a messenger to the nearest French post, to demand an explanation. This resolution brought into the history of our country, for the first time, the man of all others whom America most loves to honor, namely, George Washington. He was chosen, although not yet twenty-one years of age, as the one to perform this delicate and difficult mission. With five companions he set out on

November 10, 1753, and after a perilous journey returned January 6, 1754. The struggle could not, however, be averted by diplomacy. It commenced, continued long, and was bloody and fierce; but on October 10, 1765, the ensign of France was displaced on the ramparts of Fort Chartres by the flag of Great Britain. This fort was the depot of supplies, and the place of rendezvous for the united forces of the French, and was then the best built and most convenient fort in North America. In subsequent years the Mississippi reached and undermined its west wall; the inhabitants of Kaskaskia carried away much of the remaining portions for building material, and at the present day nothing remains of it but a ruin in the midst of a dense forest.

Although, as has been already seen, Fort Chartres was not occupied by the English until 1765, the treaty which terminated what is known as the French and Indian War had been arranged late in 1762. According to its stipulations France ceded to England all of her possessions in Canada and east of the Mississippi, and to Spain all that part of the province of Louisiana lying west of the same, which, although really belonging to Spain, remained under French laws and jurisdiction until 1768.

The Founding of St. Louis.—In 1762 M. D'Abadie, at that time director general and civil and military commandant of Louisiana, granted to a certain company the exclusive right to trade with the Indians of Missouri, and indeed of all the Northwest, for a term of eight years. At the head of this company was M. Pierre Laclede Liguest—Laclede, as he is generally known, a man of ability, foresight and experience. He left New Orleans in August, 1763, and arrived in Missouri the following November. It will be remembered that all the French settlements, except that of Ste. Genevieve, were on the east side of the river, and consequently included in the territory ceded to England. At the one small village west of the Mississippi there was no building large enough to contain one quarter of M. Laclede's merchandise. M. De Neyon, the commandant at Fort Chartres, hearing of Laclede's dilemma, offered him room for his goods until the occupation of the fort by the English. Laclede readily availed himself of this generous offer, and repaired to Fort Chartres, where he deposited his effects, and then turned his attention to finding a site, near the Missouri River, suitable for his enterprise. Ste. Genevieve he rejected both on account of its distance from that stream and its unhealthful situation. Accompanied by his stepson, a lad of fourteen, named August Chouteau, he explored the region thoroughly, and fixed upon the place of his settlement. Upon returning to the fort, he assured De Neyon and his officers that he had found a situation where he would form a settlement, which might become, hereafter, "one of the finest cities of America." Thus readily did his sagacious mind appreciate the advantages of this location. Navigation being open, early in the February of 1764, Laclede sent thirty men, in charge of Chouteau, to the place designated, with orders to clear the land, build a large shed to shelter the tools and provisions, and also erect some small cabins for the men. On the 14th of February the work was commenced. Early in April Laclede himself arrived, chose the place for his own house, laid out a plan for his village and named it Saint Louis, in honor of Louis XV, not knowing that the territory had already been transferred to Spain, and then hastened back to Fort Chartres to remove his goods, as the English garrison was daily expected.

When, in 1765, Capt. Sterling in command of the English troops, a company of highlanders, actually took possession of the fort, St. Ange, French commandant at the time, removed with his officers and men to St. Louis, which was recognized as the capital of Upper Louisiana. M. D'Abadie had died, and M. Aubry was acting governor at New Orleans. Receiving, probably, the sanction of this latter gentleman, St. Ange at once assumed the reins of government at St. Louis, and so liberal was the spirit in which he conducted affairs that a stream of immigration soon set in from Canada and Lower Louisiana.

Death of Pontiac.—At the time of the founding of St. Louis, the Ottawa chieftain, Pontiac, was enjoying his greatest fame. At the breaking out of the war between France and England, he had allied himself with the former country, which had at all times followed a conciliatory policy with the Indians, and he had achieved some brilliant exploits at the ambuscade near Pittsburgh (1755), which resulted in Braddock's defeat, and on other occasions. He had subsequently formed a confederacy of all the western tribes, and had endeavored, by one general and combined movement, to sweep the English settlers from the country west of the Alleghanies. In this effort he was so far successful that, at one time, every English fort in the west, except Niagara, Fort Pitt and Detroit, had fallen into the hands of the savages. St. Ange, hating the English and dreading their encroachments, was proportionately friendly to Pontiac, whom he invited to St. Louis in 1769. Here the chief was received in the most flattering manner, and was warmly welcomed by the principal citizens. Soon, however, it became apparent that Pontiac's plans were doomed to failure.

Tribe after tribe had forsaken him, his powerful allies, the French, were conquered, and his most trusted friends among the latter counseled him to give up the unequal contest. He endeavored to drown his disappointment in drink, and in spite of the remonstrances of St. Ange, sank lower and lower in debauchery. Finally, while in a state of intoxication, he was assassinated at Cahokia by a Kaskaskia Indian. His body was interred with great pomp near the tower at the intersection of Walnut and Fourth Streets. St. Ange, himself, lies buried near, but nothing is left to mark either grave. Houses have been built above them, and but few persons even know that these remains repose in the midst of the great city.

Spanish Rule.—The transfer of Louisiana to Spain caused sorrow to the inhabitants of the province, and at St. Louis this feeling was deepened to one of horror when it became known that Don Alexander O'Reilly had arrived at New Orleans with 3,000 men, and, upon the inhabitants of that city making armed resistance to his authority, had executed several of the ringleaders of the revolt and imprisoned others. The new commandant-general soon established his authority at New Orleans, and in 1770 sent Don Pedro Piernas to St. Louis as lieutenant-governor. This official showed himself master of the situation by treating the terrified inhabitants with the utmost consideration, securing the friendship of St. Ange, whom he made a captain of infantry, and establishing all the grants of land which the latter had bestowed. St. Ange died soon after. Piernas was succeeded by Francisco Cruzat, and he by Don Ferdinando Leyba. During the early part of Leyba's administration, Laclede died while on an expedition to New Orleans, and was buried at the mouth of the Arkansas River. His grave, also, is unknown, and probably has long ere this been washed into the stream.

The Revolutionary War.—War having already begun between Great Britain and her American colonies, Washington, who had been active in the service of England against the French, now commanded the forces opposed to English tyranny. On the breaking out of the Revolution the British held every important post in the West. The Indians, jealous of the rapid extension of American settlement westward, and aroused to action by the English, became the allies of the latter, and, while the colonies at the East were struggling against the armies of the mother country, the western frontiers were ravaged by the savages, often led by British commanders. To prevent indiscriminate slaughter in the West, some of the most daring exploits connected with American history were planned and executed. The hero of the achievements by which this region was snatched as a gem from the British crown, was Gen. George Rogers Clark, of Virginia. He had closely watched the movements of the English throughout the Northwest, and understood their plans; he also knew that the Indians were not unanimously in accord with them, and that although the forts were in control of the English, the inhabitants were mostly French, and retained much of their old hostility against their conquerors, while sympathizing with the colonies. He was convinced that American soldiers would be welcomed and aided, as far as possible, by the French settlers, and that the English garrisons once driven out, the natives might be easily awed into neutrality. Patrick Henry was governor of Virginia and at once entered heartily into Clark's plans. The latter proceeded to Pittsburgh, raised his small army west of the Alleghanies, as he well knew the colonies needed all the available men farther east, for the conflict there. His plan was to go by water as far as Fort Massac, and thence march direct to Kaskaskia. Here he intended to surprise the garrison, and after its capture to proceed to Cahokia, then to Vincennes, and lastly to Detroit. Each of these posts was in turn captured, and the plans of the English in the West entirely overthrown.

In the meantime, although the settlement at St. Louis was under the jurisdiction of Spain, it was well known that the sympathies of that country were identified with the colonies, and therefore the inhabitants of the little city were in constant dread of attacks from the Indians. Hearing rumors, also, of a threatened assault by the British, they at once began to fortify the place. A wall of brush and clay, five feet in height, with three gates, was built, encircling the town, the extremes terminating at the river. A small fort, which was afterward used as a prison, was also built. At each of the gates a piece of ordnance was mounted, and kept in constant readiness for use. These preparations were made in the summer and fall of 1779. No attack was made during the winter, and the people of St. Louis were almost beginning to hope their precautions unnecessary, when in May, bands of Ojibways, Winnebagos, Sioux and other tribes began to gather on the east side of the river, preparing to fall upon the settlement on the 26th of the month. These savages were instigated by Canadian fur traders, and commanded by officers from the British fort at Michilimackinac.

On May 25, which was the festival of Corpus Christi, a portion of the Indians crossed the river, but made no assault, an extremely fortunate circumstance, as many of the citizens, together with their wives and children, were outside of the wall, and scattered about over the prairie, gathering strawberries. The following day the entire force of savages stole silently across the river, and crept to the rear of the town, expecting to find some of the inhabitants working in the fields. Near what is now the fair grounds, at the "Cardinal Springs," they surprised the man from whom the spring was named and another person call Riviere. The former they killed, and took the latter prisoner. A few other settlers were surprised and massacred.

On account of his misconduct at this time, Leyba was removed from office and Francisco Cruzat once more placed in authority at St. Louis. During the administration of Cruzat, the town was thoroughly fortified, but was not subjected to another attack, although other settlements on the Mississippi and Missouri Rivers were often harassed by the Indians even after the close of the war.

Floods.—In 1785 occurred a sudden and remarkable rise in

the Mississippi River, causing great alarm and considerable loss of property to the inhabitants of St. Louis and the adjacent settlements. Cahokia and Kaskaskia were menaced with entire destruction. Ste. Genevieve, which was located at first in the river bottom, three miles south or southeast of its present site, was completely inundated, and the inhabitants, unwilling to risk a repetition of the disaster, removed to higher ground and founded the present town, which therefore dates from 1785. Most of the buildings in St. Louis were then situated on Main Street, and the rise of the river above the steep bank occasioned extreme anxiety and terror. The flood subsiding, however, nearly as rapidly as it had risen, the inhabitants returned to their houses, and business was speedily resumed. This year received the name of "L'annee des Grandes Eaux," or "The year of the Great Waters." Other remarkable floods occasioning loss of life and property, and involving St. Louis and other river towns of Missouri, have occasionally occurred, most destructive among which may be mentioned those of 1844, 1851, 1875 and 1881.

1785–1800.—Cruzat was succeeded in office by Manuel Perez, who bestowed a large tract of land in the vicinity of Cape Girardeau upon friendly Indians of the Pawnee and Delaware tribes, in return they agreeing to aid the young settlements in repelling the incursions of the hostile Osage Indians. Trudeau, who succeeded Perez, devised and carried out many improvements at St. Louis, and stimulated in a great measure the fur traffic, and by this means encouraged traders to penetrate the wilderness, and make further expeditions on the Missouri River. The administration of Trudeau was followed by that of Delassus, who, in 1799, ordered that a census be taken of the settlements in Upper Louisiana or Western Illinois, as Missouri was sometimes called. According to this census, the total number of inhabitants in the settlements was 6,028. Of these 4,948 were white; 197 free colored, and 883 slaves. St. Louis had a population of 925; Ste. Genevieve, 949; St. Charles, 875; New Madrid, 782; New Bourbon, 560; Cape Girardeau, 521; St. Ferdinand, 276; St. Andrew, 393; Carondelet, 184; Meramec, 115; Little Meadows, 72.

Daniel Boone, famous in the annals of Kentucky and the West, came to Louisiana about the year 1797. He renounced his allegiance to the United States, became a Spanish subject, and was appointed by Delassus commandant of the Femme Osage District. When the province was transferred to the United States, he again became an American citizen. At some time between the years 1804 and 1808 he may very probably have hunted through Howard County, and discovered the salt springs there. During the summer of 1807, Boone's sons, Nathan and Daniel M., visited these springs and there manufactured salt, but there is no evidence that the elder Boone ever resided, even temporarily, at the place. The settlement afterward made was called Boone's Lick, and a large region in that part of the State, the "Boone's Lick Country." Boone County, organized in 1820, was named after the great frontiersman, who died in September of that year at the residence of his son, on Femme Osage Creek, in St. Charles County, aged eighty-eight years.

Louisiana Purchased by the United States.—In the year 1801 Napoleon Bonaparte made a treaty with Spain, known in the annals as the treaty of San Ildefonso, the conditions of which were that Spain should surrender to France all the region known as Louisiana west of the Mississippi River, in return for certain assistance which she expected to receive from the great warrior in her European affairs. It was not, however, until 1803, that M. Laussat, a French officer, was placed in authority at New Orleans. Although Napoleon fully realized the immense value of his acquisition, it was on many accounts an occasion of perplexity. In the first place, the American Government regarded with a jealous eye this attempt of the French to re-establish themselves in Louisiana; and the English, who had control of the seas, made it extremely difficult for men and equipments to be conveyed into the country; and, rather than have it wrested from him by this powerful foe, he determined to tantalize the mother country by adding it to the possessions of the young nation, which had succeeded in maintaining its independence in the face of her authority. Accordingly, he accepted an offer made by the United States, and the transfer was accomplished during the administration of Thomas Jefferson. In December, 1803, M. Laussat, the French commandant, who had but just acquired jurisdiction of Louisiana from Spain, conveyed it to Gov. Claiborne and Gen. Wilkinson, commissioners appointed by the United

States. The price paid for this purchase was $15,000,000, including various claims, the payment of which was assumed by the American Government.

At St. Louis the French flag was in the ascendant only one day, Capt. Stoddard, the representative of France, receiving possession of the territory at the hands of Delassus, the Spanish governor, on March 9, 1804, and transferring his authority to the United States on the following day.

The District of Louisiana.—March 26, 1804, Congress passed an act separating the provinces of Louisiana into two parts—the southern designated as "The Territory of Orleans," and the northern, "The District of Louisiana." This latter included all of the province north of "Hope Encampment," a place near Chickasaw Bluffs, and embraced within its boundaries the present States of Arkansas, Missouri and Iowa, a large part of Minnesota, and all the vast region extending westward to the Pacific Ocean, excepting the territory claimed by Spain.

The executive power of the Government in the Territory of Indiana was extended over the district of Louisiana or "Upper Louisiana" as it was popularly called. Gen. William Henry Harrison, then governor of Indiana, assisted by Judges Griffin, Vanderberg and Davis, represented the authority of the United States, under the provisions of the act of 1804, and, during the following winter, courts of justice were held in the old fort, near Fifth and Walnut Streets, in St. Louis.

The Territory of Louisiana.—March 3, 1805, by another act of Congress, the Territory of Louisiana was regularly organized, and the President appointed Gen. James Wilkinson, governor, and Frederick Bates, secretary. Gov. Wilkinson, together with Judges R. J. Meigs and John B. C. Lucas, constituted the Legislature of this almost boundless territory. Gov. Wilkinson was visited in 1805, by Aaron Burr, when the latter was planning his daring conspiracy against the United States.

In 1807 Capt. Merriwether Lewis, of the famous Lewis and Clark expedition, was appointed governor, but in 1809, in Lewis County, Tenn., he committed suicide at the age of thirty-five, by shooting himself with a pistol, and President Madison designated Gen. Benjamin Howard, of Lexington, Ky., as governor in his stead. Gov. Howard served as brigadier-general in the War of 1812, and died in 1814. Howard County was named in his honor.

Lewis and Clark's Expedition.—After the purchase of Louisiana, President Jefferson, anxious to prove the value of that immense tract then in possession of the United States, planned an expedition for the purpose of exploring the country from the Mississippi to the Pacific Ocean. The expedition was organized with Merriweather Lewis, Mr. Jefferson's private secretary, at its head, assisted by Capt. William Clark, of the American army. With a small party, these indomitable explorers ascended the Missouri River as far as Jefferson, Madison and Gallatin, which they named in honor of the President, Secretary of State and Secretary of the Treasury, respectively, followed the Jefferson to its source, crossed the Rocky Mountains, navigated the Columbia River, and returned to St. Louis, in September, 1806, after an absence of two years and four months, having overcome innumerable hardships and difficulties, and traveled nearly 6,000 miles. Lewis, as has been already noted, was appointed governor of the Territory of Louisiana, which office he filled until his untimely and tragical death.

Lieut. Zebulon M. Pike also organized two successful exploring parties, one of which, in 1805, discovered the sources of the Mississippi, and the other, in the two succeeding years, the sources of the Arkansas, Kansas, Platte and Pierre Jaune (Yellowstone) Rivers, and penetrated the Spanish Provinces. Pike's Peak was named from this explorer. The county of Pike, in this State, was named in honor of Lieut. Pike, who rose to the rank of brigadier-general in the War of 1812, and was killed at York, Canada, in 1813.

Earthquakes at New Madrid.—New Madrid, rendered famous by the great earthquake of 1811–12, was, originally, one of the old Spanish forts, and lies about seventy miles below the mouth of the Ohio River. It was settled immediately after the close of the Revolutionary War by families from Virginia and the Carolinas, and was growing rapidly in wealth and population when its progress was arrested by that frightful calamity which affected not only the county of New Madrid, but also the adjacent country on both sides of the Mississippi. Streams were turned from their channels or dried up; hills, forests and plains disappeared, and lakes (one of which was sixty or seventy miles in length, and from three to twenty in breadth) were formed in their places; vast heaps of sand were scattered in various places, and whole tracts of land sank below the level of the surrounding country. Short extracts from the description of Mr. Godfrey Lesieur, who was an eye-witness of the scene, are quoted:

"The first shock was about 2 o'clock A. M., on the night of December 16, 1811, and was very hard, shaking down log houses, chimneys, etc. It was followed at intervals, from half an hour to an hour apart, by comparatively slight shocks, until about 7 o'clock in the morning, when a rumbling noise was heard in the west, not unlike distant thunder, and in an instant the earth began to totter and shake so that no persons were able to stand or walk. This lasted a minute; then the earth was observed to be rolling in waves of a few feet in height, with a visible depression between. These swells burst, throwing up large volumes of water, sand and a species of charcoal, some of which was partly covered with a substance, which, by its peculiar odor, was thought to be sulphur. Where these swells burst, large, wide and long fissures were left, running north and south parallel with each other for miles. I have seen some four or five miles in length, four and one-half feet deep on an average, and about ten feet wide.

"After this, slight shocks were felt at intervals, until January 7, 1812, when the region was again visited by an earthquake equal to the first in violence, and characterized by the same frightful results." Mr. Lesieur says further that, upon this second visitation, the inhabitants, excepting two families, fled from the country in dismay, leaving behind their stock, and even many of their household goods, all of which were appropriated by adventurers and carried away in flat-boats. The last violent shock occurred on the 17th of February, 1812.

During these terrible earthquakes, but two among the settlers were killed, both of whom were women, but many of the boatmen on the river must have perished. An act of Congress for the relief of the New Madrid sufferers was passed in 1817.

By its provisions, persons whose lands had been seriously damaged by the earthquakes were allowed to locate a like quantity upon any of the public lands of the State, provided that no claims should exceed 640 acres. This was the origin of the "New Madrid Claims," of which speculators and sharpers gained the chief benefit, the people many of them being uninformed as to their exact privileges.

For convenience of reference a short table is appended of the early settlements of Missouri, with the date of the establishment of each in cases where it has been determined.

Names of Settlements.	Dates.
Ste. Genevieve	1735(?)
St. Louis	1764
Near St. Charles	1765
Portage des Sioux	1769
New Madrid	1780
New Bourbon	1789
Potosi	1765(?)
Big River Mills, St. Francois County	1796
Near Farmington, St. Francois County	1797
Perry County	1796
Bird's Point	1800
Norfork	1800
Charleston	1801
Warren County	1801
Parkersville (Cote Sans Dessein)	1801
Loutre Island	1807
Boone's Lick	1807
Cooper's Bottom, Franklin County	1810

TERRITORIAL AND STATE ORGANIZATION.

The Territory of Missouri was organized by Congress, June 4, 1812, the first Council consisting of nine members, and the House of thirteen.* Its real boundaries were the same as those of the "Territory of Louisiana," but practically it consisted of only the settled parts of Missouri, comprising four districts, as follows: Cape Girardeau, embracing the territory between Tywappity Bottom and Apple Creek; Ste. Genevieve, extending from

---

*These members were as follows: House: St. Charles County—John Pitman and Robert Spencer; St. Louis County—David Music, Bernard G. Farrar, William C. Carr and Richard Caulk; Ste. Genevieve County—George Bullett, Richard S. Thomas and Isaac McGready; Cape Girardeau—George F. Bollinger and Stephen Byrd; New Madrid—John Schrader and Samuel Phillips. W. C. Carr became speaker and Andrew Scott clerk. Council: St. Charles County—James Flaugherty and Benjamin Emmons; St. Louis County—Auguste Chouteau, Sr., and Samuel Hammond; Ste. Genevieve—John Scott and James Maxwell; Cape Girardeau—William Neeley and George Cavener; New Madrid—Joseph Hunter.

Apple Creek to the Meramec River; St. Louis, including that part of the State between the Meramec and Missouri Rivers, and St. Charles, comprising the settled country betweeen the Missouri and Mississippi.

The legislative power of the Territory was vested in a governor, legislative council and House of Representatives. By the same act the Territory was authorized to send one delegate to Congress. In October of the same year the four districts, by proclamation of Gov. Howard, were reorganized into five counties, the fifth being called New Madrid, and included Arkansas. An election of a delegate to Congress, and members of the Territorial House of Representatives, was held in the following November. Capt. William Clark, the associate explorer of Capt. Lewis, was appointed by the President as governor, and entered upon his duties in 1813. He continued to occupy the gubernatorial chair until the admission of the State into the Union, and died in St. Louis in 1838.

Edward Hempstead was chosen the first delegate to Congress. It was mainly owing to his efforts that an act was passed by that body confirming to the people of Missouri the titles of their lands derived from Spanish grants, and also providing that "all village lots, out lots, or common field lots" held by them at the time of the cession of Louisiana to the United States, should be retained for school purposes. The real estate thus secured to the city of St. Louis alone, for educational purposes, was valued at $1,252,895.79. Col. Thomas F. Riddick, who first originated the proposition, rode to Washington on horseback to aid Mr. Hempstead in obtaining the ratification of Congress.

Growth.—In 1814 the population of the Territory was 25,000. The country was rapidly settled, and new counties were organized. The Legislature of 1816-17 incorporated a board of trustees for superintending schools in the "Town of St. Louis," the beginning of the school system of that city. At the same session the old "Bank of Missouri" was chartered, and in the fall of 1817 the two banks, "St. Louis" and "Missouri," were issuing bills, the former having gone into operation in 1814.

The first newspaper west of the Mississippi was published at St. Louis, July 12, 1808. It was called the *Missouri Gazette*, and was a diminutive sheet, measuring 12x16 inches. Although this paper has undergone several changes of title it still lives and flourishes as the *Missouri Republican*. The first newspaper west of St. Louis was the *Missouri Intelligencer*, established at Old Franklin, by Nathaniel Patton, in 1819, and subsequently removed to Fayette. In 1818 a cathedral was commenced at St. Louis, on the site of the old log church which had been erected by the early French inhabitants, and in the same year the first Protestant Church (Baptist) was built.

The first steamboat which ascended the Mississippi, above the mouth of the Ohio, was the "Gen. Pike," Capt. Jacob Read, which landed in St. Louis at the foot of Market Street August 2, 1817, and was received with every demonstration of delight. The next was the "Constitution," Capt. R.T. Guyard, which arrived in the October following. In 1819 the "Independence," Capt. Nelson, from Louisville, Ky., navigated the Missouri as far as Old Chariton, an abandoned town a short distance above Glasgow, and, returning to Franklin, took freight for Louisville. The first steamboat on the Upper Mississippi was the "Gen. Putnam," Moses D. Bates, captain, which made several trips between St. Louis, and Galena, Ill., during the summer of 1825.

In 1818 the Government of the United States projected the celebrated Yellowstone expedition, the objects of which were to ascertain whether the Missouri was navigable by steamboats, and to establish a line of forts from its mouth to the Yellowstone. This expedition left St. Louis in June, 1819. In the same year Arkansas was formed into a separate Territory.

State Organization.—In 1818, John Scott being delegate to Congress, the inhabitants of Missouri petitioned for admission into the Union. The House of Representatives passed a bill to admit the State without slavery, but, the Senate refusing to concur in this anti-slavery clause, the bill failed. Subsequently the measure was amended so as to provide for the gradual restriction of involuntary servitude, but the Senate refused to endorse any anti-slavery proviso whatever, and the House insisting on that provision, the bill again failed. In 1820, while the matter was still under discussion, Jesse B. Thomas, of Illinois, presented an amendment, which settled for the time all differences between the two Houses, and allowed Missouri to enter the Union with slavery. That amendment, famous in history as the "Missouri Compromise," is as follows:

An Act to Authorize the People of the Missouri Territory to form a Constitution and State Government, and for the Admission of such State into the Union on an equal footing with the Original States, and to Prohibit Slavery in certain Territories—Adopted March 6, 1820.

* * * * * * * * * *

Sec. 8. *And be it further enacted,* That in all that territory ceded by France to the United States, under the name of Louisiana, which lies north of thirty-six degrees and thirty minutes north latitude, not included within the limits of the State contemplated by this act, slavery and involuntary servitude, otherwise than in the punishment of crimes whereof the parties shall have been duly convicted, *shall be and is hereby forever prohibited. Provided always,* That any person escaping into the same, from whom labor or service is lawfully claimed in any State or Territory of the United States, such fugitive may be lawfully reclaimed and conveyed to the person claiming his or her labor or services as aforesaid.

Such was the "Missouri Compromise," one of the most important acts of American Legislation. The pro-slavery senators consented to this measure because they saw by the determination of the House that they would be unable otherwise to secure the admission of Missouri.

State Convention.—Under the act of Congress, the people of the Territory of Missouri, organized into fifteen counties, were authorized to hold an election in May, 1820, to choose representatives to a State convention whose object should be the framing of a constitution. Accordingly, forty-one representatives thus chosen convened at St. Louis on June 12. The following are the names of the members of the convention, together with the counties which they represented:

Cape Girardeau—Stephen Byrd, James Evans, Richard S. Thomas, Alexander Buckner, Joseph McFerran.

Cooper—Robert P. Clark, Robert Wallace, William Lillard.

Franklin—John G. Heath.

Howard—Nicholas S. Burkhartt, Duff Green, John Ray, Jonathan S. Findlay, Benjamin H. Reeves.

Jefferson—Daniel Hammond.

Lincoln—Malcolm Henry.

Montgomery—Jonathan Ramsey, James Talbott.
Madison—Nathaniel Cook.
New Madrid—Robert D. Dawson, Christopher G. Houts.
Pike—Stephen Cleaver.
St. Charles—Benjamin Emmons, Nathan Boone, Hiram H. Barber.
Ste. Genevieve—John D. Cook, Henry Dodge, John Scott, R. T. Brown.
St. Louis—David Barton, Edward Bates, Alexander McNair, William Rector, John C. Sullivan, Pierre Chouteau, Jr., Bernard Pratte, Thomas F. Riddick.
Washington—John Rice Jones, Samuel Perry, John Hutchings.
Wayne—Elijah Bettis.

David Barton was elected president of the convention and William G. Pittis, secretary.

The constitution which the convention formed took effect from the authority of the body itself, no provision having been made to submit it to the vote of the people. It withstood the mutations of parties and all efforts at material amendment from the time of its adoption till the convention of 1865.

The Clay Compromise.—November 16, Mr. Scott laid before the House of Representatives at Washington a copy of the constitution of the new State, when a fresh debate arose, first, because the constitution sanctioned slavery and, second, because one of its articles especially enjoined that such laws should be passed as might be necessary to prevent free mulattoes and negroes from coming to or settling in the new State, under any pretext whatsoever.

The perils of the political situation becoming imminent, Mr. Clay, of Kentucky, moved that twenty-three representatives, one from each State, be appointed to act jointly with the Senate committee, in an attempt to adjust the difficulty. Such a committee was chosen with Mr. Clay as its chairman. The Senate also appointed seven of its members on the joint committee, which, on February 26, 1821, reported to each House the following:

Resolved by the Senate and House of Representatives of the United States of America, in Congress Assembled, That Missouri shall be admitted into this Union on an equal footing with the original States, in all respects whatever, upon the fundamental condition that the fourth clause of the twenty-sixth section of the third article of the constitution, submitted on the part of said State to Congress, shall never be construed to authorize the passage of any law, and that no law shall be passed in conformity thereto, by which any citizen of either of the States in this Union shall be excluded from the enjoyment of any of the privileges and immunities to which such citizen is entitled under the constitution of the United States. *Provided,* That the Legislature of said State, by *a solemn public act,* shall declare the assent of the said State to the said fundamental condition, and shall transmit to the President of the United States, on or before the fourth Monday in November next, an authentic copy of the said act; upon the receipt whereof the President, by proclamation, shall announce the fact; whereupon, and without any further proceeding on the part of Congress, the admission of the said State into the Union shall be considered as complete.

The resolution was soon adopted by both Houses, and on the 26th of the following June, the Legislature of Missouri adopted an act declaring the assent of the State to the conditions of admission, and transmitted to the President a copy of the same. August 10, 1821, after a struggle of two years and a half, the admission of Missouri into the Union was announced by the proclamation of President Monroe, and the State from that day took rank as the twenty-fourth of the American Republic.

First General Assembly.—Anticipating the admission of the State into the Union a general election had been held August 28, 1820. Alex. McNair was chosen governor; Wm. H. Ashley, lieutenant-governor, and John Scott, representative to Congress. Senators and representatives to the General Assembly (fourteen of the former and forty-three of the latter) were also elected. This body convened at St. Louis in September, and elected David Barton and Thomas H. Benton United States senators, although, as the State was not formally admitted into the Union until the following August, they were not allowed to take their places until December, 1821. Mr. Benton held the position of United States senator for thirty consecutive years.

At this session of the Legislature were organized the counties of Boone, Callaway, Chariton, Cole, Gasconade, Lillard (afterward La Fayette), Perry, Ralls, Ray and Saline. The seat of government was fixed at St. Charles, but was moved, in 1826, to Jefferson City. According to the first census taken in September, 1821, the population of the State was 70,647, of whom 11,254 were slaves.

EARLY WARS.

War of 1812.—Although the inhabitants of Missouri were far distant from the principal scenes of this conflict, they participated in many engagements with the Indians, and were obliged to exercise ceaseless vigilance against their insidious foe. For several years British traders had incited the savages against the settlers, and had supplied the former with arms and ammunition. In July, 1810, W. I. Cole and two other men at Loutre Island were killed while attempting to rescue property stolen by the Pottawattomies. In 1815 the Sac and Fox Indians, who had stolen horses from the same settlement, were followed by a party of "rangers," with Capt. James Callaway, a grandson of Daniel Boone, in command. Four of the pursuers, including Capt. Callaway, were killed.

In 1813 Fort Madison, Iowa, was abandoned by its garrison, and burned to save it from Indian occupation. During the same year the scattered settlements in the present counties of Montgomery, Lincoln and Pike were often plundered by the Indians, under the renowned Black Hawk and other noted chiefs. In St. Charles County there were many massacres, but at length a number of forts were erected, which proved a sufficient protection against further outrages. The Boone's Lick country was constantly harassed by tribes, who stole horses and murdered the inhabitants. Living beyond the jurisdiction of any organized county, these pioneers built forts, and defended themselves. Sentinels kept guard while the fields were plowed, sown and harvested, and upon the appearance of danger the people were notified by means of signals, and hastened to the shelter of the forts.

At Cote Sans Dessein (now Barkersville), on the Missouri River in Callaway County, three men and two women successfully withstood a protracted and determined siege of the Indians.

Of all the murders committed by the savages, none aroused more indignation than that of Capt. Sarshell Cooper, who was shot while sitting at his own fireside in Cooper's Fort, in the Boone's Lick country, in 1814. An Indian crept to the wall of Cooper's cabin, which also formed one side of the fort, and made a small opening between the logs, through which the fatal shot was fired.

Black Hawk War.—In 1804 a treaty was concluded between the United States and the Sac and Fox Indians. One old warrior of the Sacs, however, called Black Hawk, who had fought with great bravery in the service of Great Britain during the War of 1812 had always taken exception to this treaty, pronouncing it void. In 1831 he established himself with a chosen band of braves upon the disputed territory in Illinois, ordering the whites to leave the country at once. Fifteen hundred volunteers from that State, aided by Gen. Gaines, with a company of regulars, surprised the Indians, and forced them into another treaty, by which they ceded all their lands east of the Mississippi, and agreed to remain upon the other side of the river. Soon, however, a band of these same Indians attacked a party of friendly Menominies encamped at Prairie du Chien, murdering twenty-five and wounding many others. Brig.-Gen. Atkinson, with a large detachment of regular troops from Jefferson Barracks, was sent to chastise the murderers who had thus flagrantly violated their treaty. Upon this Black Hawk, with his adherents, recrossed the Mississippi and established himself at Rock River. Keokuk was the rightful chief of the Sacs and Foxes, and with the majority of his tribes remained true to their agreement with the United States, but Black Hawk's followers were bent upon revenge and plunder. May 14, 1832, a bloody engagement occurred near Dixon's Ferry. On account of the proximity of these hostilities to the Missouri border, and fearing an Indian invasion, Gov. Miller ordered Maj.-Gen. Richard Gentry, of Columbia, this State, to raise 1,000 volunteers, prepared to start for the frontier at a moment's warning.

Accordingly on May 29, 1832, orders were issued by Gen. Gentry to Brig.-Gens. Benjamin Means, commanding the Seventh; Jonathan Riggs, the Eighth, and Jesse T. Wood, the Ninth Brigade, Third Division, to raise, the first named 400 and each of the last 300 men. Each man was "to keep in readiness a horse with the necessary equipment, and a rifle in good order, with an ample supply of ammunition." Five companies were at once raised in Boone County, and others in Callaway, Montgomery, St. Charles, Lincoln, Pike, Marion, Ralls, Clay and Monroe. Two of them, Capt. John Jamison's, of Callaway, and Capt. David M. Hickman's, of Boone, in July, 1832, were mustered into service for thirty days, and placed under command of Maj. Thomas Conyers. This detachment, accompanied by Gen. Gentry in person, arrived at Palmyra July 10, and at Fort Pike, which was situated on the Des Moines, at the present site of St. Francisville, in Clark County, five days afterward. Finding that no hostile Indians had entered Missouri, Gen. Gentry ordered work to be discontinued on Fort Matson, in the northern part of Adair County, sixty-five miles from Fort Pike, and within eight miles of the Chariton, and left for Columbia, where he arrived on July 19. Maj. Conyers' command was left at Fort Pike. On August 5 this detachment was relieved by two other companies under Capts. Sinclair Kirtley, of Boone, and Patrick Ewing, of Callaway. Maj. Conyers' remained in command of the fort. In September, the Indian troubles having apparently subsided, the troops on the northern frontier of Missouri were mustered out of service.

For nearly a year afterward, the war was continued at various points in Illinois and Iowa, until, at the decisive battle of the Bad Axe, Black Hawk was entirely defeated, and a great number of his followers killed. He himself escaped, but was soon captured and delivered to the United States officers. He was carried in triumph through a great part of the States, after which, shorn of his power, if not his ambition, he was permitted to return to his tribe. Black Hawk died at the village of his people, on the Des Moines River, in Davis County, Iowa, in 1838, aged about seventy years.

Seminole War.—Florida originally belonged to Spain. Among its aboriginal inhabitants was a humane, romantic tribe of Indians —the Seminoles. Their manners were gentle, and their language soft; but the wrongs they suffered are as deep and wicked as any ever inflicted by a civilized nation upon a weak and defenseless people. Escaping slaves found refuge in the Spanish Territory, formed settlements along the Appalachicola and Suwanee Rivers and became members of the Seminole and Creek nations, holding lands and enjoying the fruits of their labors. Spain refused to deliver up the fugitives who had thus intermarried with the Indians, and whose descendants soon became an almost indistinguishable part of the tribe. The slaveholders of Georgia were furious, and the government of that State, on several occasions, sent troops into the Creek country and laid waste villages, burned huts, and killed innocent members of the tribe. Spain resented these piratical raids, and the President of the United States was compelled to disavow any responsibility for such outrages, which nevertheless continued.

On July 27, 1816, an old fort situated on the Appalachicola, which had been built by the British during the War of 1812, and subsequently occupied by the blacks and their descendants, was blown up by forces under command of Gen. Gaines. There were in the fort 334 persons, mostly women and children, and 270 of these unfortunate creatures were instantly torn in pieces.

The Seminoles, goaded from their placid ways, attempted to retaliate; but their efforts, though gallant, were feeble. The raids upon the Seminole country and its citizens continued, and the state of affairs became a matter of serious perplexity to the general Government.

In 1835, during President Jackson's administration, renewed hostilities arose from an attempt to remove the Seminoles and Creeks to lands west of the Mississippi. The chief of the former tribe was Osceola, a half breed of great talents and audacity, who, driven to desperation by personal wrongs, as well as those inflicted upon his people, formed a conspiracy to slaughter the whites and devastate the country. The Creeks were soon conquered and set beyond the Mississippi. In 1837 Osceola was captured and soon after died, but the war continued.

In the fall of 1837 the Secretary of War issued a requisition on Gov. Boggs, of Missouri, for two regiments of mounted volunteers for the Seminole War.

The first regiment was raised chiefly in Boone and neighboring counties by Col. Gentry, and was composed of eight companies. Four companies of the second regiment were also raised and attached to the first. Of these latter, two companies were composed of Delaware and Osage Indians.

Col. Gentry's regiment left Missouri in October, 1837. The

men were taken by boat from St. Louis to New Orleans, and transported thence to Tampa Bay, Florida. On the voyage they encountered a severe storm, and several of the vessels were stranded. Many horses were lost but no men, and on the 15th of November the troops disembarked at their destination. On the 1st of December they received orders from Gen. Zachary Taylor, then commanding in Florida, to march to Okeechobee Lake, in the vicinity of which the whole force of the Seminoles was said to have collected. Having reached the Kissimee River, seventy miles distant, the cavalry scouts captured several Indians, from whom Col. Gentry learned that their main forces were near at hand, and immediately crossing the river he formed the Missouri volunteers in front, and, supporting them at a proper distance by the regular army on either flank, advanced to meet the attack. The Indians had chosen a fine position, and continued the battle with a pertinacity seldom exhibited in their method of warfare. Col. Gentry fought on foot, as did all his command, and had repulsed the enemy after several hours of severe fighting. He was gradually pushing them across a swamp, and had nearly reached the dry soil when a bullet pierced his abdomen, inflicting a fatal wound. He knew its serious nature, yet stood erect an hour afterward, and cheered his men to victory, until, at last, being compelled to desist, he was borne from the field, and expired the same night. The Missourians continued to fight several hours after the fall of their leader, until the Indians were entirely vanquished. The loss of the whites in killed and wounded was 138, most of whom were Missourians.

The forces from this State being no longer needed, they returned to their homes early in 1838. The remains of Col. Gentry, as well as those of Capt. Vanswearingen and Lieuts. Brooke and Center, of the Sixth Regular United States Infantry, were afterward brought to Jefferson Barracks and buried, the Government of the United States erecting over them a suitable monument. The country of Gentry was named in memory of the gallant commander.

After a war of eight years, during which nearly $40,000,000 had been expended, several hundred persons seized and enslaved, and hundreds of lives lost, the Seminoles and their colored kindred were removed as far as the Cherokee country, and subsequently to that of the Creeks. After persistent attempts of the latter to reduce them to a state of servitude, and after many of the exiles had been actually seized and sold into perpetual bondage, the remainder of the blacks, excepting 200 who were supposed to be so intermarried with the Seminoles as to render them safe, abandoned the country and fled to Mexico.

The Mormon War.—The origin, rapid development and prosperity of the religious sect, commonly called the Mormons, are among the most remarkable historical events of the present century. That an obscure individual, without money, education or elevated position in society, should persuade people to believe him inspired of God, and cause a book, insignificant as a literary production, to be received as a continuation of the sacred revelation, appears almost incredible. Yet in less than half a century the disciples of this personage have increased to hundreds of thousands; have founded a State in the distant wilderness, and compelled the Government of the United States to practically recognize them as an independent people.

The founder of Mormonism was Joseph Smith, a native of Vermont, who emigrated, while quite young, with his father's family to western New York. The story of the finding of the golden plates in the "Hill of Cumarah," their transcription, the printing of the Mormon Bible, the organization of the first church of the new faith, are themes not important to be considered here. It may be well to state in passing that the believers in Mormonism claim that their Bible gives a history of the peopling of the Western Continent, as the common Bible narrates the origin of the human race on the Eastern, and the Mormons accept both volumes as of Divine inspiration, calling themselves "The Church of Jesus Christ of Latter Day Saints." The common name by which they are known is that given to one of the writers of the Mormon Bible.

Having gained a number of converts, Smith, in 1831, moved to Kirtland, Ohio, and, during the same year, made a visit to Missouri in search of a location for "Zion." He found it at Independence, Jackson County, named the place "The New Jerusalem," and returned to Kirtland.

In 1832 Smith established himself with many followers in Jackson County. Here the new church acquired several thousand acres of land, which the members professed to hold in common, and published a paper called *The Morning and Evening Star*, in which were printed promises of boundless prosperity to the "Saints," and frightful denunciations against the "Gentiles." The result was a series of trifling encounters between the two parties, until, October 31, 1833, an engagement occurred near Westport, in which two citizens and one Mormon were killed.

The Gentile citizens of Jackson County now rose in arms in considerable numbers, and committed a series of acts of violence toward the Mormons. The bishop was tarred and feathered, the printing press thrown into the river, the storehouse plundered, and the "Saints" were forced to leave the county without any compensation whatever for the lands they were compelled to abandon.

The Mormons next located in Clay, Carroll and Caldwell Counties, but principally in the latter, which was organized for their benefit. They established headquarters at Far West, which was founded in 1836, and which Smith assured his followers would soon become one of the great cities of the world. As the result of the preaching of missionaries in the Eastern States, converts flocked into the country, and their settlements soon spread into Daviess and Clinton Counties, but Far West was their chief town and commercial center. Some of the Mormon settlers were good and industrious people, but many were violent and lawless, and considered that they had a right to take anything they chose from the Gentiles. As the latter were in the minority in Caldwell County, and as most of the county offices were held by "Saints," there was considerable dissatisfaction among the Gentiles, and violent deeds were committed on either side.

In Carroll County a committee of citizens waited upon the leaders of the Mormon settlement at De Witt, and notified them that they must leave the county. Mormon recruits poured into the town, and an engagement took place on the 21st of September, 1838, but no serious casualty occurred. The attacking party was now increased by reinforcements to 400 or 500 men, but, before renewing the battle, they demanded once more that the obnoxious settlers should leave the county.

Although the terms of this proposition were quite stringent, they were acceded to, and the Saints loaded their property on wagons and removed to Far West.

October 25 a skirmish took place at Crooked River, in the southwestern part of Caldwell County, where one Gentile was killed, several others wounded, and David Patten, the leader of the Danite Band or United Brothers of Gideon, and two other Mormons, were killed. The Gentiles were commanded by Capt. Sam. Bogart.

The people of Missouri now determined to be rid of the Mormons, and in 1838 Gov. Boggs issued an order to Maj.-Gen. David R. Atchison, to call out the militia of his division and proceed against the Mormons and expel them from the State or "extenuate them." A part of the First Brigade of the Missouri State Militia, under command of Gen. Alexander W. Doniphan, at once proceeded to the seat of war. Upon receipt of Gov. Boggs' exterminating order, Gen. Atchison left the field, and the command of the forces was turned over to Maj.-Gen. S. D. Lucas, of Independence, pending the arrival of Gen. John B. Clark, of Howard County. The Mormon forces, numbering about 600 men, were led by Col. George W. Hinkle.

The principal event was the massacre at Haun's mills, five miles south of the present site of Breckinridge, Caldwell County. Three militiamen were wounded and seventeen of the Mormons, two of them little boys, killed — some of them after their surrender — and their bodies were thrown into a half-finished well. This massacre, for it was nothing else, was perpetrated by 250 men from Livingston and Daviess Counties, under Col. Thomas Jennings.

When the militia appeared at Far West, where the principal Mormon forces were gathered, the Mormons surrendered, agreeing to Gen. Lucas' conditions, viz.: That they should deliver up their arms, pay the expenses of the war, surrender their prominent leaders for trial, and the remainder of the Mormons should, with their families, leave the State.

The leaders were taken before a court of inquiry at Richmond, Judge Austin A. King presiding. He remanded them to Daviess County to await the action of the grand jury on a charge of treason against the State. The Daviess County jail being poor, they were confined at Liberty. Indictments for various offenses — treason, murder, robbery, receiving stolen goods, arson, resisting legal process, etc.,— were found against Joseph Smith, Hiram Smith, Sidney Rigdon, G. W. Hinkle, Parley P. Pratt and a number of others. Sidney Rigdon was released on a writ of *habeas corpus*. The others requested a change of venue, and Judge King sent their cases to Boone County for trial. On their way to Columbia, under a military guard, Joe Smith effected his escape. It is generally believed that the guard was bribed; subsequently P. P. Pratt and others also escaped; some of the prisoners were acquitted, and the indictments dismissed against all the others. In connection with the removal of the Mormons, and according to the terms of their surrender, there were many terrible scenes. Numbers of them were poor, and had invested their all in lands from which they were about to be driven. Valuable farms were traded for an old wagon, a horse, a yoke of oxen, or anything that would furnish means of transportation. In many instances, conveyances of lands were demanded and enforced at the muzzle of the pistol or the rifle. Nearly 4,000 Mormons removed from Caldwell County to Nauvoo, Ill.

The Mexican War.—From 1821 to 1836 the vast territory between Louisiana and Mexico had been a province of the latter. It had been the policy of Spain and Mexico to keep Texas uninhabited, in order that the vigorous race of Americans might not encroach on the Mexican borders. At last, however, a large land grant was made to Moses Austin, of Connecticut, on condition that he would settle 300 American families within the limits of his domain. Afterward the grant was confirmed to his son Stephen, with the privilege of establishing 500 additional families of immigrants. Thus the foundation of Texas was laid by people of the English race.

Owing to the oppressive policy adopted by Mexico, the Texans, in 1835, raised the standard of rebellion. Many adventurers and some heroes from the United States flocked to their aid. In the first battle fought at Gonzales, 1,000 Mexicans were defeated by a Texan force numbering 500. On March 6, 1836, a

Texan fort, called the Alamo, was surrounded by a Mexican army, commanded by Pres. Santa Anna. The feeble garrison was overpowered and massacred under circumstances of great atrocity. David Crockett, an ex-congressman of Tennessee, and a famous hunter, was one of the victims of the butchery. In the next month was fought the decisive battle of San Jacinto, which gave to Texas her freedom. The independence of the new State was acknowledged by the United States, Great Britain and France.

On the 1st of March, 1844, Texas was admitted into the American Union as a sovereign State, and on the 4th of July, 1845, the Texan Legislature ratified the act of annexation. Knowing the warlike attitude of Mexico, the authorities of Texas sent an immediate and urgent request to the President to dispatch an army for their protection. Accordingly, Gen. Zachary Taylor was ordered to occupy Texas. The real issue between that State and Mexico was concerning boundaries. Texas claimed the Rio Grande as her western limit, while Mexico was determined to have the Nueces as the separating line. The territory between the two rivers was in dispute. Having made an unsuccessful attempt to settle the difficulty by negotiation, the American Government sent Gen. Taylor to Corpus Christi, at the mouth of the Nueces, where, by the beginning of November, 1845, he had concentrated a force of 4,000 or 5,000 men. In the following January Gen. Taylor was ordered to advance to the Rio Grande. He took his station opposite Matamoras and hastily erected a fortress, afterward named Fort Brown.

In April, 1846, Mexico declared war against the United States, and this was promptly followed by a counter declaration, on the part of the American Congress, against Mexico. Soon after this exchange of challenges, the Mexicans crossed the Rio Grande in strong force, headed by their famous generals, Arista and Ampudia, and, on the 8th and 9th of May, at Palo Alto and Resaca de la Palma, were met and repulsed with great slaughter by Gen. Taylor.

When the news of the battles on the Rio Grande was borne through the Union, the national spirit was everywhere aroused, and party dissensions were hushed into silence. A call was made for 50,000 volunteers, and Missouri was not backward among her sister States in responding to the appeal. The St. Louis Legion, a military organization under command of Col. A. R. Easton, quickly prepared for the field of action. Supplies were raised for them by liberal subscriptions on the part of the citizens, and in a few days they departed for the seat of war. The American forces were organized in three divisions: The Army of the West, under Gen. Kearney, to cross the Rocky Mountains and conquer the northern Mexican provinces; the Army of the Center, under Gen. Scott as commander-in-chief, to march from the Gulf coast into the heart of the enemy's country; and the Army of Occupation, commanded by Gen. Taylor, to subdue and hold the districts on the Rio Grande. About the middle of May, 1846, Gov. Edwards, of Missouri, called for mounted volunteers to join the first of these divisions, which was about to undertake an expediton to Santa Fe. By the 18th of June the full complement of companies to compose the First Regiment had arrived at Fort Leavenworth, the appointed rendezvous. These volunteers were from the counties of Jackson, Lafayette, Clay, Saline, Franklin, Cole, Howard and Callaway. Alexander W. Doniphan, of Clay, was elected colonel; C. F. Ruff, lieutenant-colonel, and William Gilpin, major. The battalion of light artillery, from St. Louis, was commanded by Capts. R. H. Weightman and A. W. Fischer, with Maj. M. L. Clark as its field officer. Battalions of infantry from Platte and Cole Counties were commanded by Capts. Murphy and W. Z. Augney, respectively. The Laclede Rangers, from St. Louis, were led by Capt. Thomas B. Henderson.

In all, Gen. Kearney had 1,658 men and sixteen pieces of ordnance. After a long and wearisome march he reached Santa Fe, and on the 18th of August captured and garrisoned the city. The whole of New Mexico submitted without resistance. With a body of 400 dragoons Kearney then continued his march toward the Pacific coast, leaving Col. Doniphan in command of New Mexico.

With a body of 700 fearless men, this latter officer made one of the most brilliant movements of the war. He undertook a march through the enemy's country from Santa Fe to Saltillo, a distance of more than 800 miles. Reaching the Rio Grande on Christmas day, he fought and gained the battle of Bracito; then crossing the river, captured El Paso, and in two months pressed his way to within twenty miles of Chihuahua. On the banks of Sacramento Creek he met the Mexicans in overwhelming numbers, and on the 28th of February completely routed them. He then marched unopposed into Chihuahua, a city of more than 40,000 inhabitants, and finally reached the division of Gen. Wool in safety.

Early in the summer of 1846 Hon. Sterling Price, a member of Congress from Missouri, resigned, and was appointed by President Polk to command another regiment of Missouri volunteers to reinforce the Army of the West. This force consisted of a full mounted regiment, one mounted extra battalion, and one extra battalion of Mormon infantry. These troops were raised in the counties of Boone, Benton, Carroll, Chariton, Linn, Livingston, Monroe, Randolph, Ste. Genevieve and St. Louis, with Lieut.-Col. David Willock's extra battalion from Marion, Ray and Platte.

Col. Price's command took up the line of march for Santa Fe over the same route pursued by Doniphan and Kearney, and arrived on September 28, three days after Kearney's departure for California.

In the winter of 1847 an insurrection against the American authority broke out in New Mexico, and on the 24th of January Col. Price met the enemy, numbering about 2,000 men, at Canada, and repulsed them with a slight loss on both sides. He totally routed them at El Embudo, on January 29. On February 3 he found the Mexicans and Indians strongly fortified at Taos, and engaged them on the following day with shot and shell. The battle raged all day, and at night the Mexicans surrendered. Price's loss in these three engagements was but fifteen killed and forty-seven wounded. Afterward, by order of Gen. Price, twenty-one of the Mexican leaders were hung.

In August, 1847, Gov. Edwards made another requisition for 1,000 infantry to follow Col. Price's command. The regiment was organized immediately, and Maj. John Dougherty, of Clay County, was chosen colonel, but before it marched the President countermanded the order under which it was raised.

Another regiment of mounted volunteers (the Third Missouri Regiment) was formed to serve during the Mexican War. It was commanded by Col. John Ralls, of Ralls County, and was mustered into service about May, 1847. A portion of this regiment went as far as El Paso, Chihuahua and Santa Cruz De Rosales, and at the latter place participated in a battle against the Mexicans under Gen. Trias. The enemy were in the town, and sheltered by breastworks, but after fighting all day were obliged to surrender with their arms, ammunition, wagons and teams. The Americans were commanded by Gen. Sterling Price.

The war was now drawing to a close. Everywhere the arms of the United States had been victorious, and on February 2, 1848, a treaty was concluded between the two belligerent nations. By the terms of settlement the boundary line between Mexico and the United States was fixed as follows: The Rio Grande from its mouth to the southern limit of New Mexico; thence westward along the southern, and northward along the western boundary of that Territory to the river Gila; thence down that river to the Colorado; thence westward to the Pacific. The whole of New Mexico and Upper California was relinquished to the United States. Mexico guaranteed the free navigation of the Gulf of California, and the Colorado River from its mouth to the confluence of the Gila. In consideration of these territorial acquisitions and privileges, the United States agreed to surrender all places held by military occupation in Mexico; to pay into the treasury of that country $15,000,000, and to assume all debts due from the Mexican Government to American citizens, said debts not to exceed $3,500,000. Thus, at last, was the territory of the United States spread out in one broad belt from ocean to ocean.

Constitutional Convention of 1845.—At the August election of 1845, sixty-six members were chosen by the people to remodel the constitution. Representation under the old constitution, which allowed each county at least one representative, and limited the whole number to 100 members in the lower branch of the General Assembly, had become very unequal. Chiefly to remedy this irregularity, but at the same time for other purposes, the convention was called.

It convened at Jefferson City, on November 17, 1845, and organized by the election of Robert W. Wells as president; Claiborne F. Jackson, vice-president, and R. Walker, secretary. Some of the most able and distinguished men of the State were members of this body. The whole organic law was reviewed, and, in many material respects, remodeled. The convention adopted (ayes, forty-nine, nays, thirteen) a new constitution, and submitted it to the people, and adjourned *sine die* January 14, 1846. During the canvass the constitution was very generally discussed by the newspapers and candidates, and finally, at the August election, rejected by about 9,000 majority, the whole number of votes cast being about 60,000.

EVENTS PRECEDING THE CIVIL WAR.

The Jackson Resolutions.—The sixteenth General Assembly of Missouri, which convened at Jefferson City, December 25, 1848, will ever be remembered for its passage of the famous "Jackson Resolutions." The occasion of these was a bill called the "Wilmot-Anti-Slavery Proviso," which had been introduced into the preceding Congress by Hon. David Wilmot of Pennsylvania, prohibiting the extension of slavery into the recently acquired Territories. Slave holders throughout the Southern States were exceedingly agitated over this measure, seeing that it must effectually put an end to the formation of new pro-slavery States, thus giving the majority of members in Congress to the anti-slavery party, and insuring the final triumph of the Free Soilers. As a result of the excitement in Missouri, Carty Wells, a Democratic State senator from Lincoln County, introduced into the Upper House of the Legislature a series of resolutions on various subjects suggested by the Wilmot Proviso, which was referred to the Senate Committee on Federal Relations. On January 15, 1849, Claiborne F. Jackson, senator from Howard County, reported from this committee to the Senate the following modification of Mr. Wells' resolutions:

Resolved, by the General Assembly of the State of Missouri, That the Federal constitution was the result of a compromise between the conflicting interests of the State which formed it, and in no part of that instrument is to be found any delegation of power to Congress to legislate on the subject of slavery, excepting some special provisions, having in view the prospective abolition of the African slave trade, made for the securing the recovery of fugitive slaves; any attempt, therefore, on the part of Congress to legislate on the subject, so as to affect the institution of slavery in the States, in the District of Columbia, or in the Territories, is, to say the least, a violation of the principles upon which that instrument was founded.

2. That the Territories acquired by the blood and treasure of the whole nation ought to be governed for the common benefit of the people of all the States, and any organization of the Territorial Governments, excluding the citizens of any part of the Union from removing to such Territories with their property, would be an exercise of power, by Congress, inconsistent with the spirit upon which our Federal compact was based, insulting to the sovereignty and dignity of the States thus affected, calculated to alienate one portion of the Union from another, and tending ultimately to disunion.

3. That the General Assembly regard the conduct of the Northern States on the subject of slavery as releasing the slave-holding States from all further adherence to the basis of compromise fixed on by the act of Congress of March 6, 1820, even if such act ever did impose any obligation upon the slave-holding States, and authorizes them to insist upon their rights under the constitution; but for the sake of harmony, and for the preservation of our Federal Union, they will sanction the application of the principles of the Missouri Compromise to the recent territorial acquisitions, if by such concession future aggressions upon the equal rights of the States may be arrested and the spirit of anti-slavery fanaticism be extinguished.

4. The right to prohibit slavery in any Territory belongs exclusively to the people thereof, and can only be exercised by them in forming their constitution for a State government, or in their sovereign capacity as an independent State.

5. That in the event of the passage of any act of Congress, conflicting with the principles herein expressed, Missouri will be found in hearty co-operation with the slave-holding States, in such measures as may be deemed necessary for our mutual protection against the encroachments of Northern fanaticism.

6. That our senators in Congress be instructed and our representatives be requested to act in conformity to the foregoing resolutions.

The resolutions were written by Hon. William B. Napton, afterward one of the judges of the supreme court.

The scope of this work forbids a detailed account of the discussion which followed the introduction of these resolutions into the General Assembly, as well as the names of the many distinguished men who took opposing sides upon the question of their adoption. The Jackson resolutions were finally adopted after much opposition, particularly in the Lower House, where a strong but unsuccessful attempt was made to modify them.

Perhaps the chief object in the introduction and passage of the resolutions was the retirement of Senator Thomas H. Benton. His course in and out of the Senate had become obnoxious to many of the Democratic politicians of the State, who determined to get rid of him. They knew he would not obey the instructions contained in the resolutions, and this would furnish an excuse for a refusal to return him for another term. There was much excitement throughout the State, and the feeling was still farther intensified by the course of Senator Benton, who appealed from the Legislature to the people, and prosecuted a canvass against the resolutions, denouncing them in powerful and passionate speeches, as tending to the dismemberment of the Union. He declared them to be in direct contradiction to the Missouri Compromise, upon which depended the safety and harmony of the nation.

That Col. Benton was right in his position, although, perhaps, intemperate in its defense, is perfectly apparent in the light of subsequent events; but his crusade against the "Jackson Resolutions" resulted in his defeat at the next election, when, after thirty years of loyal service toward his State and Nation, he was succeeded in 1851 by the Whig candidate, Henry S. Geyer, an eminent lawyer of St. Louis, who was chosen by Democratic votes.

Organization of Kansas and Nebraska.—Missouri was admitted into the Union as a slave State in the year 1820, only upon the terms of the Missouri Compromise, which forever prohibited involuntary servitude in territory north of 36° 30', now constituting Kansas, Iowa, Nebraska, Colorado, Dakota, Wyoming, Montana, Idaho and a portion of Minnesota. And now this great domain was to be organized into territorial governments. Already into these vast regions the tide of immigration was pouring, and it became necessary to provide for the future. In December, 1852, Hon. Willard P. Hall, of Missouri, introduced a bill into the United States House of Representatives, to organize the Territory of Platte, which was designed to embrace the country above mentioned. Having been referred to the Committee on Territories, that committee, in February, 1853, reported a bill to establish a territorial government in the Territory of Nebraska. As this bill did not contemplate a repeal of the Missouri Compromise, it was opposed in the House by all the Southern delegations. The only senators from the South who voted for it were David R. Atchison and Henry S. Geyer, of Missouri. On January 16, 1854, when the subject again came before the Senate, Senator Dixon, of Kentucky, gave notice that whenever the Nebraska bill should be called up, he would move an amendment to the effect that the Missouri Compromise, drawing the line of 36° 30' north latitude, and forever prohibiting slavery or involuntary servitude north of said line, should not be so construed as to apply to the Territory contemplated by the act, or to any other Territory of the United States; but that the citizens of the several States or Territories should be at liberty to take and hold their slaves within any of the Territories or States to be founded therefrom. That is to say, in plain language, that the Missouri Compromise should be made null and void. The announcement of this amendment in Congress was immediately followed by the most intense excitement throughout the country. Indeed, the introduction, in 1848, of the Wilmot Proviso, did not rouse the people in a greater degree.

On January 23, 1854, Senator Stephen A. Douglas, of Illinois, reported from the Committee on Territories a bill which provided for the organization of the region of country embraced by Mr. Hall's bill, known as the Platte country, from the Platte River, which flows through it into two Territories, namely, Kansas and Nebraska. As Senator Douglas' bill must always be an important document in history, we transcribe some part of it.

* * * * * * * * * *

SEC. 21. *And be it further enacted*, That, in order to avoid misconstruction, it is hereby declared to be the true intent and meaning of this act, so far as the question of slavery is concerned, to carry into practical operation the following propositions and principles, established by the compromise measures of 1850, to wit:

First. That all questions pertaining to slavery in the Territories, and in the new States to be formed therefrom, are to be left to the decision of the people residing therein, through their appropriate representatives.

Second. That all cases involving title to slaves and questions of personal freedom are referred to the adjudication of the local tribunals, with the right of appeal to the Supreme Court of the United States.

Third. That the provisions of the constitution and laws of the United States, in respect to fugitives from service, are to be carried into faithful execution in all the organized Territories, the same as in the States.

The section of the bill which prescribed the qualifications and mode of election of a delegate to Congress from each of the Territories was as follows:

SEC. 2. *And be it further enacted,* * * * * That the constitution and laws of the United States, which are not locally applicable, shall have the same force and effect within the said Territory of Kansas as elsewhere within the United States, except the eight sections of the act preparatory to the admission of Missouri into the Union, approved March 6, 1820, which was superseded by the principles of the legislation of 1850, commonly called the compromise measures, and is declared inoperative.

The debate which ensued upon the introduction of this bill, known as the "Kansas-Nebraska Bill," was conducted with great ability, and lasted several weeks. On February 6, Hon. S. P. Chase, a senator from Ohio, who was afterward Secretary of the Treasury under Lincoln's administration, and finally chief justice of the United States, moved to strike out so much of the bill as declared the Missouri Compromise "superseded" by the compromise of 1850, but the motion was defeated. On February 15 Mr. Douglas moved to strike out the clause objected to by Mr. Chase, and insert the following:

Which being inconsistent with the principle of non-intervention by Congress with slavery in the States and Territories, as recognized by the legislation of 1850 (commonly called the compromise measures), is hereby declared inoperative and void; it being the true intent and meaning of this act not to legislate slavery into any Territory or State, nor to exclude it therefrom, but to leave the people thereof perfectly free to form and regulate their domestic institutions in their own way, subject only to the constitution of the United States.

This amendment embodied what was afterward known as the doctrine of "squatter sovereignty." It was at once adopted by the Senate; but Mr. Chase and others, not having full confidence that it was not the true intent and meaning of the act "to legislate slavery into any Territory or State," moved to add, after the words "United States," the following:

Under which the people of the Territories, through their appropriate representatives, may, if they see fit, prohibit the existence of slavery therein.

Mr. Chase's amendment was voted down. From January until May, Mr. Douglas' report was debated in Congress. By the Kansas-Nebraska bill the Missouri Compromise was virtually repealed, and the old settlement of the slavery question overthrown at a single blow. All the bitter sectional animosities of the past were aroused in full force. The bill was violently opposed by a majority of the representatives from the East and North; but the minority, uniting with the congressmen of the South, enabled Douglas to carry his measure through Congress, and in May, 1854, the bill received the sanction of the President.

Kansas itself now became a battlefield for the contending parties; whether the new State should admit slavery or not depended upon the vote of the people. Both factions made a rush for the territory in order to secure a majority. The people of Missouri were especially interested in the situation. Apprehensive that Kansas would become a free State, and that Missouri would in the future occupy the position of a slave-holding peninsula, jutting out into a sea of free soil, with Illinois and Iowa at the east and north, and Kansas and Nebraska on the west, many of her citizens, especially on the Kansas border, became seriously alarmed for the safety of their slaves, and in the excitement of the conflict were induced without authority of law to cross over into Kansas, and, carrying ballots in one hand and arms in the other, to coerce the new State into the Union with a pro-slavery constitution.

Meanwhile the Northern States were not idle. Massachusetts had chartered a wealthy corporation, called the Emigrant Aid Company; Connecticut followed soon after with a similar company. The New York *Tribune*, edited by Horace Greeley, opened a Kansas contribution, and aid societies sprang into activity at hundreds of points in the Northwest. Thus stimulated, the people of the free States flocked to Kansas in such numbers that in a few months they constituted a decided majority of the actual settlers. The Missourians, with force and arms, attempted to carry out their measures, and prevent Northern and Eastern settlers from passing through their State, but the emigrants then wound around through Iowa, thus circumventing their plans. The struggle between the hostile parties in Kansas and on the Missouri border resulted in a series of desultory but bloody encounters, some of which assumed the proportions of battles. Large and fiercely excited public meetings were held in Missouri, and at times in some localities a reign of intolerance and proscription prevailed. This was intensified in that portion of the State bordering on Kansas.

An election held in the new State in November of 1854 resulted in the choice of a pro-slavery delegate to Congress, and, in the general territorial election of the following year, the same party was triumphant. The State Legislature thus chosen assembled at Lecompton, organized the government, and framed a constitution permitting slavery. The Free Soil party declaring the general election to have been illegal, on account of fraudulent voting, assembled in convention at Topeka, September 25, 1855, framed a constitution excluding slavery, and organized a rival government. Civil war broke out between the factions.

From the autumn of 1855 until the following summer the Territory was the scene of constant turmoil and violence. The people of the North held meetings to enlist additional settlers, cash poured into the *Tribune* fund, and food, clothing, seeds, arms and money were sent in quantities to the Free Soil settlers.

On September 8, 1856, John W. Geary, of Pennsylvania, was appointed governor. He issued a 'proclamation of peace, and promised the settlers protection in their persons, pursuits and property. They, therefore, laid down their arms. This was no sooner done than an army from the Southern States attacked Lawrence, which had before been the scene of much violence; but Gov. Geary, calling out the United States troops, finally induced the invaders to retire. On January 26, 1857, the free Legislature met at Topeka, but was dispersed by the United States marshal, who captured several members and threw them into jail at Tecumseh. The pro-slavery people now met in legislature at Lecompton and adopted a resolution calling a convention to frame another State constitution.

Gov. Geary resigned because the pro-slavery United States Senate refused to uphold some of his measures, and Robert J. Walker, of Mississippi, was appointed to succeed him. Gov. Walker guaranteed protection to the settlers on election day, rejected fraudulent returns, condemned both the Lecompton constitution and the methods of promulgation, and started for Washington to prevent Congress from accepting it. The President had officially signed the instrument before the arrival of Gov. Walker, and the latter promptly resigned. J. W. Denver, of California, was appointed to succeed him.

An election was held for the rejection or adoption of the pro-slavery clauses of the Lecompton constitution, December 21, 1856. The Free-State men did not go to the polls, and the fraudulent instrument was therefore adopted by a vote of 6,143 to 569. The pro-slavery Legislature ordered a vote for State officers under the Lecompton constitution, January 4, 1858. The settlers' Legislature then submitted that constitution to the people, as a whole, to be accepted or rejected, this election also to take place on January 4, 1858. It was rejected by a majority of 10,226. Congress, after a long discussion, again sent the Lecompton constitution to a vote of the people, and again it was rejected by a majority of 10,000 votes, on August 3, 1858. Gov. Denver then resigned, and Samuel Medary, of Ohio, succeeded him.

The settlers' Legislature submitted another constitution, which was adopted. Some portions of it proving unsatisfactory, another convention was called, and at last the new constitution, forever prohibiting slavery, was promulgated at Wyandotte, July 4, 1859, and was adopted in October by a 4,000 majority. On December 6, 1859, a State election was held under the new constitution, and Charles Robinson, who had been chosen governor under the first Topeka constitution, in 1856, was once more elected to that office. January 29, 1861, Kansas came into the Union as a free State, and ultimately Nebraska was admitted upon the same conditions.

The facts thus briefly stated constitute the civil history of the struggle in Kansas. A fratricidal war raged over her rich plains for three years. Bloodshed, robbery, devastation and fire spread like a pestilence through her humble settlements, and but a faint shadow of the fearful events of that period is cast upon these pages.

In the final adjustment of these questions in Congress, Stephen A. Douglas, of Illinois, and James S. Green, of Missouri, played a prominent part. Senator Green opposed the views of Mr. Douglas, and, as the acknowledged leader of the pro-slavery party, maintained his ground with rare ability and eloquence. Coming into the Senate, in 1857, during the discussion of the question of the admission of Kansas under the Lecompton constitution, he supported the policy of the administration in speeches distinguished not only by perspicuity of style, but by powers of argument which called forth commendations, even from those who did not share his convictions.

The Dred Scott Decision.—A few days after the inauguration of President Buchanan (1857) the supreme court of the United States delivered the celebrated opinion known in American history as "The Dred Scott Decision."

Dred Scott was a negro slave belonging to Dr. Emerson, who was a surgeon in the army of the United States. In 1834 Dr. Emerson took Scott from the State of Missouri to the military post at Rock Island, Ill., and held him there as a slave until April or May, 1836. At the time last mentioned Dr. Emerson removed Scott to Fort Snelling, Minn., and there held him until 1838. At the latter place Scott was married to a colored woman who had been taken to Fort Snelling by her master in 1835, and had been subsequently sold there to Dr. Emerson. Two children were born of this marriage, and then the whole family were taken back to St. Louis and sold. Dred thereupon brought a complaint of assault and battery against John F. A. Sandford, the purchaser of himself, his wife and children, which was tried in the United States Circuit Court for the District of Missouri.

Before beginning this suit Scott had brought another in the State courts of Missouri for his freedom, on the ground that, having been a resident of a free State and a free Territory, he thereby relieved himself from the chains of bondage and became a citizen of the United States. The inferior court gave judgment in his favor, but on a writ of error to the supreme court of the State the judgment was reversed and the case remanded for a new trial. By consent this action was continued to await decision on the suit for assault and battery against Sandford, brought in the Federal court.

At the conclusion of the trial Scott's attorney asked the court to charge the jury, on the agreed statement of facts, to find for the plaintiff. This was refused, and the jury being instructed that the law was with the defendant, was ordered so to find. The verdict accordingly was that the plaintiff, his wife and children were slaves, as alleged by Sandford, and that therefore they had no rights in the court, and no redress against their master for personal violence.

Scott's attorney filed a bill of exception to the charge of the court, and thereupon carried the case by writ of error to the United States Supreme Court. After a delay of nearly three years a decision was finally reached in March, 1857. Chief Justice Taney, speaking for the court, decided that negroes, whether free or slave, were not citizens of the United States, and that they could not become such by any process known to the constitution; that under the laws of the United States a negro could neither sue nor be sued, and that therefore the court had no jurisdiction of Dred Scott's cause; that a slave was to be regarded in the light of a personal chattel, and that he might be removed from place to place by his owner as any other piece of property; that the constitution gave to every slave holder the right of removing to or through any State or Territory with his slaves, and of returning with them, at will, to a State where slavery was recognized by law; and that therefore the Missouri Compromise of 1820, as well as the compromise measures of 1850, was unconstitutional and void. In these opinions six of the associate justices of the supreme bench—Wayne, Nelson, Grier, Daniel, Campbell and Catron—concurred; while two associates—Judges McLean and Curtis—dissented. The decision of the majority, which was accepted as the opinion of the court, gave great satisfaction to the ultra slave-holding people of the South. Observing that the control of Congress and the Government was slowly passing out of their hands by the tremendous expansion of the North, and the growth of the spirit of freedom, they hoped, before it was too late, to so wall in and hedge about their peculiar institution, that future Congresses would be unable and would not dare attempt to reach it by legislative enactments.

At the North, on the contrary, the decision excited thousands of indignant comments, and much better opposition. This indignation could not be expended in mere words, but crystallized into a well-grounded determination to resist in the free States the enforcement of the laws of the slave States which contravened or were repugnant to their own.

War Mutterings.—The presidential campaign and canvass of 1860 must ever be regarded as one of the most important and exciting in the history of the republic. Four candidates were in the field. The Republican party nominated Abraham Lincoln, on a platform in which opposition to the further extension of slavery was declared to be the vital issue. The Democratic convention, assembled at Charleston, divided on the question of slavery in the Territories, and, after a long and stormy session, the party was disrupted, and the "Southern Rights" delegates withdrew from the convention. They met first at Richmond and afterward at Baltimore, where they nominated for president John C. Breckinridge, of Kentucky. The squatter sovereignty Democrats nominated Stephen A. Douglas —the apostle of popular sovereignty. Still another—the "American" party, or Constitutional Unionists—chose John Bell, of Tennessee, as their candidate.

The contest resulted in the election of Mr. Lincoln. The leaders of the South had declared that his election would be considered as a just cause for the dissolution of the Union. The Government was under the control of the Douglas Democrats, but a majority of the cabinet and a large number of members of Congress in both Houses were supporters of Mr. Breckinridge, and the advocates of disunion. It was now evident that under the new administration all the departments of the Government must pass into the power of the Republican party. Disunion was now possible, but the opportunity would shortly be past. The attitude of President Buchanan favored the measure. He was not himself a disunionist, but he did not consider that he had the constitutional right to coerce a sovereign State. The interval, therefore, between the presidential election of November, 1860, and the inauguration of the following March was improved to its full extent by the political leaders of the South.

Secession.—December 17, 1860, a convention assembled at Charleston, S. C., passed a resolution declaring that the union hitherto existing between that State and others, under the name of the United States of America, was dissolved. The cotton-growing States were almost unanimous in support of the measure. By the 1st of February, 1861, six other States—Mississippi, Florida, Alabama, Georgia, Louisiana and Texas—had withdrawn from the Union. Nearly all the senators and representatives of those States resigned their seats in Congress, and joined the disunion cause.

In the secession conventions there was little opposition to the movement, although in some instances a large minority vote was cast. A few of the speakers denounced disunion as wrong in principle and tending to certain ruin. Alexander H. Stevens, afterward vice-president of the Confederate States, while advocating the doctrine of State sovereignty and the right of secession, spoke against the latter as a practical measure on the ground that it was impolitic and disastrous. Not a few prominent men at the South held similar views, and yet were governed by the opinion of the majority.

On the 4th day of February, 1861, delegates from six of the seceded States met at Montgomery, Ala., and formed a new government under the name of the Confederate States of America. On the 8th of the same month, the government was organized by the election of Jefferson Davis, of Mississippi, as provisional president, and Alexander H. Stevens as vice-president.

In 1850, when the representatives of the slave holders declared in Congress that, unless California should be admitted as a slave State, they would break up the Union, albeit they would do it "calmly and peaceably," Daniel Webster arose in his majesty and uttered this remarkable and prophetic warning:

"I hear with pain, anguish and distress the words secession; peaceable secession! Sir, your eyes and mine are never destined to see that miracle—the dismemberment of this vast country—without convulsion! The breaking up of the fountains of the great deep without ruffling the surface! Who is so foolish as to expect to see such a thing? Sir, he who sees these States now revolving in harmony around a common center, and expects to see them quit their places and fly off without convulsion, may look the next hour to see the heavenly bodies rush from their spheres and jostle against each other in realms of space, without producing the crash of the universe. *There can be no such thing as peaceable secession.* Peaceable secession is an utter impossibility. Is the great constitution under which we live here, covering the whole country, is it to be thawed and melted away by secession, as the snows of the mountains melt under the influence of the vernal sun, disappear almost unobserved and die off? No sir! No sir! I see it as plainly as I see the sun in heaven. *I see disruption must produce such a war as I will not describe in its two-fold character.*"

Hostilities Begun.—The American nation seemed on the verge of ruin. The Government seemed paralyzed. The army was stationed in scattered detachments on remote frontiers. The fleet was dispersed in distant seas. President Buchanan was distracted with hesitancy and the contradictory counsels of his friends. With the exception of Forts Sumter and Moultrie in Charleston Harbor, Fort Pickens near Pensacola, and Fortress Monroe in the Chesapeake, all the important posts in the seceded States had been seized and occupied by the Confederates, even before the organization of their government.

In vain had Gen. Scott, lieutenant-general of the United States army, observing the energy of the Secessionists, repeatedly urged upon the President that strong garrisons be sent to the imperiled fortresses, some of which were indifferently occupied and some not at all. Scott was not allowed to do anything to save the United States forts, or even to send a warning to the handful of soldiers who garrisoned them, until it was too late to avail. Early in January, 1861, the President made a feeble effort to reinforce and provision the garrison at Fort Sumter. The steamer "Star of the West" was sent with men and supplies, but, upon approaching Charleston harbor, it was fired upon by a Confederate battery, and was obliged to return without performing its mission.

In March Abraham Lincoln was inaugurated as President of the United States, and entered upon the duties of his office. William H. Seward, of New York, was chosen Secretary of State; Salmon P. Chase, of Ohio, Secretary of the Treasury; Simon Cameron, of Pennsylvania, Secretary of War, succeeded in the following January by Edwin M. Stanton, and Gideon Welles, Secretary of the Navy. Lincoln declared, both in his inaugural address and in his early official papers, that the efforts of the new administration would be directed to the recovery of the forts, arsenals and other public property which had been seized by the Confederate authorities, and it was with this intention that the first military preparations were made. With the second attempt of the Government to reinforce Fort Sumter came the actual beginning of hostilities.

The defenses of Charleston Harbor were held by Maj. Robert Anderson with only seventy-nine men. He had deemed it prudent to evacuate Fort Moultrie and retire to Sumter, which was situated on an island in front of the city, but at some distance. That occupancy having been decided to be "a menace to the free people of the State," Fort Sumter was attacked by Gen. Beauregard, April 12, 1861, on the order of George W. Randolph, secretary of war for the Confederacy. On the 14th, Maj. Anderson and his gallant little band were forced to surrender, and thus were the fountains of the great deep broken up, deluging the South in blood, and turning her smiling fields to desolation.

On the 15th of April, Lincoln issued a proclamation declaring the South to be in a state of rebellion, and calling for 75,000 militia "to repossess the forts, places and property seized from the Union." He also summoned both Houses of Congress to assemble in extraordinary session on July 4, 1861.

The War of the Rebellion now began in earnest. With the firing on Fort Sumter a radical change took place in the sentiments of a large portion of the Democracy of the North. Every free State, and the slave States of Delaware and Maryland, pledged men and troops to suppress the Rebellion, and such Democratic leaders as Stephen A. Douglas, Matthew H. Carpenter, Daniel S. Dickinson, John J. Crittenden and Benjamin F. Butler announced their hearty support of the President. Jefferson Davis also issued a proclamation, two days later than that of Lincoln, calling upon the "good people of the Confederacy" to rally and drive out "the invaders." On the same day Virginia seceded from the Union; on May 6 Arkansas followed her example, and then North Carolina on the 20th of the same month. In Tennessee, specially East Tennessee, there was a strong opposition to disunion, and it was not until the 8th of June that a secession ordinance could be passed. The people of Maryland were divided in their opinions, but the disunion sentiment prevailed largely. In Missouri, as will presently be seen, the movement resulted in civil war, while in Kentucky the authorities issued a proclamation of neutrality.

On the 19th of April some Massachusetts regiments, passing through Baltimore on their way to Washington, were attacked by the citizens with stones and fire-arms, and three men were killed. This was the first bloodshed of the war. On the preceding day a body of Confederate soldiers advanced on the armory of the United States at Harper's Ferry. The officer in charge destroyed a portion of the vast stores collected there, and then escaped into Pennsylvania. On the 20th of the month, another company of Virginians attacked the great navy yard at Norfolk. The Federal officers commanding fired the buildings, sank the vessels, spiked the guns, and withdrew their forces. Most of the cannons and many of the vessels were afterward recovered by the Confederates, the property thus captured amounting to fully $10,000,000.

The Southern forces poured into Virginia in such numbers that for a time the city of Washington seemed in danger. May 3 the President called for 83,000 more soldiers, whose term of enlistment should be for three years, or during the continuation of the war. Lieut.-Gen. Winfield Scott was made commander-in-chief of the United States forces. As many war ships as could be mustered were sent to blockade the Southern harbors. In the seceded States, also, there were tireless preparation and activity. Richmond was chosen as the capital of the Confederacy. Mr. Davis and the officers of his cabinet had already repaired thither, for the purpose of directing the affairs of the government and the army. So stood the opposing powers in the beginning of the summer of 1861.

It was now evident that a great war, perhaps the greatest in modern times, was about to break over the American nation.

Having thus outlined the causes of the war, and the breaking out of actual hostilities, attention may well be directed to Missouri and the part she bore in the mighty conflict.

The Attitude of Missouri.—The people of Missouri had been deeply involved in the agitation caused by the territorial questions connected with the subject of slavery. Moreover, the State was largely populated by emigrants from Kentucky, Virginia and other Southern States, or by their descendants, and naturally there was a wide-spread sympathy with the secession movement. Nevertheless there was much intelligent conservatism among the people, and they were not, in the language of Gov. Stewart's last message, to be frightened from their property by the past unfriendly legislation of the North, or dragooned into secession by the restrictive legislation of the extreme South.

The General Assembly met in Jefferson City on December 31, 1860, under peculiarly embarrassing circumstances. Ten days before it convened South Carolina had passed an ordinance of secession, and before the 20th of January four other Southern States had followed her example. Besides this, the preceding national and State canvass had resulted in returning to the State Legislature representatives of each of the four political parties into which the people were divided. There were, in each branch of the General Assembly, Breckinridge Democrats, Douglas Democrats, Union or Bell-Everett men, and Republicans, and in neither Senate nor House was any one of these parties dominant. January 4, 1861, Claiborne F. Jackson, author of the famous "Jackson Resolutions," was inaugurated as governor, having been elected by the Douglas Democrats. While Gov. Stewart's farewell message concluded with an eloquent appeal for the maintenance of the Union, as he depicted the inevitable ruin and bloodshed that must attend secession, Gov. Jackson's inaugural insisted that the interests of all the slave-holding States were identical; that in case the Union was really divided, it would be the duty and privilege of Missouri to stand by the South; that the State was in favor of remaining in the Union as long as there was any hope of maintaining the guarantees of the constitution, but that, in any event, he was utterly opposed to coercion.

Believing that Missouri was entitled to a voice in the settlement of the questions then pending in the country, he recommended the immediate call of a State convention, that the will of the people might be ascertained. Such a convention was called by Gov. Jackson, in accordance with an act of the Legislature, and met at Jefferson City, February 28, 1861. Each senatorial district sent to this convention three times as many delegates as the number of members in the State Senate to which said district was entitled. In all ninety-nine members were present, and the convention was permanently organized by the election of the following officers: Sterling Price, of Chariton County, president (he was then regarded as a decided Union man); Robert Wilson, of Andrew County, vice-president; Samuel A. Lowe, of Pettis, secretary; Robert A. Campbell, of St. Louis, assistant secretary; C. P. Anderson, of Moniteau, doorkeeper; B. W. Grover, sergeant-at-arms.

On March 9, during an adjourned meeting at St. Louis, Mr. Gamble, chairman of the Committee on Federal Relations, reported from the majority of that committee a list of resolutions, which after some amendments were adopted by the convention, which thus refused to pass the ordinance of secession.

The amended resolutions are as follows:

1. *Resolved*, That at present there is no adequate cause to impel Missouri to dissolve her connection with the Federal Union, but on the contrary, she will labor for such an adjustment of existing troubles as will secure the peace, as well as the rights and equality of all the States.

2. *Resolved*, That the people of this State are devotedly attached to the institutions of our country, and earnestly desire that by a fair and amicable adjustment all the causes of disagreement that at present unfortunately distract us as a people, may be removed, to the end that our Union may be preserved and perpetuated, and peace and harmony be restored between the North and South.

3. *Resolved*, That the people of this State deem the amendments to the Constitution of the United States, proposed by the Hon. John J. Crittenden, of Kentucky, with the extension of the same to the territory hereafter to be acquired by treaty or otherwise, a basis of adjustment which will successfully remove the causes of difference forever from the arena of national politics.

4. *Resolved*, That the people of Missouri believe the peace and quiet of the country will be promoted by a convention to propose amendments to the Constitution of the United States, and this convention therefore urges the Legislature of this State and the other States to take the proper steps for calling such a convention in pursuance of the fifth article of the constitution; and by providing by law for an election by the people of such number of delegates as are to be sent to such convention.

5. *Resolved*, That in the opinion of this convention the employment of military force by the Federal Government to coerce the submission of the seceding States, or the employment of military force by the seceding States to assail the Government of the United States, will inevitably plunge this country into civil war, and thereby entirely extinguish the hope of an amicable settlement of the fearful issues now pending before the country; we, therefore, earnestly entreat, as well the Federal Government as the seceding States, to withhold and stay the arm of military power, and on no pretense whatever bring upon the nation the horrors of civil war. And in order to the restoration of harmony and fraternal feeling between the different sections, we would recommend the policy of withdrawing the Federal troops from the forts within the borders of the seceding States, when there is danger of collision between the State and Federal troops.

The sixth and seventh resolutions we omit because they have

no reference to war questions. Two of the resolutions will attract the attention of every intelligent reader: the first, containing the explicit declaration that there was no adequate cause to impel Missouri to dissolve her connection with the Federal Union; and the fifth, wherein the convention took uncompromising ground against the employment of military force by either the seceding States or the nation.

It was with the earnest and patriotic purpose of averting civil war that the Union men of Missouri, Kentucky, Tennessee and other slave States entreated the Federal Government not to resort to military force, but after the firing upon Fort Sumter and other violent and unmistakably rebellious acts, these patriots assumed more extreme views.

Gov. Jackson and the Missouri Legislature.—Upon President Lincoln's call for 75,000 men, Simon Cameron, Secretary of War, issued a telegram to all of the loyal and doubtful States, requesting each of them to detail from the militia of the State a certain number of men, as infantry or riflemen, for a period of three months.

Missouri's quota was fixed at four regiments, which Gov. Jackson was requested to furnish. The following was his reply:

EXECUTIVE DEPARTMENT OF MISSOURI,
JEFFERSON CITY, April 17, 1861.

To the Hon. Simon Cameron, Secretary of War, Washington, D. C.,

SIR:—Your dispatch of the 15th inst., making a call on Missouri for four regiments of men for immediate service has been received. There can be, I apprehend, no doubt but these men are intended to form a part of the President's army to make war upon the people of the seceded States. Your requisition, in my judgment, is illegal, unconstitutional and revolutionary in its objects, inhuman and diabolical, and cannot be complied with. Not one man will the State of Missouri furnish to carry on such an unholy crusade.

C. F. JACKSON,
Governor of Missouri.

Pursuant to a proclamation of Gov. Jackson, the State Legislature convened in extra session May 2, 1861. In his message to that body, the governor reiterated the declaration that the interests and sympathies of Missouri were identical with those of the slave-holding States, and recommended the policy of arming the people and placing the State in an attitude of defense.

The Legislature responded by passing several important measures, among which were the following: To authorize counties to loan money, not exceeding $30,000 each, to the State; to authorize the banks of Missouri to issue $1, $2, and $3 notes to the amount of $1,500,000, instead of the same amount of larger notes; to authorize the governor to purchase or lease David Ballentine's foundry at Boonville for the manufacture of arms and the munitions of war; to authorize the governor to appoint one major-general, who, in time of insurrection, invasion, or war, should command the entire military force in the field; to authorize the governor, whenever in his opinion the security and welfare of the State might require it, to take possession of the railroad and telegraph lines within the State; to provide for the organization, government and support of the "Missouri State Guard;" and to authorize the governor to borrow $1,000,000 to arm and equip the militia of the State, to repel invasion, and protect the lives and property of the people.

MILITARY HISTORY.

Surrender of Camp Jackson.—Into the midst of this body of busy legislators dropped the news of the capture of Camp Jackson, at St. Louis.

By order of Gov. Jackson, the United States arsenal at Liberty, Clay County, had been seized April 20, 1861, and on the same day of the governor's proclamation calling an extra session of the General Assembly the following general military order was issued by Warwick Hough, then adjutant-general of Missouri:

(*General Orders No. 7.*)
HEADQUARTERS ADJUTANT-GENERAL'S OFFICE, MO.,
JEFFERSON CITY, April 22, 1861.

First. To attain a greater degree of efficiency and perfection in organization and discipline, the commanding officers of the several military districts in this State, having four or more legally organized companies therein, whose armories are within fifteen miles of each other, will assemble their respective commands at some place to be by them severally designated, on the 3d of May, and to go into an encampment for the period of six days, as provided by law. Captains of companies not organized into battalions will report the strength of their companies immediately to these headquarters, and await further orders.

Second. The quartermaster-general will procure and issue to the quartermasters of districts, for those commands not now provided for, all necessary tents and camp equipage, to enable the commanding officers thereof to carry the foregoing orders into effect.

Third. The light battery now attached to the Southwest Battalion, and one company of mounted riflemen, including all officers and soldiers belonging to the First District, will proceed forthwith to St. Louis, and report to Gen. D. M. Frost for duty. The remaining companies of said battalion will be disbanded for the pupose of assisting in the organization of companies upon that frontier. The details in the execution of the foregoing are intrusted to Lieut.-Col. John S. Bowen, commanding the battalion.

Fourth. The strength, organization and equipment of the several companies in the districts will be reported at once to these headquarters, and division inspectors will furnish all information which may be serviceable in ascertaining the condition of the State forces.

By order of the Governor.

WARWICK HOUGH,
Adjutant-General of Missouri.

Pursuant to this order, the military encampment of Camp Jackson, at Lindell's Grove, St. Louis, was organized May 3, by Brig.-Gen. Daniel M. Frost, of the Missouri Militia. Its object, as stated above, was said to be the attainment of greater efficiency in the organization and drill of the State troops, but there seemed to be reason for the suspicion, entertained by officers of the United States Army, that Gov. Jackson, Gen. Frost and their confréres had some ulterior purpose in view. This purpose was believed by many to be nothing less than the seizure of the United States arsenal at St. Louis, and the military control of the State by those who, notwithstanding the anti-secession voice of the people, were determined to link her destinies with the Confederacy.

The stars and stripes floated over Camp Jackson, yet Capt. Nathaniel Lyon, commandant of the arsenal, had in view the sentiments of Gov. Jackson's inaugural and of his more recent message to the Legislature, his response to the requisition of the Secretary of War, the seizure of the arsenal at Liberty, and the fact that two of the streets in the new camp were called "Davis" and "Beauregard," after two of the most prominent leaders of the Rebellion. Also Capt. Lyon discovered that cannon and mortars in boxes, marked "Marble," and shot and shell in barrels, had been landed at the St. Louis wharf and hauled to Camp Jackson.

On the morning of May 10, Gen. Frost, having been informed

that the United States troops were preparing for an attack upon his camp, addressed the following note to Capt. Lyon:

HEADQUARTERS CAMP JACKSON,
MISSOURI MILITIA, May 10, 1861.

Capt. N. Lyon, Commanding United States Troops in and about St. Louis Arsenal,

SIR:—I am constantly in receipt of information that you contemplate an attack upon my camp, whilst I understand that you are impressed with the idea that an attack upon the arsenal and United States troops is intended on the part of the militia of Missouri. I am greatly at a loss to know what could justify you in attacking citizens of the United States who are in the lawful performance of duties devolving upon them under the constitution in organizing and instructing the militia of the State in obedience to her laws, and therefore have been disposed to doubt the correctness of the information I have received.

I would be glad to know from you, personally, whether there is any truth in the statements that are constantly pouring into my ears. So far as regards any hostility being intendent toward the United States, its property, or representatives by any portion of my command, or as far as I can learn (and I think I am fully informed) of any other part of the State forces, I can positively say that the idea has never been entertained. On the contrary, prior to your taking command of the arsenal, I proffered to Maj. Bell, then in command of the very few troops constituting its guard, the services of myself and all my command, and if necessary, the whole power of the State, to protect the United States in the full possession of all her property. Upon Gen. Harney's taking command of this department, I made the same proffer of services to him, and authorized his adjutant-general, Capt. Williams, to communicate the fact that such had been done to the war department. I have had no occasion since to change any of the views I entertained at that time, neither of my own volition nor through orders of my constitutional commander.

I trust that after this explicit statement we may be able, by fully understanding each other, to keep far from our borders the misfortunes which so unhappily affect our common country.

This communication will be handed to you by Col. Bowen, my chief of staff, who will be able to explain anything not fully set forth in the foregoing.

I am, sir, very respectfully, your obedient servant,

BRIG.-GEN. D. M. FROST,
Commanding Camp Jackson M. V. M.

On the day of this communication, and perhaps at the very hour of its writing, Capt. Lyon was making active preparations to march upon Camp Jackson. It was said that he refused to receive the communication from Gen. Frost.

Between 2 and 3 o'clock on the afternoon of the same day Gen. Frost received a note from Capt. Lyon, as follows:

HEADQUARTERS UNITED STATES TROOPS,
ST. LOUIS, MO., May 10, 1861.

Gen. D. M. Frost, Commanding Camp Jackson,

SIR:—Your command is regarded as evidently hostile toward the Government of the United States.

It is, for the most part, made up of those secessionists who have openly avowed their hostility to the general Government, and have been plotting at the seizure of its property and the overthrow of its authority. You are openly in communication with the so-called Southern Confederacy, which is now at war with the United States, and you are receiving at your camp, from the said Confederacy, and under its flag, large supplies of the material of war, most of which is known to be the property of the United States. These extraordinary preparations plainly indicate none other than the well-known purpose of the governor of this State, under whose orders you are acting, and whose purpose, recently communicated to the Legislature, has just been responded to by that body in the most unparalleled legislation, having in direct view hostilities to the General Government and co-operation with its enemies.

In view of these considerations, and of your failure to disperse in obedience to the proclamation of the President, and of the eminent necessities of State policy and warfare, and the obligations imposed upon me by instructions from Washington, it is my duty to demand, and I do hereby demand, of you an immediate surrender of your command, with no other conditions than that all persons surrendering, under this demand, shall be humanely and kindly treated. Believing myself prepared to enforce this demand, one-half hour's time before doing so will be allowed for your compliance therewith.

Very respectfully, your obedient servant,   N. LYON,
Capt. Second Infantry, Commanding Troops.

Capt. Lyon's command numbered between 6,000 and 7,000 men, and about twenty pieces of artillery. With this force he rapidly invested Camp Jackson, planting batteries on the overlooking heights, and allowing none to pass the lines thus formed. Many of the citizens seized whatever weapons they could lay their hands upon, and rushed to the assistance of the State troops, but were, of course, foiled in their design. Men, and numbers of women and children, flocked to the neighboring hills, wishing to obtain a view of the scene, and thinking themselves out of harm's way. Upon the receipt of Capt. Lyon's communication, Gen. Frost called a hasty consultation of the officers of his staff, and as resistance seemed mere recklessness, a surrender upon the proposed terms was quickly agreed to. The State troops were therefore made prisoners of war, but an offer was made to release them on condition that they would take an oath to support the constitution of the United States, and would swear not to take up arms against the Government.

All but eight or ten men refused to accede to these terms, on the ground that having already sworn allegiance to the United States and its Government, repeating their oath would be to admit that they had been in rebellion, which they would not concede.

About half past five o'clock the prisoners of war left their camp, and entered the road, the United States soldiers enclosing them by a single file on each side of their line. Suddenly the report of fire-arms was heard from the front of the column, which was then opposite a small hill, on the left as one approaches the city. It seems that some members of the United States companies, upon being pressed by the crowd and receiving some blows from them, turned, and, without orders, discharged their pieces. No one was injured, and the offending soldiers were immediately placed under arrest. Hardly, however, had quiet been restored, when repeated volleys of musketry were heard from the extreme rear ranks, which were still at the entrance to the grove, and the crowd of spectators were seen running wildly from the spot. Many, even while escaping, were shot down, and the wounded and dying made the late beautiful field look like a battle-ground. The total number of citizens killed was twenty-eight, including two ladies; the wounded numbered about twenty-five. On the part of the Federals, one officer, Capt. C. Blandowski, and one private were killed and a dozen men wounded. As in the disturbance at the other end of the line, the arsenal troops were attacked with stones, and shots were discharged at them before they fired. Not until he himself had been seriously wounded did Capt. Blandowski give the order to fire on the mob.*

Gen. Frost's command was marched to the arsenal, and there remained, as prisoners of war, until the following day. They were then released, every man, Capt. Emmet McDonald excepted, subscribing to the following parole:

St. Louis Arsenal, May 11, 1861.

We, the undersigned, do pledge our words as gentlemen that we will not take up arms nor serve in any military capacity against the United States, during the present civil war. This parole shall be returned upon our surrendering ourselves, at any time, as prisoners of war. While we make this pledge with the full intention of observing it, we hereby protest against the injustice of its exaction.

The following letter, written by Gen. Frost to Gov. Jackson, and dated January 24, 1861, was afterward captured with other Con-

---

*In his report of the affair Gen. Lyon says: "The sad results are much to be lamented. The killing of innocent men, women and children is deplorable. There was no intention to fire upon peaceable citizens. The regular troops were over in the camp, beyond the mob, and in range of the firing. The troops manifested every forbearance, and at last discharged their guns in simply obeying the impulse, natural to all, of self-defense. If innocent men, women and children, whose curiosity placed them in a dangerous position, suffered with the guilty, it is no fault of the troops."

federate records. It pours a flood of light upon the events which transpired previous to the beginning of the war in Missouri. Maj. Bell, it will be remembered, was superseded by Capt. Lyon, as commandant at the arsenal:

ST. LOUIS, MO., January 24, 1861.

His Excellency, C. F. Jackson, Governor of Missouri,

DEAR SIR:—I have just returned from the arsenal, where I have had an interview with Maj. Bell, the commanding officer of that place. I found the Major everything that you or I could desire. He assured me that he considered that Missouri had, whenever the time came, a right to claim it as being upon her soil. He asserted his determination to defend it against any and all irresponsible mobs, come from whence they might, but at the same time gave me to understand that he would not attempt any defense against the proper State authorities.

He promised me, upon the honor of an officer and a gentleman, that he would not suffer any arms to be removed from the place without first giving me timely information; and I, in return, promised him that I would use all the force at my command to prevent him being annoyed by irresponsible persons. I at the same time gave him notice that if affairs assumed so threatening a character as to render it unsafe to leave the place in its comparatively unprotected condition, that I might come down and quarter a proper force there to protect it from the assaults of any persons whatsoever, to which he assented. In a word, the Major is with us, where he ought to be, for all his worldly wealth lies here in St. Louis (and it is very large), and then, again, his sympathies are with us.

I shall, therefore, rest perfectly easy, and use all my influence to stop the sensationalists from attracting the particular attention of the Government to this particular spot. The telegraphs you received were the sheerest "canards" of persons who, without discretion, are extremely anxious to show their zeal. I shall be thoroughly prepared with the proper force to act as emergency may require. The use of force will only be resorted to when nothing else will avail to prevent the shipment or removal of arms.

The Major informed me that he had arms for 40,000 men, with all the appliances to manufacture munitions of almost every kind.

This arsenal, if properly looked after, will be everything to our State, and I intend to look after it—very quietly, however. I have every confidence in the word of honor pledged to me by the Major, and would as soon think of doubting the oath of the best man in the community.

His idea is that it would be disgraceful to him as a military man to surrender to a mob, whilst he could do so without compromising his dignity to the State authorities. Of course I did not show him your order, but I informed him that you had authorized me to act as I might think proper to protect the public property.

He desired that I would not divulge his peculiar views, which I promised not to do except to yourself. I beg, therefore, that you will say nothing that might compromise him eventually with the General Government, for thereby I would be placed in an awkward position, whilst he would probably be removed, which would be unpleasant to our interests.

Grimsley, as you doubtless know, is an unconscionable jackass, and only desires to make himself notorious. It was through him that McLaren and George made the mistake of telegraphing a falsehood to you.

I should be pleased to hear whether you approve of the course I have adopted, and if not, I am ready to take any other that you, as my commander, may suggest.

I am, sir, most truly,
Your obedient servant,
D. M. FROST.

Upon the capture of Camp Jackson, and the consequent disastrous collision between some of the United States troops and the people, the wildest excitement prevailed throughout the State. The most sensational reports flew abroad of the brutal murder of men, women and children by an infuriated soldiery, of their charge with fixed bayonets upon an unoffending crowd of citizens, and of their committing the most horrid outrages upon these innocent victims. People in various localities rose to avenge the reported terrible slaughter, and the whole State was in a frenzy of indignation.

Final Efforts Toward Conciliation.—Two days after the capture of Camp Jackson, Brig.-Gen. William S. Harney, commandant of the department, returned to St. Louis from Washington, and issued a proclamation, in which he called upon the people to resume their accustomed peaceful vocations, and assured them that he would only use "the military force stationed in this district in the last resort to preserve the peace."

After two more days, Gen. Harney issued a second proclamation in which he characterized the "Military Bill," passed by the recent Legislature, as "an indirect secession ordinance, ignoring even the forms resorted to by other States," and as unconstitutional and void. He spoke approvingly of the overthrow of Camp Jackson, upon the ground that it had been "organized in the interests of the secessionists," the men openly wearing the dress and badge of the Southern Confederacy; and that arms had been received into the camp which had been unlawfully taken from the United States arsenal at Baton Rouge, and shipped up the river in boxes marked "marble." He declared that "no government in the world would be entitled to respect, that would tolerate for a moment, such openly treasonable preparations;" but added that it was but simple justice to suppose that there were many loyal men in the camp who were in no way responsible for its treasonable character. He disclaimed all intention of interfering with the prerogatives of the State, but expressed in plain terms that the "supreme law of the land must be obeyed, and that no subterfuges, whether in the form of legislative acts or otherwise," could be permitted to harass the law-abiding people of Missouri. He promised that his authority should be used to protect their persons and property, and that he would suppress all unlawful combinations of men formed under any pretext whatsoever.

Gen. Harney's policy was to preserve peace as long as it could be done, and the authority of the National Government preserved. Accordingly, he held a conference at St. Louis, May 21, 1861, with Gen. Sterling Price, whom Gov. Jackson had placed at the head of the Missouri State Guard, which resulted in an amicable agreement, signed by both generals, which undertook to calm the popular excitement and prevent further bloodshed.

The authorities at Washington disapproved of the Harney-Price compact, and they had already given orders that Capt. Lyon should succeed the former general in command of the department. Before, however, the order for his displacement reached him, Gen. Harney, in consequence of his agreement with Gen. Price, removed the Federal troops from the suburbs of St. Louis, Col. Sigel's regiment remaining at the arsenal. Gov. Jackson and Gen. Price, on their part, disbanded the State troops at Jefferson City and St. Joseph, and ordered them home, there to drill and receive military instruction.

Another conference was held in St. Louis between Gen. Lyon, Col. Frank P. Blair, Jr., and Maj. F. A. Conant, on one side, and Gov. C. F. Jackson, Gen. Sterling Price and Col. Thomas L. Snead, on the other. The interview lasted six hours, but resulted in nothing except to make the terrible truth evident that their differences could not be peaceably adjusted.

This final effort at conciliation having failed, Gov. Jackson and his associates left for Jefferson City the same night, burning railroad bridges and cutting the telegraph wires behind them.

Proclamation by Gov. Jackson.—On the next day (June 12) Gov. Jackson issued a proclamation, calling into active service

50,000 State Militia "for the purpose of repelling invasion, and for the protection of the lives, liberty and property of the citizens of this State." He instructed the people that their first allegiance was due to their own State; that they were "under no obligation, whatever, to obey the unconstitutional edicts of the military despotism which had enthroned itself at Washington, nor submit to the infamous and degrading sway of its wicked minions in this State." He declared that no brave and true-hearted Missourian would obey the one or submit to the other; and he called upon them to rise and "drive out ignominiously the invaders who have dared to desecrate the soil which your labors have made fruitful, and which is consecrated by your homes." This proclamation was the signal for civil war in Missouri, and immediately upon its publication active military movements within the State began.

The Legislature Again.—The "Missouri State Guard" bill was before the Legislature, and was meeting with much opposition, when the news of the attack on Camp Jackson so affected the minds of the legislators that they passed the act in less than fifteen minutes.

About 11 o'clock the same night the whole city of Jefferson was aroused by the pealing of bells and the shouts of men summoning the Legislature to the Capitol. There they went into secret session until past 3 o'clock in the morning. The cause of this sudden panic was the reception of a telegram, afterward asserted to be bogus, to the effect that 2,000 Federal troops would leave St. Louis that night for the express purpose of capturing the governor, State officers and members of the Legislature, then convened at Jefferson City. To prevent this anticipated raid the railroad bridge across the Osage River was burned, and the next day 12,000 kegs of powder were sent off in wagons to secret places of safety, while the money in the State Treasury was moved out of town to keep it out of the hands of the expected marauders. When the truth became known, comparative quiet was restored.

In accordance with the power conferred upon Gov. Jackson by an act of the Legislature before mentioned, he appointed Sterling Price major-general of the Missouri State Guard.

On the day before the final adjournment, Mr. George G. Vest, now a resident of Kansas City and a United States senator, made the following report to the House of Representatives from the Committee on Federal Relations.

WHEREAS, We have learned with astonishment and indignation that troops in the service of the Federal Government have surrounded and taken prisoners of war the encampment of State Militia lately assembled near the city of St. Louis, in pursuance of law and by command of the Governor, for the purpose alone of military instruction; and

WHEREAS, The United States troops aforesaid, assisted by a mob armed under Federal authority, have also murdered with unparalleled atrocity defenseless men, women and children, citizens of Missouri, lawfully and peacefully assembled: now, therefore,

Resolved by the House of Representatives, the Senate concurring therein, That we, the representatives of the people of Missouri, in general assembly convened, do hereby protest to the civilized world, and especially our sister States, against this illegal, unchristian and inhuman violation of our rights by the capture of our militia, assembled under the constitution of the United States, and the constitution of the State, and the murder of our defenseless people.

Resolved, Second, That whilst Missouri has been loyal to the Government, struggling for its reconstruction, and is now sincerely desirous of an honorable adjustment of existing difficulties, she has received as reward for her fidelity from persons assuming to act under Federal authority, unparalleled insult and wrong. An armed despotism, under infuriated partisan leaders, has been inaugurated in our midst, controlled by no law but passion, and actuated by the deepest hate against the people of Missouri and their institutions. Our railroads are now under military occupation. The steamboat "C. E. Hilman," engaged in transporting goods from the city of St. Louis to the city of Nashville, has been seized by Government troops within the jurisdiction of this State, and the cargo taken out. The capital of the State is openly threatened with capture, and our session is now being held in the midst of armed citizens hastily assembled for defense.

Resolved, Third, That it is the unquestioned constitutional right of the State to arm, equip and organize her militia for defense against aggression from any quarter; and the attempt of Capt. Lyon, acting, as he says, under authority from Washington, to use the exercise of this right as an excuse for his conduct evinces but too clearly a disposition upon the part of the authorities at Washington to disregard and trample upon the sacred rights of the people of Missouri.

Resolved, Fourth, That the charge of Capt. Lyon, in his letter to Gen. Frost, that the proceedings of the State authorities or of this general assembly, at any time, furnished a pretext for the course pursued by him, is entirely gratuitous and false.

Resolved, Fifth, That the governor of the State be hereby directed to make demand of the President of the United States, whether these outrages have been authorized by the Government, and for the immediate return of the arms, camp equipage and other property belonging to this State, lately taken from our military near St. Louis, and for the unconditional release of our State troops.

Resolved, Sixth, That the Government be requested to take instant action by calling forth the militia of the State for the purpose of defense; and that the people of Missouri should rally as one man to perish, if necessary, in defending their constitutional rights.

Resolved, That the governor be requested to furnish a copy of the foregoing preamble and resolutions to the President of the United States and to the governor of each of the States.

That these resolutions were passed in the House without a single dissenting vote is an evidence of the extraordinary excitement which prevailed, not only among the people, but also in the Legislature.

Immediately upon the adjournment of that body Gov. Jackson and the larger part of the State officers abandoned the capital, believing that delay would probably result in their falling into the hands of the United States militia and becoming prisoners of war. In September Gov. Jackson issued a proclamation, calling the General Assembly to meet in extra session at Neosho, Newton County, on the 21st day of October. At the time this official act was performed the governor was a fugitive from the State capital, and the State Convention, on the 31st of July, had declared his seat vacant, together with those of the members of the Legislature; and on the same day had invested Hamilton R. Gamble with the authority and obligations of Governor of Missouri.

Gov. Jackson's proclamation declared that the United States authorities had, "in violation of the constitution of the United States, waged a ruthless war upon the people of the State of Missouri, murdering our citizens, destroying our property, and, as far as in their power lay, desolating our land. I have in vain endeavored to secure your constitutional rights by peaceable means, and have only resorted to war when it became necessary to repel the most cruel and long-continued aggressions. War now exists between the State of Missouri and the Federal Government, and the state of war is incompatible with the continuance of our union of that Government. Therefore, for the purpose of giving to the representatives of the people of Missouri an opportunity of determining whether it be proper now to dissolve the constitutional bonds which binds us to the Government of the United States, when all other bonds between us are broken, I, Claiborne F. Jackson," etc.

In response to this proclamation, thirty-nine members of the

House and ten members of the Senate assembled at Neosho in October. The proceedings of the Senate, afterward captured, show that during the first few days nothing was done but bring in absent members. In order to constitute a quorum there must have been present sixty-seven members of the House and seventeen members of the Senate. As it was impossible to muster that number, Gov. Jackson's message was read to those who were present. He recommended the passage of an ordinance of secession, and also the passage of a law authorizing the election of senators and representatives to the Confederate Congress.

An act, declaring the union between Missouri and the United States dissolved, passed both houses of this fragmentary Legislature, and as far as that body was concerned the connection between the State and the General Government was broken. This Senate met again at Cassville, Barry County, October 31, 1861, and November 7, adjourning to meet at New Madrid on the first Monday in March, 1862; but that meeting was never held. Gov. Jackson's death occurred December 6, 1862, at a farmhouse on the Arkansas River, opposite Little Rock.

The State Convention—Further Transactions.—On the 31st of July, 1861, this body elected Hamilton R. Gamble, Willard P. Hall and Mordecai Oliver, respectively, Governor, Lieutenant-Governor and Secretary of State, to succeed Claiborne F. Jackson, Thomas C. Reynolds and Benjamin F. Massey, whose seats had been declared vacant.

At another session, held in St. Louis, and beginning October 10, 1861, the board of public works and the offices of State superintendent of public schools and county school commissioners were abolished, the salaries of all civil officers were reduced 20 per cent, and test oaths of loyalty for civil officers and citizens were authoritatively promulgated.

On June 2, 1862, the convention assembled at Jefferson City, declared vacant the seats of Sterling Price, late president of the convention, and of others who had joined the secessionists; laid upon the table an ordinance offered by Mr. Breckinridge providing for the gradual emancipation of the slaves in the State; passed an ordinance continuing the provisional government until August, 1864, at which time, according to arrangements already made, their successors would be elected and qualified, and provided that no person should vote at any election thereafter held in the State, under its constitution and laws, who should not previously take the following oath:

I, ———, do solemnly swear (or affirm as the case may be) that I will support, protect and defend the constitution of the United States, and the constitution of the State of Missouri, against all enemies or opposers, whether domestic or foreign; that I will bear true faith, loyalty and allegiance to the United States, and will not, directly or indirectly, give aid or comfort, or countenance to the enemies or opposers thereof, or of the provisional government of the State of Missouri, any ordinance, law or resolution of any State convention or Legislature, or of any order or organization, secret or otherwise, to the contrary notwithstanding; and that I do this with a full and honest determination, pledge and purpose, faithfully to keep and perform the same, without any mental reservation or evasion whatever. And I do solemnly swear (or affirm) that I have not since the 17th day of December, A. D. 1861, wilfully taken up arms, or levied war against the United States, or against the provisional government of the State of Missouri. So help me God.

A similar oath was prescribed for all civil officers, and for jurymen and attorneys.

On June 15, 1863, pursuant to a proclamation from Gov. Gamble, the convention met to devise measures for the gradual emancipation of the slaves. Without especially noting the action of the convention on the various propositions submitted or the several amendments to these propositions, it is enough to say that on July 1, the fifteenth day of the session, the ordinance as amended was passed. It is as follows:

Be it ordained by the people of the State of Missouri in convention assembled:

SECTION 1. The first and second clauses of the twenty-sixth section of the third article of the constitution are hereby abrogated.

SEC. 2. That slavery and involuntary servitude, except for the punishment of crime, shall cease to exist in Missouri on the 4th day of July, 1870, and all slaves within the State at that day are hereby declared to be free; *Provided, however,* That all persons emancipated by this ordinance shall remain under the control, and be subject to the authority of their late owners or their legal representatives, as servants, during the following period, to-wit: Those over forty years for and during their lives; those under twelve years of age until they arrive at the age of twenty-three years, and those of all other ages until the 4th of July, 1870. The persons or their legal representatives, who up to the moment of the emancipation were the owners of the slaves thus freed, shall, during the period for which the services of such freed men are reserved to them, have the same authority and control over the said freed men for the purpose of receiving the possession and service of the same, that are now held absolutely by the master in respect to his slave; *Provided, however,* That after the said 4th day of July, 1870, no person so held to service shall be sold to a non-resident of or removed from the State of Missouri by authority of his late owner or his legal representatives.

SEC. 3. That all slaves hereafter brought into this State, and not now belonging to citizens of this State, shall thereupon be free.

SEC. 4. All slaves removed by consent of their owners to any seceded State, after the passage by such State of an act or ordinance of secession, and hereafter brought into this State by their owners, shall thereupon be free.

SEC. 5. The General Assembly shall have no power to pass laws to emancipate slaves without the consent of their owners.

SEC. 6. After the passage of this ordinance no slaves in this State shall be subject to State, county or municipal taxes.

Wednesday, July 1, 1863, the convention, after having held various sessions, since its first meeting, February 28, 1861, adjourned *sine die*.

Emancipation Proclamation and the XIIIth Amendment.—In connection with the emancipation measures of the State of Missouri, it may not be amiss to give a brief recital of the various means by which slavery in the United States was finally obliterated.

President Lincoln's policy was for some time criticised as timid and slow. His more hardy and aggressive advisers demanded that the negroes be either emancipated or declared contraband of war at once, as the Southern armies could never be beaten while 4,000,000 of blacks, without cost or remuneration, were at home tilling the soil for the support of the whites in the field. After waiting long enough to see that the South did not want peace upon any terms save a permanent withdrawal from the Union, and recognition by the North as an independent, sovereign power, he issued a provisional proclamation of emancipation on September 22, 1862. On the 1st of January, 1863, the President issued one of the most important documents of modern times—the emancipation proclamation. This could have been defended throughout the world as an act of progressive and civilized humanity, but it was in reality a war measure, it having become necessary to strike an effective blow against the labor system at the South, and as such was fully sanctioned by the laws and usages of nations. This proclamation is here given in full:

WHEREAS, On the 22d day of September, 1862, a proclamation was issued by the President of the United States, containing among other things the following, to wit:

"That on the first day of January, 1863, all persons held as slaves within any

State, or designated part of a State, the people whereof shall then be in rebellion against the United States, shall be then, thenceforward and forever free, and the Executive Government of the United States, including the military and naval authority thereof, will recognize and maintain the freedom of such persons, and will do no act or acts to repress such persons, or any of them, in any efforts they may make for their actual freedom.

"That the Executive will, on the 1st day of January, aforesaid, by proclamation, designate the States and parts of States, if any, in which the people thereof, respectively, shall then be in rebellion against the United States, and the fact that any State, or the people thereof, shall on that day be in good faith represented in the Congress of the United States by members chosen thereto, at elections wherein a majority of the qualified voters of such State shall have participated, shall, in the absence of strong countervailing testimony, be deemed conclusive evidence that such State and the people thereof are not then in rebellion against the United States."

Now, therefore, I, Abraham Lincoln, President of the United States, by virtue of the power in me vested as commander-in-chief of the army and navy of the United States, in time of actual armed rebellion against the authority and Government of the United States, and as a fit and necessary war measure for suppressing said rebellion, do, on this 1st day of January, 1863, and, in accordance with my purpose so to do, publicly proclaim for the full period of 100 days from the day first above mentioned, order and designate, as the States and parts of States wherein the people thereof, respectively, are this day in rebellion against the United States, the following, to wit:

Arkansas, Texas, Louisiana (except the parishes of St. Bernard, Plaquemine, Jefferson, St. John, St. Charles, St. James, Ascension, Assumption, Terre Bonne, Lafourche, St. Mary, St. Martin and Orleans, including the city of New Orleans), Mississippi, Alabama, Florida, Georgia, South Carolina, North Carolina and Virginia (except the forty-eight counties designated as West Virginia, and also the counties of Berkley, Accomac, Northampton, Elizabeth City, York, Princess Ann and Norfolk, including the cities of Norfolk and Portsmouth), and which excepted parts are, for the present, left precisely as if this proclamation were not issued.

And by virtue of the power and for the purpose aforesaid I do order and declare that all persons held as slaves within said designated States and parts of States are and henceforward shall be free; and that the Executive Government of the United States, including the military and naval authorities thereof, will recognize and maintain the freedom of such persons.

And I hereby enjoin upon the people so declared to be free, to abstain from all violence, unless in necessary self-defense, and I recommend to them that in all cases, when allowed, they labor faithfully for reasonable wages.

And I further declare and make known, that such persons of suitable condition will be received into the armed service of the United States to garrison forts, positions, stations and other places, and to man vessels of all sorts in said service.

And upon this act, sincerely believed to be an act of justice, warranted by the constitution, upon military necessity, I invoke the considerate judgment of mankind and the gracious favor of Almighty God.

In testimony whereof I have hereunto set my name, and caused the seal of the United States to be affixed.

[L. S.] Done at the City of Washington, this first day of January, in the year of our Lord one thousand eight hundred and sixty-three, and of the Independence of the United States the eighty-seventh. ABRAHAM LINCOLN.
By the President:
 WILLIAM H. SEWARD,
  Secretary of State.

As the State of Missouri was loyal to the Union, and was at the time of the proclamation represented in Congress by her chosen representatives, the provisions of that document had no effect upon slavery within her borders. As has been seen, the people of the State, through their legislators and their State convention ordinances, had adopted emancipation, but that action was superseded by the Thirteenth Amendment to the constitution of the United States, which was ratified by thirty-three States, including Missouri, ratified conditionally by Alabama and Mississippi, and rejected only by Delaware and Kentucky. As the permission of three-fourths of the States was all that was necessary for the adoption of the amendment, it was declared in force by President Johnson in 1865, although Lincoln himself lived to see it proposed. It is as follows:

Article XIII.—SECTION 1. Neither slavery nor involuntary servitude, except as a punishment for crime, whereof the party shall have been duly convicted, shall exist within the United States or any place subject to their jurisdiction.

SEC. 2. Congress shall have power to enforce this article by appropriate legislation.

Thus, after an existence of more than two hundred and forty years, the institution of African slavery in the United States was swept away. Although it was the purpose of the General Government to discriminate carefully between Union and non-Union slave holders, and to sufficiently indemnify the former class against all losses occasioned by the freeing of their slaves, yet in many cases loyal men were ruined financially in this great overthrow of Southern institutions, and all classes suffered together.

Campaign of 1861—Boonville.—Jackson and Price had collected, at Boonville, a military force of from 3,000 to 4,000 men. This force was poorly armed, possessed of but a single piece of artillery, undisciplined, and deficient in organization and competent officers, yet they were eager to meet the troops, which under command of Lyon and Blair were coming up the river to attack them. On the eve of battle, Price was taken seriously ill, and was obliged to go home; therefore the Confederates marched under command of Col. John S. Marmaduke, to meet the advancing column of Lyon's forces. The latter had disembarked at Rocheport, and were advancing with six pieces of artillery in the direction of Boonville, when they encountered the State troops about midway between the two places. Capt. Totten, of the Unionists, opened the engagement by throwing a few nine-pounder explosives into the State ranks, while the infantry of the former filed obliquely, right and left, and commenced a terrific volley of musketry, which was at first vigorously returned. Col. Marmaduke was stationed in a lane, leading toward the river from the road by which the United States troops were advancing, and in a brick house on the northeast corner of the two roads. A couple of shells were thrown into the house, dispersing the State troops in great confusion. This, together with the well-directed fire of the infantry from the right and left, soon forced Col. Marmaduke's men to fall back, but they again formed in line of battle, and advanced a few feet to meet the Union forces. The cannon were now brought into requisition, and the State troops opened a galling musketry fire from a grove on the left of Lyon's center, and from a shed still further to the left.

The skirmish now became a battle. Lyon's force was 2,000 in all, but not more than 500 were at any one time engaged. There were 1,500 of the State troops, but neither were they all continually in the conflict. Lyon brought his artillery to bear with deadly effect, and a forward movement on the right decided the engagement, the State forces retreating in great disorder. Such was the confusion of this retreat that this battle is often jocularly styled "The Boonville Races."

The Federal forces took possession of "Camp Vest" and the city of Boonville. At the former there were found twenty or thirty tents, fifty guns, a large number of shoes and other clothing, a quantity of blankets and ammunition, and two secession flags.

Carthage.—The lead mines in the southwest part of the State became an object of great importance to the Confederate Government, which, hoping to secure them, dispatched large bodies of troops from Arkansas and Texas. On July 5, a scouting party, sent out by Col. Franz Sigel, encountered, about two miles from Carthage, a picket guard of the State troops, who were taken prisoners. As soon as possible Col. Sigel prepared to advance, expecting to find the State troops some distance west of the town. About half-past 9 o'clock the armies met in an open prairie, seven miles beyond Carthage. The State forces numbered perhaps 5,000 men, mostly cavalry, but had a battery of five cannon. Col. Sigel's command comprised his own regiment of two battalions, and Col. Salomon's detached regiment, with several pieces of artillery, under command of Maj. Backoff. Col. Sigel's and Col. Salomon's men numbered together 1,100. Gens. Parsons and Rains were in command of the State troops. Maj. Backoff, by direction of Col. Sigel, opened fire, and in less than two hours the battery of the opposing forces was silenced. The superior arms of the Federals enabled them to maintain a situation of comparatively little danger. The State ranks were twice broken, but rallied, and held their position until their guns gave out, when their column was again broken.

At this time a large body of the Confederate cavalry was sent back to cut off Sigel's transportation train. Seeing this movement, he ordered a retreat, and sent word for the wagons to advance as quickly as possible. By keeping up an incessant fire with the infantry, and using the artillery whenever practicable, Sigel managed to retard the advance of the cavalry, and to fall back in good order, some three and a half miles, to the baggage train. The wagons were then placed in the center of the column in such a manner that there were artillery and infantry forces both in front and rear. At this the State forces retreated, and attempted to surround the entire column, taking a position upon some bluffs overlooking a creek. There was but one road across this stream, and, to change his position without further retreat, it was necessary for Sigel to cross the hill where the State cavalry was mainly stationed.

Maj. Backoff ordered two of the artillery pieces in front to oblique to the left, and two to the right, and at the same time a corresponding movement was made from Sigel's battalion. This manœuver led the State troops into the belief that the Federals were seeking to outflank their cavalry. Accordingly the forces on the bluffs closed up to the right and left, when, on reaching a point 300 yards from them, Backoff's artillery was ordered to transverse oblique, and immediately opened a terrible cross-fire with canister. At the same time the Federal infantry charged at double quick, and in ten minutes the State troops were dispersed in every direction.

This engagement, with the manœuvering, occupied about two hours. The State cavalry was poorly armed and mounted, and, having no cannon on the bluffs, could make but little resistance to the attacks of Col. Sigel. Forty-five men and eighty horses were taken by the Federals, also a quantity of double-barreled shotguns and some revolvers and bowie-knives. The loss of the State troops was estimated at 250 or 300 men. However these forces still prevented Sigel's advance over the creek, and that officer was compelled to retreat in the direction of Carthage, the State troops following and surrounding the column on three sides, although kept at a distance by the infantry fire.

Sigel's command reached Carthage at half past six o'clock, and at once attempted to enter the woods about a mile distant. This movement the State cavalry resisted, knowing that they could do nothing in the timber. An effort to rally the cavalry to a charge was made, which brought the whole of Sigel's infantry into action. After some hard fighting that officer got his men into the woods and forced the State troops to relinquish the pursuit. The latter returned to Carthage intending to renew the battle in the morning. In this last engagement the State troops lost ten killed and sixty-four wounded. The dispatchers of Col. Sigel placed his loss during the whole day at thirteen killed and thirty-one wounded.

Notwithstanding the terrible fatigue of the day—his men having been in action nearly twelve hours—Sigel continued his retreat. A forced march was made to Sarcoxie, in the southeast corner of the county (Jasper), a distance of twelve or fourteen miles. There the Federal troops went into camp at 3 o'clock in the morning. On the following afternoon the retreat was continued to Mount Vernon, Lawrence County, where, for a time, Sigel established his headquarters.

The Western Department.—On July 3, 1861, the Western Department was created, comprising Illinois and the States and Territories west of the Mississippi and east of the Rocky Mountains, including New Mexico. The headquarters of this department were at St. Louis, where, previous to its establishment, Gen. Harney, and, afterward, Gen. Lyon, were in command. Gen. John C. Fremont, who was a son-in-law of Senator Benton, and had been a candidate for the presidency in 1856, was appointed to the command of the new department, and assumed the duties of his office on the 26th of July.

The authorities at Washington, perplexed by the disastrous defeat at Bull Run, were so absorbed with the defenses of the National Capital, and with military operations at the East, as to be unable to give necessary aid to the Western Department. Fremont finally obtained $100,000 from the National sub-treasurer at St. Louis, with which he proceeded to secure the re-enlistment of many of the three-months' men, whose terms had expired, and to fortify the city against any probable attack. Harassed by a lack of resources, Fremont was soon placed in a dilemma, occasioned by the exigencies of the campaign in Missouri. The Confederate general, Pillow, was reported to be advancing with a large number of troops against Cairo and Bird's Point, while Gen. Hardee was pushing into the interior of Missouri to annoy Gen. Lyon's flank and rear. In addition to all this, Lieut.-Gov. Reynolds, Gov. Jackson being temporarily absent, elated with the Confederate victory at Bull Run, issued a proclamation to the people of Missouri, in which he alluded to the State convention as merely a tool in the hands of their enemies, assured them that peace and security could only be obtained through union with the South, and called upon them to rally as one man to the standard of the State, and aid Gen. Pillow in expelling the invader from their borders.

In view of this variety of changes, Gen. Fremont decided to secure Bird's Point against the attack of Gen. Pillow, but upon sending an expedition to that place, found that the menace against it was merely intended as a diversion.

Meanwhile, after the battle of Boonville, Gen. Lyon, with a force of nearly 3,000 men, four pieces of artillery and a long baggage train, left that place, and followed in pursuit of the State troops, who were reported to have fled to Syracuse and beyond. At Grand River, a branch of the Osage, in Henry County, he was reinforced by 3,000 Kansas troops under command of Maj. S. D. Sturgis. When within eighty miles of Springfield, Lyon heard of Sigel's battle at Carthage, and determined to change his course and march to his relief. Notwithstanding the intensely hot weather, and the fatigue of his infantry, early on the morning of July 10 Lyon's army moved from their encampment and forced their way among the hills, gorges and forests that lay in their path. After they had proceeded fifty miles a messenger from Sigel brought definite information of the desperate encounter at Carthage, and that Sigel's little army was now at Springfield. Therefore Lyon, marching more leisurely, accomplished the remaining thirty miles of the journey in two days.

Encamped near Springfield, he now prepared to meet the enemy, who were his superior in numbers and constantly increasing. It was now that he repeatedly called upon Gen. Fremont for those reinforcements which the latter failed to supply.

Near the close of July, Gen. Lyon was informed of the concentration of the Confederate forces at Cassville, and of their design of attacking his camp. Therefore, although their numbers were much greater than those of his army, he determined to anticipate their attack by an advance of his own troops. Late on the afternoon of August 1, his entire army, consisting of 5,500 foot, 400 horse and 18 guns, moved toward Cassville, and bivouacked that night on Cave Creek, ten miles south of Springfield. The next morning they marched to Dug Springs, in Stone County, nineteen miles southwest of Springfield. Here they encountered and defeated a body of Confederates under Gen. Rains.

Wilson's Creek.—On August 6, Gen. Lyon returned with his army to Springfield. The entire Confederate force was now concentrated near Crane Creek, in the northern part of Stone County. Believing that Lyon's army was much larger than their own, a disagreement arose between Price and McCulloch as to the expediency of an advance toward Springfield, the former counseling a forward, and the later a retrograde movement. Finally an order was received from Maj.-Gen. Polk, ordering an advance upon Lyon. A council was at once held, in which McCulloch expressed his willingness to march upon Springfield, provided he were granted the chief command. Price, to whom that distinction, perhaps, rightfully belonged, consented to the terms of McCulloch, hoping that Lyon might be defeated and driven from the State. A little after midnight on Sunday, August 4, they took up the line of march, and reached Wilson's Creek, ten miles southwest of Springfield, on the 9th. Here they encamped, determining at 9 o'clock that night to march in four separate columns against Springfield, surround the place, and begin a simultaneous attack at daybreak. A threatened storm caused Gen. McCulloch to countermand his order, and morning found his entire army, consisting of 5,300 infantry, fifteen guns, and 6,000 cavalry, besides a large number of unarmed horsemen, encamped upon the field. But the night was neither too dark nor stormy for Gen. Lyon. At 5 o'clock P. M., of August 9, he marched in two columns from Springfield, making a detour to the right, and, notwithstanding the darkness and storm, at 1 o'clock found himself within sight of the Confederate guard fires. Here he called a halt, and his soldiers lay on their arms until dawn, when they formed in battle line and advanced. Lyon's effective force was 5,200 men, including infantry and cavalry, and three batteries of sixteen guns. The two columns of the Federal army were commanded by Lyon and Sigel, and their early attack was a complete surprise to the Confederates, McCulloch, trusting for security to the darkness and storm, having withdrawn his advanced pickets.

The Federal forces in command of Lyon formed a line of battle at daybreak, closely followed by Totten's battery, supported by a strong reserve, and with skirmishers thrown out in front. After driving in the enemy's outposts, a ravine was crossed and a high ridge gained, when a large force of Confederate skirmishers came in view. Very severe fighting ensued, and it became evident that Lyon's column would soon reach the stronghold, where the main battle would take place. A few shells cleared the front, and the First Missouri and First Kansas moved forward, supported by the First Iowa and Totten's battery. The Second Kansas, Capt. Steele's battalion and Lieut. Dubois' battery, were held in reserve, so as to bear upon a powerful battery of the enemy, which was stationed in front, on the opposite side of Wilson's Creek. The Confederates now rallied in large force near the foot of the slope, opposite Lyon's left wing, and along the slope in his front and to his right. During this time, Capt. Plummer, with four companies of infantry, had moved down a ridge a few hundred yards to Lyon's left, and found at its terminus a large body of the enemy's infantry, which arrested further progress in that direction. Directly artillery firing was begun at the point, about two miles distant, where it was expected that Sigel's column would encounter the enemy.

Lyon's whole line now moved with great impetuosity toward the Confederate position; and the roar of musketry increased and became continuous. Totten's battery came into action, as rapidly as the nature of the ground would permit, and made great havoc in the opposing ranks. After half an hour's fierce fighting the Confederates retired in great confusion, leaving Gen. Lyon in possession of the field. Meanwhile, Capt. Plummer had been compelled to fall back, but Lieut. Dubois' battery, supported by Capt. Steele's battalion, opened upon the enemy in that direction, and soon drove them from the cornfield, where they had intrenched themselves. There was now a momentary cessation of firing along the whole line, except on the right, where the First Missouri was still engaged against superior numbers. The Second Kansas was ordered to the support of this regiment, which must otherwise have been destroyed while unflinchingly holding its position. During this time Capt. Steele's battalion, which had been detailed to the support of Dubois' battery, was brought forward to the support of Totten's, and soon the Confederate force reappeared along Lyon's entire front, marching toward each flank. The battle again began with great fury, and became general along the whole line. The ranks of the opposing sides were sometimes within thirty or forty yards of each other, when charges upon Totten's battery were made. For more than an hour the conflict was carried on with great slaughter on both sides, and so equally balanced were the opposing forces that neither was gaining any decisive advantage.

Early in this desperate engagement, Gen. Lyon's horse was

killed, and he himself received a wound in the leg and one in the head. He then mounted another horse, and, swinging his hat, called upon the nearest troops to follow him. The second Kansas gallantly responded, but their commander, Col. Mitchell, soon fell severely wounded, and, at about the same time, Gen. Lyon received a mortal wound in or near the heart. Maj. Sturgis then succeeded to the command. The Confederates had been driven back, and for twenty minutes there was a lull in the battle, during which Sturgis summoned his officers for a consultation. Lyon's column had been dreadfully shattered, and the leader killed. For nearly thirty hours the men had been without water, and a supply could not be had short of Springfield, which was ten or twelve miles away. Their ammunition was nearly gone, and should they, by slackening fire, reveal this fact to the enemy, annihilation seemed inevitable.

Sigel, meanwhile, had not been heard from; but the consultation of officers was soon brought to a close by the advance of a heavy column from the direction whence Sigel's guns had been at first heard. These troops carried a banner resembling the American flag, and their dress resembled that of Sigel's brigade. Hoping to effect a junction with that officer, Sturgis formed his line for an advance. Suddenly from a hill in Sturgis' front a battery began to pour into his line shrapnel and canister, and at this moment the on-coming Confederate forces, for such they were, displayed their true colors, and the fiercest engagement of the day immediately commenced along the entire Union lines. Totten's battery, in the center, supported by the Iowa and regular troops, was the main object of attack. The Confederates were often within twenty feet of the battery, and the smoke of the opposing lines was so intermingled as to appear made by the same guns. Notwithstanding the complete rout of the Confederate front, they continued to hold the field. Finally, therefore, the Federal forces were ordered to retreat. They moved slowly to the open prairie, about two miles from the battlefield, and thence to Springfield, which they reached at 5 o'clock that afternoon. Their total loss was 223 killed, 721 wounded, and 292 missing.

Sigel's column, in the meantime, had marched within a mile

of McCulloch's camp at daybreak, and planted four pieces of artillery on the left, the infantry advancing toward the point where the Fayetteville road crosses Wilson's Creek, and the two cavalry companies guarding his right and left. His artillery fire was so destructive that the enemy were soon driven from their tents, and retired toward the northeast part of the valley. The Third and Fifth Missouri Infantry (Union) had passed the creek, and formed almost in the center of the camp. As the enemy were now rallying in front, Sigel ordered the artillery to be brought forward and formed in battery across the valley, with the Third and Fifth to the left and the cavalry to the right. At the end of half an hour the enemy retreated into the woods and up the adjoining hills. By the firing in the direction of Gen. Lyon's column, it now became evident that he had engaged the enemy along the whole line; therefore, to give him the greatest possible assistance, Sigel left his position in the camp and advanced to attack the enemy's line of battle in the rear. In pursuance of this design, Sigel's column struck the Fayetteville road, and, following it to Sharpe's farm, planted his artillery on the plateau, and the two infantry regiments on the right and left, across the road, while the cavalry was stationed on its flanks. The firing in the direction of Lyon's column had then almost entirely ceased. Supposing that Lyon had repulsed the Confederates, and that his forces were coming up the road, the commanders of the Third and Fifth Regiments gave orders not to fire upon troops advancing from that direction. Very unexpectedly two Confederate batteries opened fire upon them, one in front on the Fayetteville road, and the other from the hill, where it was supposed Lyon's forces were victorious, while a strong column of infantry, mistaken for the Iowa regiment, advanced from the Fayetteville road and attacked Sigel's right. Consternation and frightful confusion at once ensued. Sigel's men, thinking that by some mistake Lyon's troops were firing upon them, could hardly be induced to serve their guns until it was too late. The Confederates arrived within a few paces of Sigel's cannon, killed the horses, turned the flanks of the infantry, and forced them to fly. In this retreat Sigel lost five cannon, of which three were spiked, and the colors of the Third Regiment.

The total Federal loss was 258 killed, 873 wounded, and 186 missing; in all, 1,317. The Confederate loss was 279 killed, 951 wounded, and 68 prisoners; total, 1,298. Upon the arrival of the shattered Federal forces at Springfield, the command of the whole was entrusted to Col. Sigel, who ordered a retreat to Rolla, Phelps County, 125 miles distant. The retreating army reached this place August 19, having safely conducted a Government train five miles in length, and valued at $1,500,000.

After the Federal defeat at Wilson's Creek, Gov. Gamble issued a proclamation calling into service 42,000 of the State militia to serve for six months, unless peace in the State should be sooner restored.

Martial Law Declared.—Gen. Fremont, on the 30th of August, inaugurated a new remedy for the lawlessness which prevailed, and the almost absolute impotence of the civil authority. He declared martial law and appointed J. McKinstry, major United States army, provost marshal-general of the State.

Capture of Lexington.—Contrary to the expectations of both armies, McCulloch and Price failed to pursue their victory at Wilson's Creek by following Sigel in his retreat to Rolla, and McCulloch soon left Missouri with all his forces. Taking advantage of the favorable impression made upon the people by his success, Gen. Price issued a proclamation in which he declared that his army had been organized for the maintenance of the rights, dignity and honor of Missouri, and was kept in the field for these purposes alone. The citizens of the State now flocked to his standard in considerable numbers, and in a few weeks he had collected a large force. He now pressed northward across the State to Lexington, on the Missouri River. This place was defended by a force of Federals, 2,600 strong, commanded by Col. Mulligan. In anticipation of an attack, intrenchments had been thrown upon Masonic College Hill, an eminence overlooking the Missouri River. Mulligan's fortifications were most skillfully planned, but his men had only about forty rounds of ammunition each, six small brass cannon and two howitzers, the latter of which were useless because of the lack of shells. At dawn of September 12, Gen. Price drove in the Union pickets, and, from a position within easy range of Mulligan's intrenchments, opened a cannonade from four different points. The assault and defense were kept up during the entire day, when Price withdrew to await the arrival of his wagon train and reinforcements. Mulligan's men worked night and day to strengthen their fortifications, and anxiously expected reinforcements, for which a courier had been dispatched to Jefferson City. This messenger was captured on the way, and, of course, no relief came.

On the morning of the 18th, Gen. Price, who had been reinforced, and now had from 15,000 to 25,000 men, began a final attack upon Mulligan's works, cutting off the communication of the beleaguered garrison with the city, stopping their supply of water, seizing a steamboat laden with stores, and occupying a building which commanded the position of the Union forces. A most stubborn defense was made, which continued for fifty-two hours. During the afternoon of the 20th, Gen. Price procured numerous bales of hemp, and with these, wetted to resist hot shot, he caused movable breastworks to be constructed, behind which a large body of the Confederates advanced within ten rods of Mulligan's works. The latter officer saw that further resistance was madness. To retreat was impossible. His men had no water except that which had been caught in blankets during a passing shower, and afterward wrung out; and the stench from the carcasses of horses and mules killed within the intrenchments was insufferable. Accordingly the white flag was raised, and the siege of Lexington was ended. The men laid down their arms and became prisoners of war. As the fruits of this victory there fell into the hands of Gen. Price six cannon, two mortars, over 3,000 stand of infantry arms, a large number of sabers, about 750 horses, wagons, teams, ammunition, and $100,000 worth of commissary stores. On the Union side 40 men were killed and 120 wounded. The Confederate loss was 20 killed and 65 wounded.

Fremont in the Field.—Gen. Fremont, deeply chagrined at the Federal reverses, and fearing that Gen. Price would advance upon the State capital, or intrench himself at some central point upon the Missouri River, determined to take the field in person, with the hope of defeating Price before McCulloch, who had been recruiting troops in Arkansas, could return to his aid.

With this intention he directed toward Southwestern Missouri an army of more than 20,000 men, arranged in five divisions, under command of Gens. Hunter, Pope, Sigel, McKinstry and Asboth. These troops were accompanied by eighty-six pieces of artillery, many of which were rifle cannon. On the 28th of September Fremont, with his famous body-guard, commanded by Maj. Zagonyi, a Hungarian, reached Jefferson City, and commenced vigorous measures to overturn the plans of Gen. Price, and drive him from the State. On the 30th of the month Price abandoned Lexington, leaving a small force of 500 men to guard such prisoners as had not been paroled. On the 16th of October Maj. White, with his "Prairie Scouts," consisting of 185 cavalrymen, surprised this garrison, releasing the Union prisoners, capturing seventy of the Confederates, and dispersing the rest. He then rejoined Fremont's army.

Springfield.—Maj. White was now ordered by Gen. Sigel to reconnoiter near Springfield, and if advisable to attack the Confederate force in camp there. The major was seriously ill at the time, but immediately set his command in motion, accompanying them in a carriage.

On the evening of the same day, October 24, he was overtaken by Maj. Zagonyi, with the "body guard," and he, under orders from Fremont, took command of the combined force. The Confederates, mostly cavalry, and numbering something more than 1,000, were encamped about a mile west of Springfield, on the Mount Vernon road, and were under command of Lieut.-Col. Cloud. The attack of Zagonyi proved a complete surprise. His men dashed down a lane under fire of the enemy, who had hastily formed a line along its north side. At this first onset a large number of the Confederates ran in every direction, but the remainder stood their ground. The Union soldiers swept past the Confederate camp, demolished a rail fence, entered the field where the enemy then were, and formed in line in a ravine about 200 yards away. They again charged with drawn sabres, but were repulsed with considerable loss. Falling back to the ravine they repeated the charge a second and third time with a like result. The Union loss in the engagement was: Zagonyi's "body guard," 15 killed, 27 wounded and 10 taken prisoners—52; White's "Prairie Scouts" killed, wounded and prisoners, 33; total 85.

After the engagement the Confederates withdrew to Price's headquarters at Neosho, and Zagonyi also fell back until he met Sigel's advance.

Gen. Fremont was just upon the eve of an attack upon Price, who, it was reported, reinforced by McCulloch, was moving on Springfield with 40,000 men, when he was superseded by Gen. Hunter. The latter, after retreating to St. Louis, was in turn superseded by Gen. Halleck, on the 18th of November.

Belmont.—The only remaining movement of importance was at Belmont, on the Mississippi. The Confederate general, Polk, acting under orders of his government, had, notwithstanding that State's neutrality, entered Kentucky with an army, and had captured the town of Columbus. Batteries planted here commanded the Mississippi. The Confederates gathered in force at Belmont, on the opposite bank. In order to dislodge them, Gen. Fremont sent Gen. Ulysses S. Grant, with a brigade of 3,000 Illinois and Iowa troops, into Missouri, by way of Cairo. On the 7th of November, Grant made a vigorous and successful attack on the Confederate camp, but Gen. Polk sent reinforcements across the river, the guns of Columbus were brought to bear on the Union position, and Grant was obliged to retreat. The total loss on the Federal side was 108 killed, 353 wounded and 121 missing; total, 582. The Confederate loss was 104 killed, 419 wounded and 117 missing; total, 641.

In addition to the engagements already described, quite a large number of raids, surprises and skirmishes—some of them important enough to be accounted battles—occurred in Missouri during 1861. They will be found mentioned in chronological order in the list of battles on another page.

The Campaign of 1862.—The beginning of the year found Missouri comparatively quiet. Gen. Price had concentrated about 12,000 men at Springfield, intending to remain there all winter, but Gen. Halleck massed his forces, comprising the troops of Asboth, Sigel, Davis and Prentiss, at Lebanon, under command of Gen. Curtis. On February 11, this army moved against Springfield, and on the following night Gen. Price retreated to Cassville. Curtis pursuing him, he withdrew still further across the Arkansas line to Cross Hollows, thence to Sugar Creek, where, reinforced by McCulloch, he gave battle and was defeated February 20. Price again retreated to Cove Creek, and then halted, leaving Missouri with no large organized Confederate force within her borders. Nevertheless, it was evident that the rebel general, sheltered in the defiles of the "Boston Mountains," was only gathering strength for more vigorous operations; therefore, Curtis retraced his steps, and fell back to Pea Ridge, among the mountains in the northwestern part of Arkansas. Here he received intelligence that Price and McCulloch had been reinforced by Gen. Van Dorn, and that their combined force under command of the latter officer would soon attack his position.

Battle of Pea Ridge—An Elkhorn Tavern.—This engagement commenced on the morning of the 6th of March, 1862. The Confederate force aggregated about 25,000 men as follows: McCulloch's troops, from Arkansas, Louisiana and Texas, 13,000; Gen. Pike's command, consisting of Choctaw, Cherokee, Chickasaw and other Indians, and some white troops, 4,000; Price's Missouri troops, 8,000. The Federal force consisted of 10,500 men, including cavalry and infantry, forty-nine pieces of artillery and one mountain howitzer.

After a hard-fought battle, which lasted for two days, the Federals were victorious. The Confederate generals, McCulloch and McIntosh, were both killed. Van Dorn withdrew to the interior of Arkansas, and Curtis marched slowly southward. The Federal loss in the battle of Pea Ridge was 203 killed, 972 wounded, and 176 taken prisoners; total, 1,351; Confederate loss about the same.

Various War Measures.—Meanwhile, in Missouri, Provost-Marshal General Farrar issued an order requiring the publishers of newspapers in the State, with the exception of St. Louis city papers, to furnish a copy of each issue, for inspection at the marshal's office.

Gen. Halleck issued an order requiring the officers of the Mercantile Library Association and of the Chamber of Commerce to subscribe to the oath prescribed by the convention ordinance of October 6, 1861, under peril of arrest and imprisonment. The same order also forbade the display of secession flags in the hands of women or on carriages—the carriages to be confiscated and the women arrested. A similar order was issued to the presidents and directors of all railroads in the State, and to the president, professors, curators and other officers of the State University at Columbia. This order required all clerks, agents and civil employes in the service of the United States to take the oath prescribed by act of Congress, and recommended that all clergymen, teachers, officers of benevolent institutions, and all engaged in business and trade, who were loyal to the Union, should voluntarily take the convention oath, in order that their patriotism might be known.

At different times men were tried and condemned to be shot upon charges of railroad wrecking and bridge burning, but these sentences were commuted to imprisonment, or, in some cases, the culprits were released upon their taking the oath of allegiance, and giving bond in the sum of $2,000 each for future loyalty to the Government.

Edmund J. Ellis, of Columbia, editor and proprietor of *The Boone County Standard*, was found guilty, and sentenced to banishment from the State during the war, on the several charges of giving information to the enemy, encouraging resistance to the Federal Government, and inciting persons to rebellion against the same. His printing materials were confiscated and sold.

Early in April, Gen. Halleck went to Corinth, Miss., and left Maj-Gen. Schofield in command at St. Louis.

Operations Against Guerrillas—Col. Jo. C. Porter.—Gov. Gamble, desiring to repress the numerous guerrilla organizations in the State, authorized Gen. Schofield to organize the State militia into companies, regiments and brigades, and to call a force into the field sufficient to quell the marauders and secure the people of the State in their persons and property. In the series of skirmishes and fights which occurred between the State militia and the Confederate guerrillas, the most brilliant and important were those connected with the pursuit and final overthrow of Col. Jo. C. Porter.

His force was first engaged July 1, at Cherry Grove, Schuyler County, by Col. Lipscomb, with about 450 of the State Militia. After a small fight the Confederates retreated, and were pursued as far as Newark, Knox County. The next important encounter with Porter's forces was at Pearce's Mills, on the Middle Fabius, Scotland County, where, on the 19th of July, a pursuing force, under Maj. John Y. Clopper, of the Merrill Horse, and Maj. John F. Benjamin, of the Eleventh Missouri State Militia, was ambuscaded, and sustained a loss of eighty-three men, while the Confederates lost but half a dozen. Porter, however, retreated toward the west and south, and in less than twenty-four hours was at Novelty, Knox County, sixty-four miles distant. Still going southward, they passed through Marion County to Florida, in Monroe, where they attacked and defeated a small detachment of the Third Iowa Cavalry, under Maj. H. C. Caldwell, and then hurried on to the heavily-wooded country near Brown's Spring, ten miles north of Fulton, in Callaway County. Ascertaining their position, Col. Guitar, of the Ninth Missouri State Militia, started in pursuit, July 27, with about 200 men and two pieces of artillery. On the preceding day Lieut.-Col. Shaffer, of Merrill's Horse, left Columbia upon the same errand, with 100 men, and was joined at Sturgeon by Maj. Clopper, with as many more. Maj. Caldwell, with a detachment of the Third Iowa, also started from Mexico. These two latter columns marched toward Mount Zion Church, in the northeast part of Boone County, believing that Porter was encamped there. Not finding the object of their search, they pursued their way into Callaway County, and, on the afternoon of the 28th, heard Guitar's cannon four or five miles distant. Shaffer and Caldwell hastened forward, and arrived in time to assist in the hard-fought battle of Moore's Mill, July 28, wherein Porter was defeated with a loss of 32 killed and 135 wounded, while Guitar lost 13 killed and 55 wounded.

Battle of Kirksville.—Porter now retreated northward, through Monroe into Marion County. Here he received a large number of recruits. On the 1st of August he attacked and captured Newark, Knox County, with its garrison of seventy-five men, under Capt. Wesley Lair, of the Eleventh Missouri State Militia, and pushed northward to Short's Well, in the Southern part of Scotland, where he was joined by a considerable detachment under Col. Cyrus Franklin and Lieut.-Col. Frisby H. McCullough. The rebel forces were closely pursued by Col. John McNeil. Porter and Franklin turned west from Short's Well, and reached Kirksville on the morning of August 6, a few hours in advance of their pursuers, and, ordering the citizens to evacuate the town, posted their troops in the courthouse, seminary, stores and private residences, and, thus entrenched, awaited the coming Unionists. Porter had about 2,800 men, all mounted, but many were without arms, and nearly all without experience.

Col. McNeil, approaching from the eastern side of the town, drew up his forces before it. Not knowing the exact position of the enemy, he ordered ten men, under Lieut. John N. Cowdry, of Merrill's Horse, to ride through the town and discover their places of concealment. They obeyed the order, and the rebels in their eagerness fired upon them from houses, stables and other places affording them protection from the missiles which were shortly to be poured upon the town. McNeil now opened the battle with his cannon, and, under cover of his artillery fire, advanced his dismounted men, and soon the Confederates began to give way.

In three hours the town was in possession of McNeil, and the forces of Porter and Franklin were in full retreat toward the Chariton River. The Confederate loss in this engagement was between 200 and 300 killed, wounded and captured; the Federal loss was 6 killed and 33 wounded.

Compton's Ferry—Yellow Creek.—On the following day Col. Guitar, who had been ill at Jefferson City, entered upon preparations for the pursuit of a considerable rebel force in Chariton County, under Col. J. A. Poindexter, and, on the 8th of August, landed from a steamer a considerable force at Glasgow. He overtook Poindexter at 9 o'clock on the night of the 11th, at Compton's Ferry, on Grand River, in Carroll County. Part of Poindexter's men had crossed the river before his arrival, but a large number, with all their baggage, horses, wagons, etc., had yet to cross. Guitar ordered a charge, and at the same time opened upon the fleeing rebels with two pieces of artillery. The result was a great panic and considerable destruction. Many of the Confederates, in their eagerness to escape, threw away their guns, and forced their horses into the river, but the animals in many instances, became unmanageable, and returned to the same shore whence they started. Some were drowned. A large number of prisoners, and all the baggage, together with horses, mules, guns and wagons, were captured.

Poindexter marched as swiftly as possible to the northward, reaching the Hannibal & St. Joseph Railroad at Utica on Tuesday morning, the 12th. Near here he was intercepted and driven back by Gen. Lyon. Retreating south he was met by Guitar on the 13th, at Yellow Creek, in Chariton County, and again routed, his band being scattered and broken up. Guitar then returned to Jefferson City and was promoted by Gov. Gamble to be brigadier-general of Enrolled Missouri Militia.

Battle at Independence.—The next important engagement in the State occurred at Independence very early in the morning of August 11. The town was garrisoned by about 450 Federal troops, comprising infantry and cavalry, under Lieut.-Col. J. T. Buell. The Confederates, commanded by Col. John T. Hughes, of Clinton County, and G. W. Thompson, numbered from 600 to 800. They were fairly inside the town, and had commenced a vigorous attack before their approach was suspected. Col. Buell was at once surrounded at his headquarters, thus preventing all communication between himself and his men; nevertheless his soldiers fought bravely; but so completely were they surprised that the best they could do was to retreat into the fields, where they formed for defense behind a stone wall. While the rebels were charging upon this position Col. Hughes was killed. Col. Buell, finding that his camp was in the hands of the enemy, and that extrication was hopeless, raised the white flag and surrendered the post. Both sides suffered heavy losses.

Battles of Lone Jack and Newtonia.—At Lone Jack, a village in Jackson County, a rebel force (3,000 strong) under Cols. John T. Coffee, Vard. Cockerill, S. D. Jackman and D. C. Hunter, attacked 800 State militia under Maj. Emory Foster, of the Seventeenth Missouri State Militia on August 16. The Federal loss was 43 killed, 154 wounded and 75 missing; the Confederate casualties were about the same. The Federals were defeated and lost two pieces of artillery. The rebels, hearing their adversaries were to be reinforced, retreated southward.

On September 13, 1862, an engagement took place at Newtonia, Newton County, between about 5,000 Kansas, Wisconsin, Missouri and Indian troops, under Gen. Salomon, and a Confederate force of 8,000 or 10,000 under Col. D. H. Cooper. Numbers were killed and wounded on both sides, and the Federals were compelled to retreat as far as Sarcoxie, fifteen miles distant.

Execution of Rebel Prisoners.—At Macon, Mo., on the 25th of September, ten rebel prisoners were executed on the charge of repeated violations of their paroles, and on October 18 a similar number was shot at Palmyra, in retaliation for the abduction and murder of Andrew Allsman, a Unionist of Marion County. After the battle of Kirksville, sixteen were executed for violating their paroles, and Col. F. H. McCullough was shot for recruiting within the lines.

Battle of Cane Hill, Arkansas—The last great battle of the year in which Missourians had a part was fought at Cane Hill, near Fayetteville, Ark., on Sunday, December 6, 1862. The Confederate forces under Gen. Hindman, of Arkansas, and Marmaduke, of Missouri, were defeated by the Unionists under Gen. Blunt, of Kansas. The following is the official report of the engagement, sent by Gen. Blunt to Maj.-Gen. Curtis, commandant of the department of Missouri:

PRAIRIE GROVE, December 10, 1862.

Maj.-Gen. S. R. Curtis.

The enemy did not stop in their flight until they had crossed the Boston Mountains, and are probably ere this across the Arkansas River. The enemy's killed and wounded is between 1,500 and 2,000—a large proportion of them killed. One hundred of their wounded have died since the battle, and a large proportion of the others are wounded mortally, showing the terrible effects of my artillery. My casualties will be about 200 wounded. Most of the wounded will recover. The enemy have left their wounded on my hands, and most of their dead, uncared for. They are being buried by my command. Hindman admitted his force to be 28,000. Maj. Hubbard, who was a prisoner with them all day of the fight, counted twenty regiments of infantry and twenty pieces of artillery. They had no train with them, and muffled the wheels of their artillery in making their retreat. Four caissons filled with ammunition were taken from the enemy. The Twentieth Regiment of Wisconsin Volunteers, in addition to those mentioned yesterday, suffered severely in charging one of the enemy's batteries, which they took, but were unable to hold.

JAMES G. BLUNT,
Brigadier-General.

The Campaign of 1863.—Battles of Springfield, Hartsville and Cape Girardeau.—In the early part of this year, the Confederates, led by Gens. Marmaduke and Price, resumed activity in Arkansas and Southern Missouri. On the 8th of January, with a force of 2,500 or 3,000 men and three pieces of artillery, Gen. J. S. Marmaduke attacked Springfield, which was occupied by Federal troops under Gen. E. B. Brown, commander of the Southwestern Department of Missouri. The fighting continued from 1 o'clock P. M. until after dark. Gen. Brown having been severely wounded, the command devolved upon Col. B. Crabb. The Confederates retreated the following morning, going to Marshfield and Hartsville. Their loss was 42 killed and 60 wounded, who were left on the field. The Federal loss was 18 killed and 110 wounded.

Three days afterward, at the town of Hartsville, Gen. Marmaduke, having united near Marshfield with a force under Col. Jo. C. Porter, and moving thence southward, attacked a Federal force under Col. Samuel Merrill, of the Twenty-first Iowa, and after a bloody little engagement drove them from the field.

On April 26, Gen. Marmaduke attacked the post at Cape Girardeau, on the Mississippi, but the garrison, under Gen. John McNeil, succeeded in driving the Confederates away.

During the last week in August, Col. Woodson, of the Third Cavalry Missouri State Militia, surprised and captured Gen. Jeff. Thompson, known as the "Swamp Fox," together with his staff officers, at Pocahontas, Ark. The prisoners were sent to St. Louis, and committed to Gratiot prison.

Order No. 11.—On the 25th of August, Gen. Thomas Ewing, of the Eleventh Kansas Infantry Volunteers, afterward a Democratic member of Congress from Ohio, issued the following order, which, as it was productive of much suffering at the time in the counties indicated, and has been commemorated by George C. Bingham in the celebrated painting entitled: "Order No. 11," we copy in full:

General Orders No. 11:

HEADQUARTERS DISTRICT OF THE BORDER,
KANSAS CITY, Mo., August 25, 1863.

First. All persons living in Cass, Jackson and Bates Counties, Mo., and in that part of Vernon included in this district, except those living within one mile of the limits of Independence, Hickman's Mills, Pleasant Hill and Harrisonville, and except those in that part of Kaw Township, Jackson County, north of Brush Creek and west of the Big Blue, embracing Kansas City and Westport, are hereby ordered to remove from their present residences within fifteen days from the date thereof.

Those who, within that time, establish their loyalty to the satisfaction of the commanding officer of the military station nearest their present places of residence will receive from him certificates stating the fact of their loyalty, and the names of the witnesses by whom it can be shown. All who receive such certificate will be permitted to remove to any military station in this district, or to any part of the State of Kansas, except the counties on the eastern border of the State. All others shall remove out of this district.

Officers commanding companies and detachments, serving in the counties named, will see that this paragraph is promptly obeyed.

Second. All grain and hay in the field, or under shelter, in the district from which the inhabitants are required to remove, within reach of military stations, after the 9th day of September next, will be taken to such stations and turned over to the proper officers there, and report of the amount so turned over made to district headquarters, specifying the names of all loyal owners and the amount of such produce taken from them. All grain and hay found in such district after the 9th of September next, not convenient to such stations, will be destroyed.

Third. The provisions of General Orders No. 10, from these headquarters, will be at once vigorously executed by officers commanding in the parts of the district, and at the stations not subject to paragraph first of this order, and especially in the towns of Independence, Westport and Kansas City.

Fourth. Paragraph three, General Orders No. 10, is revoked as to all who have borne arms against the Government in this district since August 20, 1863.

By order of Brig.-Gen. Ewing.   H. HANNAHS, *Adjt.*

Gen. Schofield, at that time commandant of the Department of Missouri, has since the war approved and defended this order, on the ground that a savage guerrilla warfare had raged on the border for two years, nearly depopulating the farming districts on the Missouri side, and that all the inhabitants who remained were obliged, whether rebel sympathizers or not, to furnish shelter and supplies for bands of marauding outlaws. He said that it was imperative that this border war should be suppressed, and that the fiendish massacre of 140 persons at Lawrence, Kas., on August 13, by the guerrilla Quantrell and his band, rendered immediate and decisive action necessary in order to prevent a succession of such horrors.

To increase the military force in the district was impracticable, and the only alternative was to remove the means by which these guerrillas were sustained. He stated, further, that no serious inconvenience was inflicted upon any one by the execution of the order, but that the necessities of the poor people were provided for, and none were permitted to suffer.

In reply to this statement of Gen. Schofield, which appeared in the St. Louis daily *Republican* of February 21, 1877, Hon. George C. Bingham, an old citizen of Jackson County, and a strong Union man during the war, prepared a counter statement, which was published in the same paper on the 26th of the month. He denounced the order as an act of purely arbitrary power, directed against a disarmed and defenseless population. He declared that it put an end to the predatory raids of Kansas "red-legs and jay-hawkers," by simply giving them all that they desired at once, that it gave up the country to Confederate bushwhackers, who, until the close of the war, stopped stages, robbed mails and prevented any one wearing a Federal uniform from entering the district. Mr. Bingham says he was in Kansas City when the order was enforced, and that he knew personally of the sufferings of the unfortunate victims. Men were shot down while obeying the order, and their effects seized by their murderers; dense columns of smoke rising in every direction marked the conflagration of dwellings; large trains of wagons, extending over the prairies for miles, moved toward Kansas, freighted with every description of household furniture and clothing belonging to the exiles; women and little children, barefooted and bareheaded, exposed to burning heat and choking dust, tramped wearily along, to whom neither aid nor protection were afforded by the authorities who had driven them from their homes, and who were indebted to the charity of steamboat conductors who took them to places of safety.

Mr. Bingham admitted that guerrilla warfare had been waged for two years in the counties embraced by the order, but denied that this region was by any means depopulated, or that the remaining farmers were supporting these outlaws. He said that the larger portion of the marauders were Kansas "jay-hawkers and red-legs," with no authority of law either military or civil, yet countenanced and protected by Gen. Ewing and his predecessors from the State of Kansas; that the others, constituting the more desperate class, were chiefly Missouri bushwhackers, acting under Confederate authority; that the inhabitants of the counties had been disarmed, as Gen. Schofield admitted, and were unable to resist the demands made upon them, but that the bushwhackers were insignificant in numbers compared with the Federal troops who were stationed there, and that twenty if not fifty times as much produce was furnished to the latter as to the former.

To this reply of Mr. Bingham neither Gen. Schofield nor Gen. Ewing made any response.

Order No. 11 belongs to that extensive list of war measures which, wise or unwise, necessary or unnecessary, was viewed in a very different light by those who were, on one hand, personally aggrieved and injured, and by those who, on the other hand, were looking from afar at the great end in view, namely, the overthrow of the Rebellion. In the border States, where Unionists and Disunionists lived side by side, numerous complexities arose, heightened by personal animosities and old family feuds; and in many cases loss of life, and especially loss of property, fell upon partisans indiscriminately, verifying the old, sad maxim that where transgression enters, the innocent must often suffer with the guilty.

Shelby's Raid.—In September Gen. Blunt drove the Confederate forces under Gen. Cabell and the Creek chief, Stand Watie, into the Choctaw reservation, and took possession of Fort Smith. As the autumn advanced and Cabell's supplies began to run low, a part of his command under Col. Jo. O. Shelby undertook a raid into Missouri. They crossed the Arkansas River, a little east of Fort Smith, and pushed rapidly northward as far as Crooked Prairie, in the southwestern part of this State, when they were joined by Col. Coffee. At Boonville, where Shelby expected to meet a large number of recruits, but was disappointed, his men secured from stores and dwelling houses $100,000 worth of property, after which they moved westward. On October 12 and 13, however, Gen. Brown encountered these forces at Marshall and defeated them, with a loss of fifty men killed, wounded and prisoners. Shelby hastily returned to Arkansas.

The Campaign of 1864.—Several sanguinary engagements were fought in Missouri during this, the closing year of the war. The Union troops, chiefly Missouri State Militia and Enrolled

Missouri Militia, were engaged in the effort, at many times unsuccessful, to defend the lives and property of the people from the roving bands of bushwhackers and guerrillas that infested all parts of the State, but particularly the western and river counties.

Late in January Gen. Rosecrans arrived at St. Louis, succeeding Gen. Schofield as commander of the Department of Missouri. No event of importance occurred until the following autumn, when Gen. Price made his last grand raid into the State with the intention of capturing St. Louis, and other important points.

Having been informed early in September of Price's meditated invasion, Rosecrans forwarded the information to headquarters, and Gen. A. J. Smith, then ascending the Mississippi with about 6,000 troops, was ordered to proceed to St. Louis. Gen. Rosecrans had previous to this only about 6,500 mounted men in his whole department, and these were scattered at various points—at Springfield, Pilot Knob, Jefferson City, Rolla and St. Louis, guarding military depots and railway bridges against the hordes of guerrillas who swarmed through the country. These troops were concentrated as quickly as possible when Price's intended route was ascertained, but he had already entered Southeastern Missouri, and reached Pilot Knob, before he was met by any considerable opposition. At that place a single brigade was stationed under command of Gen. Thomas Ewing. This force was intrenched in a little fort with some rude earthworks, but it made a gallant resistance, and repulsed two assaults of the Confederates, inflicting upon them a loss of 1,000 men. Gen. Price's men now took positions which commanded the entire fort, and Gen. Ewing, seeing that further resistance was hopeless, spiked his guns, blew up his magazine, and retreated, by night, toward Rolla, where Gen. McNeil was stationed. After accomplishing a march of sixty miles in thirty-nine hours, the exhausted troops were overtaken at Harrison by a large force under Shelby. Although short of ammunition, Gen. Ewing held his ground for thirty hours, when he was reinforced by troops sent from Rolla, after which he drove Shelby away, and continued his retreat in safety.

At St. Louis, Gen. Smith's infantry, 4,000 or 5,000 strong, was joined by eight regiments of the Enrolled Militia of the State, and six regiments of Illinois Militia. At Jefferson City Gen. E. B. Brown had been reinforced by Gen. C. B. Fisk with all available troops north of the Missouri River, and the citizens of that region promptly aiding the military, the capital was soon well fortified.

Gen. Price advanced by way of Potosi to the Meramec River; crossed it, and took position at Richwoods, within forty miles of St. Louis. Evidently fearing to attack that city, he burned the bridge at Moselle, and then pushed rapidly toward the capital of the State, followed by Gen. Smith and his entire command. Gen. Price, after having burned bridges behind him, and done all in his power to hinder his pursuers, arrived before Jefferson City on the 7th of October. Gen. McNeil and J. B. Sanborn, with a force of mounted men, chiefly Missouri State Militia, had just reached there by a forced march from Rolla. Squads of cavalry had been sent out to guard the fords and ferries on the Osage River, and, if not able to prevent the Confederates from crossing, to give timely warning of their approach. The railroad bridge across the river nine miles east of the city had been burned.

Several small engagements and skirmishes took place, and the Confederates partly surrounded the city with a semi-circular line nearly four miles in length, the wings resting on the Missouri River. Finding the place well prepared for an attack, Price sent his trains westward and followed with his army. A large force now started in pursuit of the Confederates, led by Federal cavalry under immediate command of Gen. Alfred Pleasanton, who arrived at Jefferson City on the day of Price's departure.

The latter general, growing bold as he marched westward, sent Gens. Jo. Shelby and John B. Clark, Jr., to attack Glasgow on the Missouri River, in Howard County. The town was garrisoned by a part of the Forty-third Missouri, and small detachments of the Ninth Missouri State Militia and Seventeenth Illinois Cavalry, under command of Col. Chester Harding. After a spirited resistance Col. Harding was obliged to surrender.

His assailants then marched back and joined their main army, which was still hastening westward. Gen. Price left Lexington just as Pleasanton's advance reached that place, October 20. At Little Blue Creek he met Blunt's Kansas troops, under command of Gen. Curtis, who, after a sharp fight which lasted for several hours, fell back to the Big Blue Creek and there awaited another attack. Meanwhile, Pleasanton reached the Little Blue, and found the bridge destroyed and the Confederate rear-guard prepared for battle. They were soon driven away, and Pleasanton continued his course to Westport, then occupied by the enemy. He captured the place by a brilliant charge in which he routed the Confederates, and took two of their guns.

Gen. Price had expected to receive at least 20,000 recruits during the progress of this raid, and perhaps to permanently occupy the State; instead, only about 6,000 Missourians came to his assistance, and he fled into Arkansas as rapidly as possible, having accomplished nothing of importance.

The Affair near Rocheport.—September 23, 1864, a train of Government wagons started from Sturgeon, Boone County, for Rocheport, in charge of seventy men of the Third Missouri State Militia, under Capt. McFadin. The train stopped near sunset at a pond about seven miles northeast of Rocheport, in order that the horses might be watered. Here it was suddenly attacked by 150 guerrillas under George Todd, who put the escort to flight, robbed the wagons of everything that they could conveniently carry away, and burned what remained. Eleven Federal soldiers were killed, and three negroes.

The Centralia Massacre.—Among the revolting and horrible crimes of the war the Centralia massacre stands prominent for its dastardly and cold-blooded atrocity. Monday night, September 26, Anderson's guerrillas, in numbers estimated from 200 to 400, encamped about three miles southeast of Centralia, which is situated on the North Missouri Railroad, in Boone County. About 10 o'clock Tuesday morning, 75 or 100 of this band went into the town, and commenced plundering the stores and depot, breaking open boxes and trunks, and appropriating whatever suited them. At 11 o'clock the stage-coach arrived from Columbia with eight or nine passengers. These gentlemen being unarmed were quickly relieved of their money and valuables, but were allowed to go to the hotel. At 11:30 the passenger train from St. Louis came in sight. Immediately the guerrillas formed into line, and as the train neared the depot, commenced throwing obstructions on the track and firing at the engineer. The cars having been stopped, the robbers rushed upon the passengers, men, women and children, taking money, watches and jewelry, together with the contents of trunks, and valuables from the express car. Twenty-three Federal soldiers who were on board the train were marched into town, placed in lines, and shot down. The guerrillas burned the railroad depot and six cars standing near. After murdering the soldiers and robbing the passengers and the citizens of the town generally, they set fire to the rifled train, and started it on the road toward Sturgeon. It ran about three miles, and then stopping was entirely consumed. Meanwhile the frightened passengers, glad to escape with their lives, went on their way as best they could, in wagons, on horseback, and on foot.

About 3 o'clock of the same afternoon Maj. A. V. E. Johnson, of Col. Kutzner's regiment of Missouri Volunteers (the Thirty-ninth), arrived at Centralia with 155 mounted infantry. An engagement took place in an open field southeast of the town. Maj. Johnson's men, being armed with long guns, were ordered to dismount. Their horses became unmanageable, and many of them ran away, leaving the soldiers on foot in the middle of the prairie. They had fired but one volley when the guerrillas dashed among them, splendidly mounted, and carrying three or four revolvers apiece. Part of Johnson's men who were still on horseback attempted to escape, but were overtaken and shot down. Maj. Johnson himself was killed, together with 122 men of his small command. Four or five of the remaining few were wounded. The guerrillas had but three killed and seven wounded.

After the murderers had left town the citizens of Centralia gathered the dead bodies together, and placed them near the railroad. Many of them were taken to Mexico for burial that very evening, and seventy-nine were interred in a trench in the eastern part of town. Afterward this trench was enclosed by a fence, and at the head of it was placed a limestone monument, fifteen feet high, with the following inscription:

" The remains of Companies A, G and H, Thirty-ninth Regiment, Missouri Volunteer Infantry, who were killed in action at Centralia, Mo., on the 27th day of September, 1864, are interred here." Since the close of the war the remains have been disinterred and re-buried in one common grave in the National Cemetery at Jefferson City.

Death of Bill Anderson.—After the horrible massacre at Centralia, the subsequent burning of Danville and the depots at New Florence, High Hill and Renick, Bill Anderson and the most of his men went into Ray County. On the 26th of October, Lieut.-Col. S. P. Cox, of the Thirty-third Enrolled Missouri Militia, learning Anderson's whereabouts, made a forced march to meet him. On the following day, just one month after the Centralia massacre, Col. Cox came in contact with the guerrilla pickets, and drove them before him into the woods. He then dismounted his men, threw an infantry force into the forest, and sent forward a cavalry advance which soon engaged Anderson's main body and fell back. The guerrillas now charged, and Anderson was killed, while his men were forced to retreat at full speed, hotly pursued by the Union cavalry. Upon the body of Anderson was found $300 in gold, $150 in treasury notes, six revolvers, and several orders from Gen. Price.

Early in December, 1864, Gen. Rosecrans was relieved of the command of the Department of Missouri, and Gen. Granville M. Dodge, of Iowa, succeeded him.

List of Battles in Missouri.—Necessarily there has been omitted from this brief review even a mention of many of the minor battles of the Civil War, which were fought upon the soil of Missouri. For convenient reference a complete list of these engagements, together with the dates at which they were fought, is herewith appended:

1861—Potosi, May 14; Boonville, June 17; Carthage, July 5; Monroe Station, July 10; Overton's Run, near Fulton, July 17; Dug Springs, August 2; Athens, August 5; Wilson's Creek, August 10; Morton, August 20; Bennett's Mills, September; Drywood Creek, September 7; Norfolk, September 10; Lexington, September 12, 20; Blue Mills Landing, September 17; Glasgow Mistake, September 20; Osceola, September 25; Shanghai, October 13; Lebanon, October 13; Big River Bridge, October 15; Linn Creek, October 16; Fredericktown, October 21; Springfield, October 25; Belmont, November 7; Piketon, November 8; Little Blue, November 10; Clark's Station, November 11; Mount Zion Church, December 28.

1862—Silver Creek, January 15; New Madrid, February 28; Pea Ridge, Ark., March 6; Neosho, April 22; Cherry Grove, July 1; Pierce's Mill, July 18; Rose Hill, July 10; Florida, July 22; Moore's Mill, July 28; Chariton River, July 30; Newark, August 1; Kirksville, August 6; Compton's Ferry, August 8; Independence, August 11; Yellow Creek, August 13; Lone Jack, August 16; Newtonia, September 13.

1863—Springfield, January 8; Cape Girardeau, April 29; Marshall, October 13.

1864—Pilot Knob, September 27; Moreau River, October 7; Prince's Ford, October 5; Glasgow, October 8; Little Blue Creek, October 20; Big Blue, October 22; Westport, October 23; Newtonia, October 28; Albany, October 27; near Rocheport, September 23; Centralia, September 27.

POLITICAL REVIEW SINCE 1865.

The delegates chosen to the State Constitutional Convention assembled in Mercantile Library Hall, St. Louis, Friday, January 6, 1865. The objects of the convention were: First, "to consider such amendments to the constitution of the State as might be deemed necessary for the emancipation of slaves;" and second, "such amendments to the constitution of the State as might be deemed necessary to preserve in purity the elective franchise to loyal citizens, and such other amendments as might be deemed essential to the promotion of the public good."

On January 11, the following ordinance was passed by the Convention:

AN ORDINANCE ABOLISHING SLAVERY IN MISSOURI.

Be it ordained by the People of the State of Missouri, in Convention Assembled, That hereafter, in this State, there shall be neither slavery nor involuntary servitude, except in punishment of crime, whereof the party shall have been duly convicted; and all persons held to service or labor as slaves are hereby declared free.

Emancipation in Missouri was thus established by law, although it had practically existed for some time previous.

The Drake Constitution.—It soon became apparent that mere amendments to the constitution would not satisfy the leading members of the convention, prominent among whom was Mr. Drake, of St. Louis, who had been chosen vice-president. A complete remodeling of the organic laws of the State seemed to many not to fall within the authority of the convention; moreover, they believed that the time had not come for that dispassionate and statesmanlike legislation which so important a measure demanded. However, the convention proceeded with its sweeping work of reform, until it had made new provisions in every article of the fundamental law. Section 3 of Article XI, on the "Right of Suffrage," which was the object of the most angry and exciting debate in the convention, and a prolific source of strife and division afterward, is here transcribed.

SEC. 3. At any election held by the people under this constitution, or in pursuance of any law of this State, or under any ordinance or by-law of any municipal corporation, no person shall be deemed a qualified voter who has ever been in armed hostility to the United States, or to the lawful authorities thereof, or to the Government of this State; or has ever given aid, comfort, countenance or support to persons engaged in any such hostility; or has ever in any manner adhered to the enemies, foreign or domestic, of the United States, either by contributing to them, or by unlawfully sending within their lines, money, goods, letters, or information; or has ever disloyally held communication with such enemies; or has ever advised or aided any person to enter the service of such enemies; or has ever by act or word manifested his adherence to the cause of such enemies, or his desire for their triumph over the armies of the United States; or his sympathy with those engaged in exciting or carrying on rebellion against the United States; or has ever, except under overpowering compulsion, submitted to the authority, or been in the service of these so-called "Confederate States of America;" or has ever left this State, and gone within the lines of the armies of the so-called "Confederate States of America," with the purpose of adhering to said States or armies; or has ever been a member of, or connected with any order, society or organization inimical to the Government of the United States, or to the Government of this State; or has ever been engaged in guerrilla warfare against loyal inhabitants of the United States, or in that description of marauding commonly known as "bushwhacking;" or has ever knowingly and willingly harbored, aided or countenanced any person so engaged; or has ever come into or left this State for the purpose of avoiding enrollment for or draft into the military service of the United States; or has ever, with a view to avoid enrollment in the militia of this State, or to escape the performance of duty therein, or for any other purpose, enrolled himself, or authorized himself to be enrolled, by or before any officer, as disloyal or as a Southern sympathizer, or in any other terms indicating his disaffection to the Government of the United States in its contest with rebellion, or his sympathy with those engaged in such rebellion; or having ever voted at any election by the people in this State, or in any other of the United States, or in any of their Territories, or under the United States, shall thereafter have sought or received, under claim of alienage, the protection of any foreign government, through any consul or other officer thereof, in order to secure exemption from military duty, in the militia of this State, or in the army of the United States; nor shall any such person be capable of holding, in this State, any office of honor, trust or profit under its authority; or of being an officer, councilman, director, trustee, or other manager of any corporation, public or private, now existing, or hereafter established by its authority; or of acting as a professor or teacher in any educational institution, or in any common or other school; or of holding any real estate or other property in trust for the use of any church, religious society or congregation. But the foregoing provisions in relation to acts done against the United States shall not apply to any person not a citizen thereof, who shall have committed such acts while in the service of some foreign country at war with the United States, and who has, since such acts, been naturalized, or may hereafter be naturalized, under the laws of the United States, and the oath of loyalty hereinafter prescribed, when taken by any such persons, shall be considered as taken in such sense.

Section 4 provided for a registration of the names of qualified voters, and Section 5 required that the oath indicated in the third section should be taken by every voter at the time of his registration. Taking the oath should not, however, be deemed conclusive evidence of the right of a person to vote, supposing such right could be otherwise disproved. This section also provided that evidence for or against the right of any person to vote should be heard and passed upon by the registering officers and not by the judges of election.

These officers should keep a list of the names of rejected voters, and the same were to be certified to the judges of elections who were to receive the ballot of any such rejected voter, marking the same as a rejected vote; but even with these precautions the vote was not to be received unless the party casting it should, at the time, take the oath of loyalty.

Under the ninth section no person was permitted to practice law, "or be competent as a bishop, priest, deacon, minister, elder or other clergyman of any religious persuasion, sect or denomination, to teach or preach, unless such person shall have first taken, subscribed and filed said oath."

While the article upon the "Executive Department" was pending, an effort was made to introduce an amendment, by which any citizen of the State, white or colored, male or female, would be eligible to the office of governor, but the amendment was rejected by a tie vote, as also a similar proposition in reference to the "Legislative Department."

It is but just to say, in this connection, that the new constitution, objectionable and stringent as it was in many particulars, was admirable in respect to its provisions for public instruction, and was conceded to be so by its bitterest enemies.

The constitution was adopted April 8, and two days afterward the convention adjourned *sine die*.

An election had been appointed for the 6th of June, 1865, to submit the new constitution to the people for their indorsement or rejection, but it had also been provided that no person should vote at that election except those who would be qualified as voters under the second article thereof. The canvass which followed was naturally one of the greatest bitterness.

Although the war was nominally over, and all the strongholds of the Rebellion were in the hands of the United States authorities, yet there were fragmentary guerrilla bands still roaming through various sections of the country, and the war spirit continued in undiminished force. Multitudes of taxpayers in the State, not a few of whom were honored and influential citizens, and had been non-combatants during the war, were disfranchised by the third section, and denied the privilege of voting upon the adoption or rejection of the code of laws which was to govern them and their children. On the other hand, it was maintained with vigor that citizens who had attempted to destroy their government, who had committed treason either by open deeds of rebellion, or by encouragement, sympathy and aid given to those in rebellion, had forfeited all right to assist in conducting the affairs of State. The election resulted in a majority of 1,862 for the constitution, which accordingly went into effect July 4, 1865.

The next General Assembly, which convened at Jefferson City on November 1, proceeded to enact a registry law, which, on account of its stringency, occasioned much violence and disorder in its enforcement. The "Ousting Ordinance," for vacating certain civil offices, was also attended with unpleasant results.

That portion of the ninth section in regard to ministers, lawyers and teachers, excited so much trouble in the State that B. Gratz Brown, Carl Schurz, and other leading Republicans, set on foot December, 1866, a movement which had for its object universal amnesty and enfranchisement. The movement soon became popular throughout the State, and, in his message to the Twenty-Fourth General Assembly, January, 1867, Gov. Fletcher recommended an amendment to the constitution, striking out the ninth section of the second article. At this session of the Legislature a constitutional amendment was submitted to the people proposing to strike the word "white" from the eighteenth section of the second article, and thus inaugurate negro suffrage in Missouri. While this amendment was under consideration in the House, Mr. Orrick of St. Charles proposed to strike out not only the word "white" but also the word "male." This effort in behalf of female suffrage was rejected; and at the election of the people in November, 1868, negro suffrage was also defeated by a majority of 18,817 votes.

The adjourned session of the Twenty-fifth General Assembly, which met on January 5, 1870, accomplished important work in several directions.

Gov. Joseph W. McClurg recommended in his message the ratification of the Fifteenth Amendment to the constitution of the United States, passed by Congress on February 27, 1869, and transmitted to the General Assembly at the same time a copy of the amendment, as follows:

Article XV.—SECTION 1. The right of citizens of the United States to vote shall not be denied or abridged by the United States or by any State on account of race, color or previous condition of servitude.
SEC. 2. The Congress shall have power to enforce this article by appropriate legislation.

Immediately upon the reading of the amendment, a joint resolution ratifying it was introduced into the Senate, and was speedily adopted by both Houses of the Legislature.

Divisions in the Republican Party.—The differences of opinion regarding universal amnesty and enfranchisement were rapidly assuming the proportions of discord and disintegration; and the Republican party in the State became divided in sentiment as well as in name, being known respectively as Radicals and Liberals; the former maintaining a severe, and the latter a more magnanimous policy towards those who had complicity with the Rebellion. The Democrats, owing to the stringent registry laws, were in a hopeless minority, and so attached themselves to the Liberal Republicans, believing that by this course they might best aid their disfranchised brethren, and eventually gain control of State politics. The State Nominating Convention, which met at Jefferson City on August 31, 1870, witnessed the final division of the Republicans. The platforms of the two branches of the party differed chiefly in regard to enfranchisement, and the articles embodying their respective sentiments were as follows:

MAJORITY OR LIBERAL PLATFORM.

Fourth. That the time has come when the requirements of public safety, upon which alone the disfranchisement of a large number of citizens could be justified, has clearly ceased to exist, and this convention, therefore, true to the solemn pledges recorded in our National and State platforms, declares itself unequivocally in favor of the adoption of the constitutional amendments, commonly called the suffrage and office-holding amendments, believing that under existing circumstances the removal of political disabilities, as well as the extension of equal political rights and privileges to all classes of citizens, without distinction, is demanded by every consideration of good faith, patriotism and sound policy, and essential to the integrity of republican institutions, to the welfare of the State, and to the honor and preservation of the Republican party.

MINORITY OR RADICAL PLATFORM.

Third. That we are in favor of re-enfranchising those justly disfranchised for participation in the late Rebellion, as soon as it can be done with safety to the State, and that we concur in the propriety of the Legislature having submitted to the whole people of the State the question whether such time has now arrived; upon which question we recognize the right of any member of the party to vote his honest convictions.

The two reports being before the convention, the report of the minority was adopted, whereupon about 250 delegates, friends of the majority report, led by Mr. Schurz, withdrew, organized a separate convention, and nominated a full State ticket, with B. Gratz Brown as a candidate for governor. The other convention also nominated a full ticket, headed by Joseph W. McClurg for governor, at that time incumbent of the office.

The election of November, 1870, resulted in the choice of the B. Gratz Brown ticket by a majority of over 40,000 Liberal and

Democratic votes. This election marks the period at which the Republicans, who had been for eight years in the ascendency, surrendered the power which they have since been unable to regain.

Amendments to the State Constitution.—At an adjourned session of the Twenty-sixth General Assembly, which convened December 6, 1871, two constitutional amendments had been submitted to the votes of the people.

These were ratified at the November election in 1872. The first increased the number of supreme court judges from three to five, fixing their term of office at ten years, and providing that two additional judges should be elected at the general election in 1872, and one judge at each general election, every two years thereafter.

The second provided that no part of the public school fund should ever be invested in the stock or bonds or other obligations of any other State, or of any county, city, town or corporation; that the stock of the bank of the State of Missouri, held for school purposes, and all other stocks belonging to any school or university fund, should be sold in such manner and at such time as the General Assembly should prescribe; and the proceeds thereof, and the proceeds of the sales of any lands or other property which belonged or might hereafter belong to said school fund, should be invested in the bonds of the State of Missouri, or of the United States, and that all county school funds should be loaned upon good and sufficient and unincumbered real estate security, with personal security in addition thereto.

Revision of the State Constitution.—During an adjourned session of the Legislature, which met on January 7, 1874, a law had been passed authorizing a vote of the people to be taken at the general election in November, 1874, for and against calling a convention to revise and amend the constitution of the State. This convention was agreed to by a majority of only 283. An election for delegates took place on January 26, 1875. On May 5, of the same year, the convention assembled at the capital. It consisted of sixty-eight members, sixty of whom were Democrats, six Republicans, and two Liberals. A thorough revision of the entire organic law was made, both in committee and in convention. Every department of the State Government passed under review, and many important changes were made, which can not be discussed here, but they are familiar to every well-informed citizen of the State.

The bill of rights occasioned much discussion. County representation, which has been a feature of every State constitution, including the first, was still maintained in spite of opposition. Carefully prepared and stringent limitations on the powers of the General Assembly were engrafted on the new instrument. Sessions of the Legislature were made biennial, and the gubernatorial term changed from two or four years. The formation of new counties was made extremely difficult or impossible. The power of the Legislature, and of counties, cities, towns and all other municipalities, to levy taxes and contract debts, was hedged about with limitations and safeguards. Extra mileage and perquisites to officials were laid under embargo. The system of free public schools, embracing a liberal policy for the maintenance of the State University, received recognition in the article on education. The final vote on the adoption of the constitution as a whole stood—ayes, 60; noes, 0; absent, 8. October 30, 1875, the people ratified the constitution by a majority of 76,688, and on the 30th of November, 1875, it became the supreme law.

Gov. Crittenden's Administration.—In 1880, Thomas T. Crittenden, of Johnson County, received the Democratic nomination for governor of Missouri, and was elected in November of that year. Gov. Crittenden's competitors for the nomination were Gen. John S. Marmaduke, of St. Louis, and John A. Hockaday, of Callaway County. In his inaugural address, he recommended refunding at a lower rate of interest all that part of the State debt which could be thus refunded; some measures for the relief of the docket of the supreme court of the State, and a compromise of the indebtedness of several counties. He also condemned in the strongest terms the doctrine of repudiation.

Gov. Crittenden is by birth a Kentuckian—a direct descendant of the old Crittenden stock so long and deservedly prominent and popular in the State of Kentucky. Though himself a slaveholder, at the outbreak of the Civil War he espoused the cause of the Union, and no braver officer than he ever faced an enemy. At the close of the war he was found in the front rank of the conservative portion of the people, who contended that peace should prevail, and the bitter animosities of the past be forgotten.

He was sent to Congress, where, in more than one instance he proved his integrity. Throughout his entire career, no stain of venality adhered to his fair name, and no act of violence characterized his discharge of any duty.

Under his guiding hand the credit of the State advanced to a par with that of the Federal Government; the debt of the State gradually diminished, and all of her educational interests fostered and nourished.

When Gov. Crittenden took charge of the helm of State, a portion of the border was infested with a lawless band of thieves and murderers, known as the "James Gang," who murdered without pity, and robbed without regard to person. He resolved to disband them. Soon some of the most desperate of the gang were in the hands of the officers, and, in one instance, when resistance and rescue were threatened, Gov. Crittenden attended the trial in person, with a few chosen friends, determined to defend the supremacy of the law with his life if necessary.

One by one, the members of this gang were hunted down and sent to the penitentiary, and finally Jesse James was shot at St. Joseph by the "Ford Boys," former comrades, who had been employed to capture him.

The Election of 1884.—The campaign of 1884, both Nationally and in the State, was the most hotly contested of any this country has ever seen. In Missouri an alliance was effected between the Republican and Greenback parties, and a ticket headed by the name of Nicholas Ford, of St. Joseph, and called the "Anti-Bourbon ticket," was put into the field against the Democracy, headed by Gen. John S. Marmaduke, of St. Louis. A third party known as the Prohibitionists, exercised considerable influence in the canvass. The "Anti-Bourbon" party made their fight against the record of the Democrats, who had been in uninterrupted power for twelve years, and especially against the tendency of the Democracy to recognize and reward men who had been in rebellion during the Civil War. This plea, owing to the nomination of Marmaduke, who had been a Confederate general, was of considerable service to the opponents of Democracy, and came near securing the defeat of the party. The campaign on the part of the Democrats was mainly a defensive one; while John A. Brooks, the Prohibition candidate, urged that neither Ford nor Marmaduke should be elected, pledging himself in favor of submitting a constitutional amendment to prohibit the manufacture and sale of intoxicating liquors. Mr. Brooks made a strong fight, and polled nearly 10,000 votes. Marmaduke was elected by a majority of less than 2,000, although the Cleveland electors carried the State by about 30,000. All of the Democratic State ticket was elected by varying majorities, and also twelve out of fourteen congressmen were chosen by the same party.

Notwithstanding the opposition manifested toward him Gov. Marmaduke made an excellent career as an Executive, discharging his duties in an impartial, conservative manner. On Tuesday, December 27, 1887, news of the sudden and serious illness of the governor was spread over the country. This was soon followed, on the evening of December 28, by tidings of his death.

Lieut.-Gov. Morehouse subsequently qualified as governor of the State, and is the present incumbent of the position.

The Early Courts.—As the District of Louisiana was for many years under the dominion of Spain, it became necessary for the early lawyers to acquaint themselves with Spanish civil and criminal laws. This they uniformly did, and even after the district came into the possession of the United States the rules which obtained in the Spanish and French courts were still clung to. Until the district was purchased by the United States, the administration or execution of the laws was in the hands of the civil and military commandants, who in most instances were both ill-informed and arbitrary. In 1804 Congress extended the executive power of the Territory of Indiana over that of Louisiana, and the execution of the laws of what is now Missouri fell to William Henry Harrison, governor, and Griffin, Vanderburg and Davis, judges. The first courts were held in the winter of 1804–05, in the old fort near the junction of Fifth and Walnut

Streets, St. Louis, and were called courts of common pleas. In March, 1805, the District of Louisiana was changed to the Territory of Louisiana, and James Wilkinson became governor; Frederick Bates, secretary; and James Wilkinson, Return J. Meigs and J. B. C. Lucas, judges of the superior court of the Territory. At this time the executive officers were in the old government building called *La Place d' Armes*, St. Louis. The districts of the Territory were changed to counties, Territorial courts superseded the commandants, and the rules of the English common law soon banished those of France and Spain. Courts of common pleas were established by the Territorial Legislature in 1813. Since the formation of the State Government the constitution and the Legislature have provided the number and character of the State courts.

EDUCATION.

The history of popular education in Missouri, previous to the Rebellion, is similar to that of every other State upon which the shadow of slavery rested. That institution and free popular education were incompatible. It is true that almost every slave State established some sort of common school system, but its provisions were always so defective, the funds for its support always so small and inadequate as to render it practically useless. Free schools were called "pauper schools," and were not attended by the children of the upper classes of whites. The idea of a system of free education for rich and poor alike—a common school—was unthought of as to bringing it into practical use.

Many laws were passed by the Missouri Legislature for the establishment and regulation of free schools, but all were almost totally defective in not providing sufficient funds to put them into effective operation, and in not rendering them of sufficient importance to secure attendance and countenance from the upper classes. In the act of Congress, authorizing the people of Missouri Territory to form a constitution and State Government, the sixteenth section of each township or its equivalent was devoted to the purpose of supporting schools in each township. The first act of the Legislature on the subject of education was approved January 17, 1825. This law enacted that each congressional township should form a school district to be under the control of the county court in all matters pertaining to schools. It also declared that all rents of school lands and fines, penalties and forfeitures, occurring under the provisions of this act, should be set apart for a school fund. On January 26, 1833, the Legislature authorized the governor to appoint three suitable persons whose duty it should be to prepare a system of common primary school instruction, as nearly uniform as possible throughout the State, and to make a report to the next meeting of the Legislature. This committee made a report, but its suggestions were not acted upon by the Legislature. This body, however, at its next session, passed "an act to regulate the sale of the sixteenth sections, and to provide for the organization and regulation of common schools." The Governor, Secretary of State, Auditor, Treasurer and Attorney-General were constituted a board of commissioners for literary purposes. Its provisions required a school to be taught in each incorporated district, for six months during the year. It was similar in its details to the law of 1825, but so imperfect and impracticable as to render its repeal necessary.

February 6, 1836, the first movement was made for the endowment of a common school fund. An act was passed directing the governor to invest the principal and interest of the saline fund, and all additions thereafter made to it, and all the money received by the State from the United States, by virtue of the provisions of the act of Congress passed June 23, 1836, in some safe and productive stock, to continue, remain, and be known as "The Common School Fund," and when said fund should amount to $500,000 or more, the interests and profits accruing thereon should be applied to pay teachers in the common schools in such manner as the General Assembly should direct. No system of school laws was enacted until the next session, February 9, 1839, about two years later. Its provisions were substantially as follows: The school fund was to consist of all the moneys heretofore deposited under the act of Congress of January 23, 1836, the proceeds of the saline funds, the proceeds of all lands then or thereafter vested in the State by escheat, by purchase or by forfeiture for taxes; and the interest and proceeds of such moneys until a distribution should be ordered. The office of State superintendent of common schools was created and its duties defined. The superintendent was given a general oversight of the schools of the State, and was required to make a distribution of school moneys among the several counties in which there were any schools, in proportion to the number of white children between the ages of six and eighteen years.

This law received several amendments, and on February 24 a new system was adopted, of which the following is a synopsis: At its head was the State superintendent, elected biennially by the people. Each county had a commissioner of common schools, whose duty it was to grant certificates of qualifications to teachers, apportion school moneys and visit schools. Each congressional township was constituted a school township which could be divided into as many school districts, not exceeding four, as the inhabitants might desire. Each district was placed under the control of three trustees who employed teachers, levied taxes, voted bills, etc. Twenty-five per cent of the State revenue, and the dividends arising from the funds invested in the Bank of the State of Missouri, were apportioned to the counties in proportion to the number of children between the ages of five and twenty years. This, with the county funds coming from the interest on the moneys arising from the sale of the sixteenth sections, from fines and penalties, etc., and the income from the proceeds of the sale of swamp and overflowed lands, constituted the fund annually appropriated for the payment of teachers.

In 1858 the capital of the State school fund amounted to about $681,000, of which $20,000 was invested in Missouri State bonds and the remainder in stock of the Bank of Missouri. The first distribution of school money was made in 1842, when only thirteen counties received any portion of it, they being the only ones in which schools had been organized. They were Benton, Boone, Clark, Cole, Cooper, Greene, La Fayette, Livingston, Marion, Monroe, Ralls, Saline and Shelby. The amount apportioned at that time was only $1,999.60. In 1845 it had increased to $16,481.80; in 1850 to $27,751.52; in 1855, under the new law, which was much better than the preceding ones, it was $178,082.79.

The constitution of no State of the Union contains more liberal and enlightened provisions relative to popular education than that of Missouri, adopted in 1875. During the past sixty years not a line can be found upon her statute books inimical to the cause; and in nearly every gubernatorial message from 1824 to the present time have been earnest and effective arguments in favor of a broad and liberal system of public instruction. The people of the State have taxed themselves freely for the support of the system; and the amount of her available and productive permanent school fund at this time surpasses that of nearly every other State in the Union. In 1886 it was as follows:

Certificates of indebtedness at 6 per cent	$2,909,000 00
Certificates of indebtedness at 5 per cent	225,000 00
In treasury to credit of State School Fund	414 80
Total amount to credit of State School Fund	3,134,414 80
University or Seminary Fund	519,095 08
County Public School Fund	3,300,668 39
Township Public School Fund	3,441,048 16
Special School Fund	71,455 44
Fines, penalties, forfeitures, etc.	121,279 94
Total	$10,587,961 81

Before the establishment of the free-school system, education throughout the State was obtained wholly from private institutions of learning. The University of Missouri was founded about the time the State was admitted to the Federal Union, when two townships of land were granted for the support of a seminary of learning. In 1832 this land was sold for less than $75,000, but by 1839 this amount had grown to over $100,000. In the latter year the site was selected for the university at Columbia, which offered a bonus of $117,500 to secure the location—a remarkable offering for that day. The corner-stone was laid in 1840, and John H. Lathrop, D. D., became the first president. To this institution the following departments have since been added: Normal department, 1868; agricultural and mechanical college, 1870; schools of mines and metallurgy, 1871, at Rolla; college of law, 1872; medical college, 1873; department of analytical and applied chemistry, 1873; architecture, engineering, mechanical and fine arts, etc. The State may well be proud of this institution.

St. Louis University was established in 1829, and has become one of the best educational institutions of the country. Since the war the State has founded an educational institution for colored people—Lincoln Institute, at Jefferson City—which is supported by an annual appropriation. Several normal colleges have also been established by the Legislature, which contribute materially toward the elevation of the standard of education in the State. In nearly every county is a seminary, academy, college or university, supported by tuition or endowments, and controlled by some sectarian organization, or by a non-sectarian association.

In 1817 the Legislature incorporated the board of trustees of the St. Louis public schools, and this was the commencement of the present system. The first board was Gen. William Clarke, William C. Carr, Thomas H. Benton, Bernard Pratt, Auguste Chouteau, Alexander McNair and John P. Cabanne. Much should have been, and was, expected of this board, owing to their prominence and ability; but they did little or nothing, and it was not until twenty years later that the system sprang into life.

RELIGION.

Churches—Baptist.—The First Baptist Church organized in what is now the State of Missouri was founded near the present site of Jackson, Cape Girardeau County, in 1806, under the labors of Rev. D. Green. The growth of the denomination has been marked. It has gone steadily on in its increase, until now it marshals a great host, and it is still rapidly enlarging in numbers, and advancing in intelligence and general thrift. The annual report of the Baptist General Association of Missouri, for 1875, gives the following statistics: 61 district associations; 1,400 churches; 824 ordained ministers; 89,650 members. The Bible and Publication Society, with headquarters at Philadelphia, has a branch house at St. Louis, which has become one of the chief book establishments of the State. The Baptist periodicals of the State are the *Central Baptist* and *Ford's Repository*, both published in St. Louis. The Baptist seats of learning in Missouri are William Jewell College, Liberty; Stephens' College, Columbia; Mount Pleasant College, Huntsville; Baptist Female

College, Lexington; La Grange College, La Grange: Baptist College, Louisiana; Liberty Female College, Liberty; St. Louis Seminary for Young Ladies, Jenning's Station; Fairview Female Seminary, Jackson; Boonville Seminary for Young Ladies North Grand River College, Edinburgh; Ingleside Academy, Palmyra.

Christian.—This is one of the largest denominations in Missouri; it has more than 500 churches, and nearly 100,000 members. The literary institutions of the denomination are Christian College, Columbia; Christian University, Canton; Woodland College, Independence; Christian Orphan Asylum, Camden Point. The publications of this denomination in Missouri are *The Christian, The Little Watchman, The Little Sower,* and *The Morning Watch,* all published at St. Louis.

Congregational.—The first Trinitarian Congregational Church was organized in St. Louis, in 1852, Rev. T. M. Post, D. D., pastor. The church in Hannibal was organized in 1859. In 1864-65 fifteen churches were organized in towns on the Hannibal & St. Joseph Railroad. In 1875 the denomination had 5 district associations, 70 churches, 41 ministers and 3,363 members. There are two Congregational colleges in the State—Thayer College, at Kidder, and Drury College, at Springfield.

Episcopal.—The first service of the Protestant Episcopal Church in Missouri was held October 24, 1819, and Christ Church, St. Louis, was organized as a parish November 1, of the same year. The Rev. John Ward, previously of Lexington, Ky., was the first rector. Six persons united in the first service. In 1875 there were in the city of St. Louis 12 parishes and missions, and as many clergymen; while, taking all parts of the State, there were about 5,000 communicants, 51 ministers, 48 church buildings, 57 Sunday-schools with 4,000 scholars, and 475 teachers. The denomination controlled 4 secular schools. The Diocese of Missouri is conterminous with the State of Missouri.

Friends.—The following are the approximate statistics of this denomination in Missouri: Number of organizations and edifices, 4; sittings, 1,100; value of property, $4,800.

Israelite.—There is scarcely a county in the State of Missouri where at least one dozen Jewish families are not settled. Jefferson City, Sedalia, Springfield, Rolla, Washington, Macon City, Louisiana, Hannibal, and several other places, have wealthy, influential Jewish citizens, but too few in number to form independent religious communities. In St. Louis, St. Joseph and Kansas City they have established congregations, Sabbath-schools, houses of worship and institutions of charity. The oldest Hebrew congregation in Missouri was organized in 1838, at St. Louis. The following summary gives an approximate statement of the Israelite congregations in Missouri: Congregations, 8; members, 557; ministers, 8; houses of worship, 7; Sabbath-schools, 7; with 12 teachers and 574 scholars.

Lutheran.—The first Lutheran Church organized in Missouri was founded in St. Louis in 1839. The number of churches is now about 92. The Lutheran educational institutions of the State are Concordia College and a high school, both at St. Louis. The charitable institutions are the Lutheran Hospital and Asylum at St. Louis, and the Lutheran Orphans' Home in St. Louis County. At St. Louis are also located the Lutheran Central Bible Society, and the Lutheran Book Concern of the German Evangelical Lutheran Synod of Missouri, Ohio and other States. The following Lutheran periodicals are published in St. Louis: *Der Lutheraner, Die Abendschule, Lehreund Wehre,* and the *Evangel Lutheran Schublatt German Evangelical.* There are, in Missouri, perhaps 45 churches of this denomination, comprising 7,500 members. The *Friedensbote* is the name of a newspaper published under its patronage. Evangelical Missouri College is the theological seat of learning in this synod, and is located in Warren County.

Methodist Episcopal.—The Methodist Episcopal Church in Missouri dates from an early period in the history of the State. Indeed, several societies were formed before it became a State, and these were a part of the old Illinois Conference. When the separation of 1844–45 took place, and the Methodist Episcopal Church South was formed, the societies in Missouri were broken up with few exceptions, and the members either joined that organization or remained unable to effect a reorganization of their own until 1848, when the Missouri Conference resumed its sessions. During the Civil War the preachers and members were driven from nearly all the stations and districts. There were probably less than 3,000 persons in actual fellowship in 1861 and 1862. In May, 1862, the general conference added Arkansas to the Missouri Conference, and it bore the name of "The Missouri and Arkansas Conference," until 1868, when it was divided, the societies north of the Missouri River retaining the old name, Missouri Conference; and the societies south of the river, and those in Arkansas, being formed into the "St. Louis Conference." In 1872 the societies in Missouri, south of the river, became the St. Louis Conference, those in Arkansas, the Arkansas Conference. The two conferences of Missouri now comprise about 375 churches and 30,000 members. They have several flourishing schools and colleges, the principal of which are Lewis College, Glasgow; Johnson College, Macon City, and Carleton Institute, in Southeast Missouri. The Western Book Depository is doing a large business in St. Louis, and its agents also publish the *Central Christian Advocate.*

Methodist Episcopal Church South.—The first preaching by a Protestant minister in this State was by a Methodist local preacher, John Clark by name, who resided where Alton now stands, and who occasionally crossed the river to a settlement of Americans near Florissant. The first regularly appointed Methodist preacher was Rev. John Travis, who received an appointment from Bishop Asbury in 1806. He formed two circuits, and at the end of the year returned 100 members. These circuits were called "Missouri" and "Meramec," and at the conference of 1807, Jesse Walker was sent to supply the former, and Edmund Wilcox the latter.

From this time preachers were regularly appointed, and in 1820 there were, in Missouri, 21 traveling preachers and 2,079 members. In 1821 Methodism proper was introduced into St. Louis by Rev. Jesse Walker, who secured the erection of a small house of worship on the corner of what is now Fourth and Myrtle Streets, and returned 127 members.

OFFICIAL.

Missouri Officials—Under the French Government.—Commandant.—April 9, 1682, Robert Cavalier de La Salle.

Governors.—1698 to July 22, 1701, Sauvalle; 1701 to May 17, 1713, Bienville; 1713 to March 9, 1717, Lamothe Cadillac; 1717 to March 9, 1718, Del'Epinay; 1718 to January 16, 1724, Bienville; 1724 to 1726, Boisbriant; 1726 to 1733, Perier; 1733 to May 10, 1743, Bienville; 1743 to February 9, 1753, Vaudreuil; 1753 to June 29, 1763, Kerlerec; 1763 to February 4, 1765, D'Abadie; February, 1765, M. Aubry, acting.

Commandant.—July 17, 1765, to May 20, 1770, Louis St. Ange de Bellerive, *de facto*.

Under the Spanish Government.—*Lieutenant Governors.*—May 20, 1770, to May 19, 1775, Pedro Piernas; 1775 to June 17, 1778, Francisco Cruzat; 1778 to June 8, 1780, Fernando De Leyba; 1780 to September 24, 1780, Silvio Franc. Cartabona; 1780 to November 27, 1787, Franc. Cruzat; 1787 to July 21, 1792, Manuel Perez; 1792 to August 29, 1799, Zenon Trudeau; 1799, to March 9, 1804, C. Dehault Delassus.

Under the United States Government.—*Commandant*—March 10, 1804, to October 1, 1804, Capt. Amos Stoddard, who was also agent and commissioner of the French Government for one day, from March 9 to March 10, 1804.

Under the District of Louisiana.—*Governor*—October 1, 1804, to March 3, 1805, William Henry Harrison. The District of Louisiana was at this time attached to the Territory of Indiana, of which Gen. Harrison was governor.

Under the Territory of Louisiana.—*Governors*—1805 to 1806, Gen. James Wilkinson; last part of 1806, Joseph Brown, acting; May, 1807 to October 1807, Frederick Bates, acting; 1807 to September, 1809, Merriwether Lewis; September, 1809, to September 19, 1810, Frederick Bates, acting; 1810 to November 29, 1812, Benjamin Howard, acting; 1812 to December 7, 1812, Frederick Bates, secretary and acting governor.

Territorial Officers.—*Governors*—Frederick Bates, secretary and acting governor, 1812–13; William Clark, 1813–20.

Delegates to Congress.—Edward Hempstead, 1811–14; Rufus Easton, 1814–17; John Scott, 1817–20.

Officers of State Government.—*Governors*—Alexander McNair, 1820–1824; Frederick Bates, 1824–25; Abraham J. Williams, vice Bates, 1825; John Miller, *vice* Bates, 1826–28; John

Miller, 1828-32; Dunklin resigned; appointed surveyor-general of the United States, 1832-36; L. W. Boggs, *vice* Dunklin, 1836; Lilburn W. Boggs, 1836-40; Thomas Reynolds (died 1844) 1840-44; M. M. Marmaduke, *vice* Reynolds; John C. Edwards, 1844-48; Austin A. King, 1848-52; Sterling Price, 1852-56; Trusten Polk, resigned 1856-57; Hancock Jackson, *vice* Polk, 1857; Robert M. Stewart, *vice* Polk, 1857-60; C. F. Jackson (1860), office vacated by ordinance; Hamilton R. Gamble, *vice* Jackson—Gov. Gamble died, 1864; Willard P. Hall, *vice* Gamble, 1864; Thomas C. Fletcher, 1864-68; Joseph W. McClurg, 1868-70; B. Gratz Brown, 1870-72; Silas Woodson, 1872-74; Charles H. Hardin, 1874-76; John S. Phelps, 1876-80; Thomas T. Crittenden, 1880-84; John S. Marmaduke (died 1887), 1884-88; A. P. Morehouse, *vice* Marmaduke.

Lieutenant Governors.—William H. Ashley, 1820-24; Benjamin H. Reeves, 1824-28; Daniel Dunklin, 1828-32; Lilburn W. Boggs, 1832-36; Franklin Cannon, 1836-40; M. M. Marmaduke, 1840-44; James Young, 1844-48; Thomas L. Rice, 1848-52; Wilson Brown, 1852-55; Hancock Jackson, 1855-56; Thomas C. Reynolds, 1860-61; Willard P. Hall, 1861-64; George Smith, 1864-68; Edwin O. Stanard, 1868-70; Joseph J. Gravelly, 1870-72; Charles P. Johnson, 1872-74; Norman J. Coleman, 1874-76; Henry C. Brockmeyer, 1876-80; Robert A. Campbell, 1880-84; A. P. Morehouse (appointed governor), 1884.

Secretaries of State.—Joshua Barton, 1820-21; William G. Pettis, 1821-24; Hamilton R. Gamble, 1824-26; Spencer Pettis, 1826-28; P. H. McBride, 1829-30; John C. Edwards (term expired 1835; re-appointed 1837, resigned 1837), 1830-37; Peter G. Glover, 1837-39; James L. Minor, 1839-45; F. H. Martin, 1845-49; Ephraim B. Ewing, 1849-52; John M. Richardson, 1852-56; Benjamin F. Massey (re-elected 1860 for four years), 1856-60; Mordecai Oliver, 1861-64; Francis Rodman (re-elected 1868 for two years), 1864-68; Eugene F. Weigel (re-elected 1872 for two years), 1870-72; Michael K. McGrath (re-elected 1884 for four years), 1874-84.

State Treasurers.—Peter Didier, 1820-21; Nathaniel Simonds, 1821-28; James Earickson, 1829-33; John Walker, 1833-38;

Abraham McClellan, 1838–43; Peter G. Glover, 1843–51; A. W. Morrison, 1851–60; George C. Bingham, 1862–64; William Bishop, 1864–68; William Q. Dallmeyer, 1868–70; Samuel Hays, 1872; Harvey W. Salmon, 1872–74; Joseph W. Mercer, 1874–76; Elijah Gates, 1876–80; Philip E. Chappell, 1880–84; J. M. Seibert (present incumbent), 1884.

Attorney-Generals.—Edward Bates, 1820–21; Rufus Easton, 1821–26; Robert W. Wells, 1826–36; William B. Napton, 1836–39; S. M. Bay, 1839–45; B. F. Stringfellow, 1845–49; William A. Robards, 1849–51; James B. Gardenhire, 1851–56; Ephraim W. Ewing, 1856–59; James P. Knott, 1859–61; Aikman Welch, 1861–64; Thomas T. Crittenden, 1864; Robert F. Wingate, 1864–68; Horace P. Johnson, 1868–70; A. J. Baker, 1870–72; Henry C. Ewing, 1872–74; John A. Hockaday, 1874–76; Jackson L. Smith, 1876–80; D. H. McIntire, 1880–84; D. G. Boone (present incumbent), 1884.

Auditors of Public Accounts.—William Christie, 1820–21; William V. Rector, 1821–23; Elias Barcroft, 1823–33; Henry Shurlds, 1833–35; Peter G. Glover, 1835–37; Hiram H. Baber, 1837–45; William Monroe, 1845; J. R. McDermon, 1845–48; George W. Miller, 1848–49; Wilson Brown, 1849–52; William H. Buffington, 1852–60; William S. Moseley, 1860–64; Alonzo Thompson, 1864–68: Daniel M. Draper, 1868–72; George B. Clark, 1872–74; Thomas Holladay, 1874–80; John Walker (re-elected in 1884, for four years), 1880–84.

Judges of Supreme Court.—Matthias McGirk, 1822–41; John D. Cooke, 1822–23; John R. Jones, 1822–24; Rufus Pettibone, 1823–25; George Tompkins, 1824–45; Robert Wash, 1825–37; John C. Edwards, 1837–39; William Scott (appointed 1841 until meeting of General Assembly in place of McGirk resigned; reappointed), 1843; P. H. McBride, 1845; William B. Napton, 1849–52; John F. Ryland, 1849–51; John H. Birch, 1849–51; William Scott, John F. Ryland and Hamilton R. Gamble (elected by the people for six years), 1851; Hamilton R. Gamble (resigned), 1854; Abiel Leonard (elected to fill vacancy of Gamble); William B. Napton (vacated by failure to file oath); William Scott and John C. Richardson (resigned, elected August, for six years), 1857; E. B. Ewing to fill Richardson's resignation), 1859; Barton Bates (appointed), 1862; W. V. N. Bay, (appointed), 1862; John D. S. Dryden (appointed), 1862; Barton Bates, 1863-65; W. V. N. Bay (elected), 1863; John D. S. Dryden (elected), 1863; David Wagner (appointed), 1865; Wallace L. Lovelace (appointed), 1865; Nathaniel Holmes (appointed), 1865; Thomas J. C. Fagg (appointed), 1866; James Baker (appointed), 1868; David Wagner (elected), 1868-70; Philemon Bliss, 1868-70, Warren Currier, 1868-71; Washington Adams (appointed to fill Currier's place, who resigned), 1871; Ephraim B. Ewing (elected), 1872; Thomas A. Sherwood (elected), 1872; W. B. Napton (appointed in place of Ewing, deceased), 1873; Edward A. Lewis (appointed in place of Adams, resigned), 1874; Warwich Hough (elected), 1874; William B. Napton (elected), 1874-80; John W. Henry, 1876-86; Robert D. Ray succeeded William B. Napton, 1880; Elijah H. Norton (appointed in 1876), elected, 1878; T. A. Sherwood (re-elected), 1882; F. M. Black, 1884.

United States Senators.—T. H. Benton, 1820-50; D. Barton, 1820-30; Alexander Buckner, 1830-33; L. F. Linn, 1833-43; D. R. Atchison, 1843-55; H. S. Geyer, 1851-57; James S. Green, 1857-61; T. Polk, 1857-63; Waldo P. Johnson, 1861; Robert Wilson, 1861; B. Gratz Brown (for unexpired term of Johnson), 1863; J. B. Henderson, 1863-69; Charles D. Drake, 1867-70; Carl Schurz, 1869-75; D. F. Jewett (in place of Drake, resigned), 1870; F. P. Blair, 1871-77; L. V. Bogy, 1873; James Shields (elected for unexpired term of Bogy), 1879; D. H. Armstrong (appointed for unexpired term of Bogy); F. M. Cockrell (re-elected 1881), 1875-81; George G. Vest (re-elected in 1885 for six years), 1879-1885.

Representatives to Congress.—John Scott, 1820-26; E. Bates, 1826-28; Spencer Pettis, 1828-31; William H. Ashley, 1831-36; John Bull, 1832-34; Albert G. Harrison, 1834-39; John Miller, 1836-42; John Jameson (re-elected 1846 for two years), 1839-44; John C. Edwards, 1840-42; James M. Hughes, 1842-44; James H. Relfe, 1842-46; James B. Bowlin, 1842-50; Gustavus M. Bower, 1842-44; Sterling Price, 1844-46; William McDaniel, 1846; Leonard H. Sims, 1844–46; John S. Phelps, 1844–60; James S. Green (re-elected 1856, resigned), 1846–50; Willard P. Hall, 1846–53; William V. N. Bay, 1848–61; John F. Darby, 1850–53; Gilchrist Porter, 1850–57; John G. Miller, 1850–56; Alfred W. Lamb, 1852–54; Thomas H. Benton, 1852–54; Mordecai Oliver, 1852–57; James J. Lindley, 1852–56; Samuel Caruthers, 1852–58; Thomas P. Akers (to fill unexpired term of J. G. Miller, deceased), 1855; Francis P. Blair, Jr. (re-elected 1860, resigned), 1856; Thomas L. Anderson, 1856–60; James Craig, 1856–60; Silas H. Woodson, 1856–60; John B. Clark, Sr., 1857–61; J. Richard Barrett, 1860; John W. Noel, 1858–63, James S. Rollins, 1860–64; Elijah H. Norton, 1860–63; John W. Reid, 1860–61; William A. Hall, 1862–64; Thomas L. Price (in place of Reid, expelled), 1862; Henry T. Blow, 1862–66; Sempronious T. Boyd (elected in 1862, and again in 1868, for two years); Joseph W. McClurg, 1862–66; Austin A. King, 1862–64; Benjamin F. Loan, 1862–69; John G. Scott (in place of Noel, deceased), 1863; John Hogan, 1864–66; Thomas F. Noel, 1864–67; John R. Kelsoe, 1864–66; Robert T. Van Horn, 1864–71; John F. Benjamin, 1864–71; George W. Anderson, 1864–66; William A. Pile, 1866–68; C. A. Newcomb, 1866–68; Joseph J. Gravelly, 1866–68; James R. McCormack, 1866–73; John H. Stover (in place of McClurg, resigned), 1867; Erastus Wells, 1868–82; G. A. Finkelnburg, 1868–71; Samuel S. Burdett, 1868–71; Joel F. Asper, 1868–70; David P. Dyer, 1868–70; Harrison E. Havens, 1870–75; Isaac C. Parker, 1870–75; James G. Blair, 1870–72; Andrew King, 1870–72; Edwin O. Stanard, 1872–74; William H. Stone, 1872–78; Robert A. Hatcher (elected), 1872; Richard B. Bland, 1872; Thomas T. Crittenden, 1872–74; Ira B. Hyde, 1872–74; John B. Clark, Jr., 1872–78; John M. Glover, 1872; Aylett H. Buckner, 1872; Edward C. Kerr, 1874–78; Charles H. Morgan, 1874; John F. Phillips, 1874; B. J. Franklin, 1874; David Rea, 1874; Rezin A. DeBolt, 1874; Anthony Ittner, 1876; Nathan Cole, 1876; Robert A. Hatcher, 1876–78; R. P. Bland, 1876–78; A. H. Buckner, 1876–78; J. B. Clark, Jr., 1876–78; T. T. Crittenden, 1876–78; B. J. Franklin, 1876–78; John M.

Glover, 1876–78; Robert A. Hatcher, 1876–78; Charles H. Morgan (re-elected in 1881 and 1882), 1876–78; L. S. Metcalf, 1876–78; H. M. Pollard, 1876–78; David Rea, 1876–78; S. L. Sawyer, 1878–80; N. Ford, 1878–82; G. F. Rothwell, 1878–82; John B. Clark, Jr., 1878–82; W. H. Hatch (re-elected in 1884), 1878–84; A. H. Buckner (re-elected in 1882), 1878–82; M. L. Clardy (re-elected in 1882 and 1884), 1878–82; R. G. Frost, 1878–82; L. W. Davis (re-elected in 1882), 1878–82; R. P. Bland (re-elected in 1882 and 1884), 1878–82; J. R. Waddell, 1878–80; T. Allen, 1880–82; R. Hazeltine, 1880–82; T. M. Rice, 1880–82; R. T. Van Horn, 1880–82; J. G. Burrows, 1880–82; A. M. Alexander, 1882–84; Alex. M. Dockery (re-elected in 1884), 1882–84; James N. Burnes (re-elected in 1884) 1882–84; Alexander Graves, 1882–84; John Cosgrove, 1882–84; John J. O'Neill (re-elected in 1884), 1882–84; James O. Broadhead, 1882–84; R. W. Fyan, 1882–84; John B. Hale, 1884; William Warner, 1884; John T. Heard, 1884; J. E. Hutton, 1884; John M. Glover, 1884; William J. Stone, 1884; William H. Wade, 1884; William Dawson, 1884.

Congressmen Elected in 1886; Terms Expire in 1889.—First William H. Hatch; Second District, Charles H. Mansur; Third District, Alex. M. Dockery; Fourth District, James N. Burnes; Fifth District, William Warner; Sixth District, John T. Heard; Seventh District, John E. Hutton; Eighth District, John J. O'Neill; Ninth District, John M. Glover; Tenth District, Martin L. Clardy: Eleventh District, Richard P. Bland; Twelfth District, William J. Stone; Thirteenth District, William H. Wade; Fourteenth District, James L. Walker.

The supreme judge elected in 1886 was Theodore Brace, in room of John W. Henry; the superintendent of public schools was William E. Coleman, re-elected.

Missouri's Delegations in the Confederate Congress.—1861–63—Senate, John B. Clark, Sr., R. L. Y. Peyton. House, W. M. Cooke, Thomas A. Harris, Aaron H. Conrow, Casper W. Bell, George G. Vest, Thomas W. Freeman, John Hyer.

1864–65—Senate, Waldo P. Johnson, Rev. L. M. Lewis. House, Thomas L. Snead, N. L. Norton, John B. Clark, Sr., A.

H. Conrow, George G. Vest, Peter S. Wilkes and Robert A. Hatcher.

Rebel Governors.—1861-62—Claiborne F. Jackson; lieutenant-governor, Thomas C. Reynolds.

1862-65—Thomas C. Reynolds; lieutenant-governor, vacancy.

Presidential Elections.—Following is the aggregate vote of the State at every presidential election since the admission of Missouri into the Union:

1824—Andrew Jackson, Republican, 987; John Quincy Adams, Coalition, 311; Henry Clay, Republican, 1,401; Clay's majority, 103. Total vote, 12,699. Number of electoral votes, 3.

1828—Andrew Jackson, Democrat, 8,232; John Quincy Adams, National Republican, 3,422; Jackson's majority, 4,810. Total vote, 11,654. Number of electors, 3.

1832—Andrew Jackson, Democrat, had a majority over Henry Clay, National Republican, of 5,192. Number of electors, 4.

1836—Martin Van Buren, Democrat, 10,995; William H. Harrison and Hugh L. White, Fusion, 8,337; Van Buren's majority, 2,658. Total vote, 19,332. Number of electors, 4.

1840—Martin Van Buren, Democrat, 29,760; William Henry Harrison, Whig, 22,972; Van Buren's majority, 6,788. Total vote, 52,732. Number of electors, 4.

1844—James K. Polk, Democrat, 41,369; Henry Clay, Whig, 31,251; Polk's majority, 10,118. Total vote, 72,620. Number of electors, 7.

1848—Lewis Cass, Democrat, 40,077; Zachary Taylor, Whig, 32,671; Cass's majority, 7,406. Total vote, 72,748. Number of electors, 7.

1852—Franklin Pierce, Democrat, 38,353; Winfield Scott, Whig, 29,984; Pierce's majority, 8,369. Total vote, 68,337. Number of electors, 9.

1856—James Buchanan, Democrat, 58,164; Millard Fillmore, American, 48,524; Buchanan's majority, 9,640. Total vote, 106,688. Number of electors, 9.

1860—Stephen A. Douglas, Democrat, 58,801; John Bell, Union, 58,372; John C. Breckinridge, Democrat, 31,317; Abraham Lincoln, Republican, 17,028; Douglas' plurality over Bell, 429. Total vote, 165,518. Number of electors, 9.

1864—Abraham Lincoln, Republican, 72,750; George B. McClellan, Democrat, 31,678; Lincoln's majority, 41,072. Total vote, 104,428. Number of electors, 11.

1868—U. S. Grant, Republican, 86,860; Horatio Seymour, Democrat, 65,628; Grant's majority, 21,232. Total vote, 152,488. Number of electors, 11.

1872—Horace Greeley, Liberal Republican, 151,434; U. S. Grant, Republican, 119,196; Charles O'Conor, Democrat, 2,429; Greeley's majority, 29,809. Total vote, 273,059. Number of electors, 15.

1876—Samuel J. Tilden, Democrat, 203,077; R. B. Hayes, Republican, 145,029; Peter Cooper, Greenbacker, 3,498; Green Clay Smith, Temperance, 64; scattering, 97; Tilden over all, 54,389. Total vote, 351,765. Number of electors, 15.

1880—Winfield S. Hancock, Democrat, 208,609; James A. Garfield, Republican, 153,567; James B. Weaver, Greenbacker, 35,045; Hancock's plurality, 55,042. Total vote, 397,221. Number of electors, 15.

1884—Grover Cleveland, Democrat, 235,988; James G. Blaine, Republican, and Benjamin F. Butler, Greenbacker, (Fusion electors) 202,929; John P. St. John, Prohibition, 2,153; Cleveland's plurality, 30,906. Total vote, 441,070. Number of electors, 16.

In 1884 the vote for governor resulted: John S. Marmaduke, Democrat, 218,885; Nicholas Ford, Fusion, 207,939; John A. Brooks, Prohibition, 10,426; Marmaduke over Ford, 10,946; over all, 520. Total vote, 437,250.

THE VOTE BY COUNTIES AT THE PRESIDENTIAL ELECTIONS OF 1836-40-44.

COUNTIES.	1836.		1840.		1844.	
	Harrison and White, Whig.	Van Buren, Democrat.	Harrison, Whig.	Van Buren, Democrat.	Clay, Whig.	Polk, Democrat.
Adair					204	450
Andrew					384	941
Audrain			131	122	175	163
Barry		55	88	436	142	478
Bates					206	307
Buchanan			340	1,118	599	1,162
Benton	4	75	150	501	252	664
Boone	714	567	1,112	500	1,190	602
Callaway	446	616	881	626	940	793
Camden					70	247
Caldwell			133	154	129	212
Cape Girardeau	140	485	455	764	518	914
Carroll	33	142	112	182	242	311
Chariton	84	188	246	391	371	602
Clark			240	206	225	220
Clay	282	347	457	649	765	552
Clinton	48	129	127	288	310	567
Cole	73	576	348	962	418	1,122
Cooper			778	694	901	783
Crawford	59	86	240	264	237	367
Dade					255	690
Daviess			170	264	318	446
Decatur (now Ozark)					57	208
Franklin	133	338	355	552	386	796
Gasconade	81	115	136	636	71	326
Greene	11	140	279	452	351	817
Grundy					346	365
Henry (called Rives in 1836-40)	40	108	291	421	280	283
Holt					185	378
Howard	354	619	753	901	1,013	969
Jackson	183	489	457	711	614	852
Jasper					155	242
Jefferson	89	138	298	321	327	349
Johnson	78	240	255	374	367	511
La Fayette	165	294	500	475	820	576
Lewis	197	298	542	602	380	403
Lincoln	275	236	462	543	578	683
Linn			93	235	269	494
Livingston			249	487	198	351
Macon			374	500	327	457
Madison			152	275	183	399
Marion	343	338	827	534	1,017	721
Miller			21	317	74	369
Monroe	280	317	815	618	792	578
Montgomery	169	92	334	262	359	232
Morgan	51	216	167	494	262	544
New Madrid			363	194	298	208
Newton			178	630	189	663

THE VOTE BY COUNTIES AT THE PRESIDENTIAL ELECTIONS OF 1836-40-44.—*Concluded.*

COUNTIES.	1836.		1840.		1844.	
	Harrison and White, Whig.	Van Buren, Democrat.	Harrison, Whig.	Van Buren, Democrat.	Clay, Whig.	Polk, Democrat.
Niangua (now Dallas).......	......	......	......	......	76	345
Osage.......................	......	......	......	......	120	434
Platte.......................	......	......	459	968	900	1,386
Perry	17	173	319	339	385	463
Pettis	64	161	156	262	228	319
Pike	405	415	732	746	861	809
Polk	65	80	241	860	278	636
Pulaski.....................	49	230	196	720	86	325
Ralls.......................	122	151	400	335	422	322
Randolph....................	195	399	515	405	596	571
Ray.........................	232	221	432	563	599	734
Ripley	2	70	15	325	31	266
St. Charles.................	282	237	586	459	480	503
St. Clair...................	......	......	......	......	177	342
St. Francois................	144	197	221	199	301	234
Ste. Genevieve..............	47	97	170	223	198	245
St. Louis	843	618	2,515	1,874	3,688	3,329
Saline......................	135	178	375	322	591	446
Scotland	......	......	......	......	317	442
Scott.......................	......	......	284	500	258	480
Shannon.....................	......	......	......	......	57	271
Shelby......................	31	63	283	226	244	209
Stoddard....................	17	170	69	308	115	323
Taney.......................	......	......	41	258	36	297
Van Buren (now Cass)........	......	......	208	360	257	443
Warren	150	376	342	348	364	341
Washington	245	311	479	514	613	588
Wayne.	......	......	57	211	86	366
Wright......................	......	......	......	......	97	486
Total.......................	7,337	10,995	22,972	29,760	31,251	41,369

PRESIDENTIAL ELECTION, 1848.

COUNTIES.	Taylor Whig.	Cass Democrat.	COUNTIES.	Taylor Whig.	Cass Democrat.
Adair	110	200	Marion	1,046	797
Andrew	384	689	Mercer	144	183
Atchison	77	136	Miller	76	373
Audrain	185	166	Mississippi	133	181
Barry	55	217	Moniteau	161	466
Bates	146	186	Monroe	807	561
Benton	208	382	Montgomery	379	186
Boone	1,102	588	Morgan	167	842
Buchanan	704	1,055	New Madrid	323	168
Caldwell	128	168	Newton	161	461
Callaway	349	631	Nodaway	43	148
Camden	155	282	Osage	92	312
Cape Girardeau	485	709	Oregon	7	111
Carroll	266	298	Ozark	69	113
Cass (Van Buren)	270	410	Perry	322	889
Cedar	116	271	Pettis	230	265
Chari'	414	577	Pike	793	784
Clark	284	242	Platte	1,102	1,494
Clay	626	418	Polk	231	516
Clinton	290	286	Pulaski	124	241
Cole	277	581	Putnam	74	120
Cooper	813	633	Ralls	397	299
Crawford	263	275	Randolph	607	508
Dade	166	306	Ray	509	626
Dallas	105	288	Reynolds	21	148
Daviess	269	358	Ripley	14	154
De Kalb	37	146	St. Charles	477	569
Franklin	339	680	St. Clair	148	163
Gasconade	87	349	St. Francois	285	274
Gentry	152	396	Ste. Genevieve	142	168
Greene	401	825	St. Louis	4,827	4,778
Grundy	225	187	Saline	586	438
Harrison	63	144	Schuyler	204	192
Henry	274	239	Scotland	181	240
Hickory	98	224	Scott	147	217
Holt	148	248	Shannon	35	54
Howard	801	888	Shelby	175	263
Jackson	695	954	Stoddard	97	196
Jasper	161	294	Sullivan	154	250
Jefferson	246	311	Taney	54	325
Johnson	334	451	Texas	82	185
Knox	196	197	Warren	351	336
La Fayette	915	585	Washington	473	423
Lawrence	170	374	Wayne	91	245
Lewis	479	479	Wright	72	181
Lincoln	566	696			
Linn	230	297	Total	32,671	40,077
Livingston	195	373			
Macon	360	470	Majority		7,406
Madison	231	377			

HISTORY OF MISSOURI. 165

VOTE BY COUNTIES AT THE PRESIDENTIAL ELECTIONS OF 1852-56-60.

COUNTIES.	1852.		1856.		1860.			
	Scott, Whig.	Pierce, Democrat.	Fillmore, American.	Buchanan, Democrat.	Douglas, Democrat.	Bell, Union.	Breckinridge, Democrat.	Lincoln, Republican.
Adair	113	201	283	410	616	298	339	185
Andrew	466	784	428	889	819	677	319	97
Atchison	106	150	132	345	645	165	63	68
Audrain	200	160	565	521	289	580	206	1
Barry	72	253	148	488	257	333	286	1
Barton			53	64	107	76	93	28
Bates	104	116	255	409	511	386	348	30
Benton	167	328	159	467	574	306	100	74
Bollinger	28	112	199	413	250	166	99	23
Boone	1,112	613	1,329	958	578	1,671	652	12
Buchanan	712	857	768	1,036	1,626	1,287	614	452
Butler	16	26	34	143	235	88	17	1
Caldwell	157	209	237	295	263	367	186	43
Callaway	670	493	1,095	805	839	1,306	472	15
Camden	67	109	210	269	269	224	132	6
Cape Girardeau	328	487	664	898	543	651	325	175
Carroll	239	286	399	659	752	552	276	3
Carter					4	16	83	
Cass	228	337	596	561	242	715	607	23
Cedar	65	162	163	391	324	266	277	4
Chariton	348	498	440	559	692	608	295	1
Christian					120	342	308	
Clark	325	289	721	587	542	752	497	277
Clay	626	406	756	675	528	1,045	305	
Clinton	283	290	406	397	368	674	314	11
Cole	216	462	259	552	430	226	487	114
Cooper	645	535	787	778	988	952	281	20
Crawford	240	278	460	434	169	353	192	35
Dade	175	276	333	418	283	406	305	8
Dallas	102	344	132	454	225	288	172	20
Daviess	296	351	380	572	692	545	265	33
Dent	74	96	77	396	207	243	338	7
De Kalb	66	167	172	336	239	243	213	7
Dunklin			101	147	150	209	79	
Douglas								
Franklin	277	619	531	846	888	577	108	494
Gasconade	89	304	220	403	188	157	51	433
Gentry	133	233	396	757	873	517	259	201
Greene	484	920	1,003	1,029	298	986	414	42
Grundy	215	184	350	335	416	507	190	129
Harrison	111	164	318	495	910	319	50	297
Henry	266	245	402	369	623	703	232	16
Hickory	75	294	130	333	298	197	143	15
Holt	189	291	240	409	453	348	171	202
Howard	675	762	798	867	939	920	247	1
Howell					136	176	91	
Iron					349	194	36	108
Jackson	728	858	894	1,168	1,095	1,473	943	191
Jasper	169	355	294	398	407	424	192	38
Jefferson	172	310	528	387	490	416	155	149
Johnson	360	456	844	540	617	1,224	527	18

VOTES BY COUNTIES AT THE PRESIDENTIAL ELECTIONS OF 1852-56-60.—*Continued.*

COUNTIES.	1852. Scott, Whig.	1852. Pierce, Democrat.	1856. Fillmore, American.	1856. Buchanan, Democrat.	1860. Douglas, Democrat.	1860. Bell, Union.	1860. Breckinridge, Democrat.	1860. Lincoln, Republican.
Knox	210	255	391	471	687	520	301	161
Laclede	71	184	225	321	189	335	276	6
La Fayette	303	532	1,293	654	774	1,577	371	24
Lawrence	168	390	358	574	138	445	516	59
Lewis	398	408	642	761	468	833	597	43
Lincoln	440	587	572	846	806	725	396	3
Linn	249	282	383	400	521	546	219	105
Livingston	251	321	430	501	401	578	470	20
McDonald	63	194	61	299	206	188	194	3
Mason	355	473	435	934	1,176	655	414	134
Madison	117	259	355	418	305	226	98	9
Maries			67	246	98	95	309	7
Marion	894	751	1,321	727	1,240	1,386	432	235
Mercer	186	186	417	450	682	491	169	80
Miller	62	279	108	224	94	193	495	23
Mississippi	117	168	317	327	233	305	185	1
Moniteau	189	353	387	427	476	546	332	87
Monroe	760	611	1,012	762	680	1,086	408	8
Montgomery	386	265	603	365	612	658	83	45
Morgan	133	278	227	403	550	321	204	18
New Madrid	93	32	295	234	117	223	160	
Newton	107	323	236	528	654	406	255	22
Nodaway	61	111	183	438	546	265	274	147
Oregon	11	95	37	324	66	45	245	2
Osage	143	372	219	412	235	190	208	258
Ozark	32	57	51	149	81	69	155	
Pemiscot	57	34	111	119	118	154	70	
Perry	171	213	207	586	467	217	63	189
Pettis	245	301	432	319	369	615	211	9
Phelps					254	199	430	37
Pike	803	758	1,131	1,113	1,117	1,300	420	15
Platte	910	1,060	1,040	1,263	845	1,208	877	6
Polk	260	504	412	662	125	730	477	4
Pulaski	39	169	68	268	107	62	281	7
Putnam	135	156	257	448	590	369	246	111
Ralls	341	278	534	369	391	582	149	1
Randolph	476	502	606	595	360	821	520	
Ray	483	618	744	874	881	1,006	333	9
Reynolds	5	98	82	114	123	38	85	4
Ripley	16	83	41	306	78	74	232	
St. Charles	378	598	588	772	832	619	64	534
St. Clair	149	225	210	347	344	338	294	1
St. Francois	250	529	401	541	592	421	141	19
Ste. Genevieve	122	165	308	356	351	217	72	48
St. Louis	4,298	5,826	6,834	5,534	9,264	4,931	610	9,945
Saline	514	443	858	599	563	1,035	366	
Schuyler	177	222	287	472	455	267	251	14
Scotland	216	283	352	632	741	436	187	197
Scott	59	97	345	222	215	243	192	6
Shannon		9	14	40	27	38	127	2
Shelby	207	328	432	373	476	702	293	90
Stoddard	116	177	151	315	230	385	198	

VOTE BY COUNTIES AT THE PRESIDENTIAL ELECTIONS OF 1852-56-60.—*Concluded.*

COUNTIES.	1852.		1856.		1860.			
	Scott, Whig.	Pierce, Democrat.	Fillmore, American.	Buchanan, Democrat.	Douglas, Democrat.	Bell, Union.	Breckinridge, Democrat.	Lincoln, Republican.
Stone	17	94	3	137	83	31	112	.....
Sullivan	127	277	260	553	557	373	575	83
Taney	11	168	34	388	97	43	287	.....
Texas	95	167	91	479	61	194	511	6
Vernon	63	153	172	302	151	207	381	.....
Warren	301	301	378	369	510	307	89	95
Washington	360	334	487	578	635	493	62	28
Wayne	.....	144	100	287	185	245	290	3
Webster	.....	.....	189	468	172	335	376	7
Wright	95	167	64	267	44	128	369	.....
Total	29,984	38,353	48,524	58,164	58,801	58,372	31,317	17,028

VOTE BY COUNTIES AT THE PRESIDENTIAL ELECTIONS OF 1864-68-72.

COUNTIES.	1864.		1868.		1872.	
	Lincoln, Republican.	McClellan, Democrat.	Grant, Republican.	Seymour, Democrat.	Greeley, Liberal Republican and Democrat.	Grant, Republican.
Adair	797	162	930	288	961	1,427
Andrew	1,141	60	1,412	515	1,382	1,604
Atchison	639	7	781	183	912	1,001
Audrain	126	392	312	279	1,575	673
Barry	197	17	371	322	759	687
Barton	23	.....	277	229	570	603
Bates	27	13	732	620	1,746	1,499
Benton	574	21	705	329	807	912
Bollinger	243	12	331	79	661	409
Boone	262	813	177	171	3,199	993
Buchanan	1,914	810	1,971	1,873	3,552	2,571
Butler	.....	.....	.....	.....	404	188
Caldwell	496	88	844	374	875	1,330
Callaway	274	965	202	382	2,718	721
Camden	468	1	406	132	403	564
Cape Girardeau	1,213	551	1,009	835	1,283	1,104
Carroll	285	113	967	810	1,699	1,480
Carter	.....	.....	33	40	126	30
Cass	76	105	1,010	1,160	2,012	1,453
Cedar	297	.....	630	294	743	772
Chariton	363	2	799	834	2,342	1,342
Christian	557	5	573	123	253	663
Clark	997	128	1,080	302	1,254	1,288
Clay	216	777	293	314	2,207	528

VOTE BY COUNTIES AT THE PRESIDENTIAL ELECTIONS OF 1864-68-72.—*Continued.*

COUNTIES.	1864.		1868.		1872.	
	Lincoln, Republican.	McClellan, Democrat.	Grant, Republican.	Seymour, Democrat.	Greeley, Liberal Republican and Democrat.	Grant, Republican.
Clinton.............	297	492	585	644	1,418	975
Cole................	1,256	502	861	752	1,322	1,146
Cooper..............	939	381	972	486	2,179	1,432
Crawford............	297	307	385	431	677	524
Dade................	507	4	734	144	701	962
Dallas..............	243	12	620	199	451	791
Daviess.............	775	286	1,089	703	1,349	1,405
De Kalb.............	400	197	597	257	841	1,017
Dent................	107	1	214	161	515	394
Douglas.............	189	2	445	23		
Dunklin.............					807	112
Franklin............	1,717	401	1,624	1,146	1,582	1,725
Gasconade...........	862	185	1,074	135	276	878
Gentry..............	525	281	769	443	1,181	1,029
Greene..............	2,223	346	1,304	740	1,666	2,082
Grundy..............	983	17	1,082	306	774	1,423
Harrison............	1,252	212	1,428	475	1,115	1,750
Henry...............	465	232	980	710	2,124	1,526
Hickory.............	365	1	479	112	249	655
Holt................	673	81	1,080	137	844	1,377
Howard..............	534	6	171	1,256	1,972	873
Howell..............			170	22	350	383
Iron................	535	2	308	209	600	377
Jackson.............	602	557	1,441	3,052	4,475	2,814
Jasper..............	46	2	1,099	444	1,338	2,092
Jefferson...........	915	323	796	833	1,240	878
Johnson.............	832	224	1,512	861	2,504	2,299
Knox................	669	348	759	342	1,161	850
Laclede.............	659	50	400	372	825	556
La Fayette..........	346	395	709	543	2,984	1,523
Lawrence............	833		850	397	1,098	1,199
Lewis...............	774	533	830	825	1,708	1,109
Lincoln.............	542	357	459	393	1,537	645
Linn................	907	135	1,216	650	1,478	1,686
Livingston..........	442	497	1,127	788	1,745	1,571
Macon...............	1,757	23	1,221	1,114	2,335	1,745
Madison.............	240	14	217	161	724	340
Maries..............	215	244	145	315	439	253
Marion..............	828	375	973	703	2,598	1,685
McDonald............	26		193	41	157	143
Mercer..............	1,158	3	1,082	379	527	1,201
Miller..............	555	111	573	157	716	865
Mississippi.........	108	257	20	328	725	308
Moniteau............	866	434	781	349	1,275	986
Monroe..............	158	597	174	1,302	2,559	453
Montgomery..........	530	225	703	481	1,289	1,062
Morgan..............	348	264	586	378	895	657
New Madrid..........	99	9	10	342	796	243
Newton..............	212	1	778	208	1,036	1,158

VOTE BY COUNTIES AT THE PRESIDENTIAL ELECTIONS OF 1864-68-72.—*Concluded.*

COUNTIES.	1864. Lincoln, Republican.	1864. McClellan, Democrat.	1868. Grant, Republican.	1868. Seymour, Democrat.	1872. Greeley, Liberal Republican and Democrat.	1872. Grant, Republican.
Nodaway	829	9	1,104	588	1,503	1,683
Oregon			5	229	445	54
Osage	764	679	634	664	209	770
Ozark	38		156	56	135	288
Pemiscot			3	147	476	10
Perry	509	116	602	570	621	725
Pettis	879	396	1,022	797	1,965	1,675
Phelps	985	263	530	405	906	696
Pike	1,143	930	1,008	1,619	2,578	1,740
Platte	496	882	567	758	2,148	936
Polk	870	5	892	413	998	1,172
Pulaski	105	28	176	199	534	324
Putnam	1,292	47	1,255	248		
Ralls	292	194	225	194	1,177	391
Randolph	484	327	223	1,412	2,212	870
Ray	531	798	769	534	2,257	1,161
Reynolds	7	20	53	138	400	125
Ripley			45	108	314	97
Saline	170	98	602	377	2,790	1,283
Schuyler	546	191	509	240	788	792
Scotland	612	533	775	707	1,130	874
Scott	155	186	247	230	804	444
Shannon			4	172	242	20
Shelby	866	216	579	305	1,281	884
St. Charles	1,438	394	1,542	1,099	1,672	1,559
St. Clair	223	1	570	315	1,159	1,027
St. Francois	246	134	254	377	1,028	442
Ste. Genevieve	423	217	246	607	634	384
St. Louis	14,027	8,882	16,182	13,491	19,899	16,701
Stoddard	111	6	222	117	660	319
Stone	100		177	103	122	348
Sullivan	1,074	52	926	568	1,119	1,133
Taney	29		208	52	201	389
Texas	37	10	202	99	838	481
Vernon			341	581	1,344	601
Warren	948	271	851	367	567	1,007
Washington	788	239	419	722	878	641
Wayne	343	187			565	354
Webster	533	192	548	334	808	763
Worth	346	121	369	349	446	531
Wright	65	2	298	100	484	553
Total	72,750	31,678	86,860	65,628	151,434	119,196
Majority	41,072		*21,232		32,238	

*In 1868 the State authorities rejected the returns from the counties of Dunklin, Jackson, Monroe, Oregon, Platte, Ripley, Shannon and Wayne, together with portions of other counties bringing about the following as the final declared result: Grant, 83,887; Seymour, 58,905. Grant's majority, 24,982.

VOTE BY COUNTIES AT THE PRESIDENTIAL ELECTIONS OF 1876-80-84.

COUNTIES.	1876.			1880.			1884.	
	Tilden, Democrat.	Hayes, Republican.	Cooper, Greenbacker.	Hancock, Democrat.	Garfield, Republican.	Weaver, Greenbacker.	Cleveland, Democrat.	Blaine and Butler, Fusion.
Adair...............	1,192	1,604	24	1,269	1,657	329	1,443	2,041
Andrew.............	1,503	1,590	56	1,571	1,781	121	1,707	1,985
Atchison............	1,117	1,156	143	1,261	1,228	490	1,345	1,680
Audrain............	2,268	836	......	2,322	983	530	3,034	1,554
Barry..............	1,001	1,000	13	1,163	970	327	1,586	1,662
Barton.............	760	710	41	942	519	712	1,837	1,715
Bates...............	2,071	1,478	2	2,949	1,897	245	3,785	3,004
Benton.............	851	1,096	......	962	1,204	164	1,289	1,531
Bollinger...........	998	572	......	1,068	629	117	1,241	891
Boone..............	3,845	1,181	4	3,269	1,170	418	3,569	1,364
Buchanan...........	4,136	2,496	74	4,693	3,817	391	5,236	3,879
Butler.............	696	230	......	746	275	96	900	491
Caldwell...........	1,058	1,383	115	1,139	1,369	373	1,343	1,850
Callaway...........	3,493	976	4	3,369	1,184	110	3,420	1,347
Camden............	540	638	......	507	563	197	608	808
Cape Girardeau.....	1,836	1,417	7	1,869	1,641	102	2,084	2,078
Carroll............	2,403	1,977	28	2,404	2,039	409	2,898	2,774
Carter.............	209	80	17	238	80	50	284	132
Cass...............	2,277	1,440	14	2,710	1,710	275	3,057	2,107
Cedar..............	904	921	......	900	926	258	1,562	1,449
Chariton...........	3,165	1,719	28	2,899	1,617	548	3,287	2,194
Christian...........	494	929	4	438	791	529	700	1,536
Clark..............	1,581	1,494	8	1,570	1,503	120	1,652	1,599
Clay...............	2,844	508	57	2,969	589	193	3,179	916
Clinton............	1,756	1,019	81	2,061	1,237	187	2,164	1,636
Cole...............	1,529	1,099	......	1,384	1,338	55	1,526	1,513
Cooper.............	2,331	1,770	......	2,189	1,730	372	2,475	2,223
Crawford...........	1,036	754	......	1,099	805	69	1,106	1,053
Dade...............	893	1,305	38	902	1,227	238	1,268	1,692
Dallas..............	652	761	33	487	654	555	687	1,363
Daviess............	1,848	1,663	4	2,047	1,796	285	2,180	2,213
De Kalb............	1,083	1,110	62	1,305	1,238	221	1,501	1,645
Dent...............	826	446	......	1,073	707	35	1,171	798
Douglas............	136	744	47	163	497	556	388	1,182
Dunklin............	1,148	93	......	1,333	182	......	1,527	382
Franklin...........	2,294	2,149	2	2,260	2,647	78	2,290	2,931
Gasconade..........	558	1,158	......	487	1,512	......	548	1,523
Gentry.............	1,461	1,138	15	1,982	1,377	334	2,155	1,800
Greene.............	2,315	2,565	146	1,912	2,198	1,286	3,190	3,793
Grundy............	1,113	1,810	......	1,102	1,917	124	1,203	2,126
Harrison...........	1,373	2,013	4	1,586	2,097	239	1,688	2,410
Henry..............	2,380	1,499	1	2,821	1,694	306	3,292	2,280
Hickory............	390	631	......	436	675	252	626	1,063
Holt...............	1,815	1,628	18	1,297	1,605	212	1,475	1,957
Howard............	2,871	1,048	1	2,047	1,166	513	2,286	1,256
Howell.............	495	458	......	726	457	305	1,369	1,116
Iron................	805	386	......	854	565	......	786	545
Jackson............	5,438	2,909	490	6,703	5,123	782	9,551	9,281
Jasper..............	2,905	3,138	520	2,533	2,874	1,114	3,318	4,124

VOTE BY COUNTIES AT THE PRESIDENTIAL ELECTIONS OF 1876-80-84.—*Continued.*

COUNTIES.	1876.			1880.			1884.	
	Tilden, Democrat.	Hayes, Republican.	Cooper, Greenbacker.	Hancock, Democrat.	Garfield, Republican.	Weaver, Greenbacker.	Cleveland, Democrat.	Blaine and Butler, Fusion.
Jefferson,............	1,853	1,157	......	2,012	1,501	69	2,272	1,858
Johnson.............	2,734	2,183	6	2,795	2,400	318	3,324	3,052
Knox...............	1,538	1,165	......	1,468	574	765	1,619	1,319
Laclede.............	1,009	731	11	960	365	774	1,208	1,283
La Fayette.........	3,281	1,734	......	3,163	1,822	102	3,697	2,586
Lawrence...........	1,137	1,180	339	1,476	1,567	337	1,947	2,103
Lewis...............	2,059	1,320	......	1,928	1,152	152	2,129	1,363
Lincoln.............	2,294	1,004	10	2,089	790	634	2,243	1,321
Linn................	1,914	1,878	14	2,049	1,991	182	2,157	2,268
Livingston..........	2,013	1,616	150	1,859	1,165	1,268	2,030	2,227
McDonald...........	715	400	2	706	213	471	1,040	710
Macon...............	2,776	1,752	288	2,880	1,726	844	3,100	2,619
Madison.............	1,277	447	3	952	391	1	931	478
Maries...............	840	251	....	924	288	58	957	425
Marion..............	3,099	1,723	3	3,086	1,811	87	3,251	2,172
Mercer...............	960	1,501	22	990	1,573	231	964	1,811
Miller...............	662	836	9	757	970	167	1,047	1,360
Mississippi..........	1,195	458	......	1,137	525	118	1,222	722
Moniteau...........	1,607	1,142	.....	1,323	853	643	1,408	1,448
Monroe..............	3,422	589	......	3,488	671	120	3,485	801
Montgomery........	1,809	1,411	29	1,721	1,329	343	1,930	1,641
Morgan..............	1,038	748	......	950	798	57	1,141	1,014
New Madrid........	1,042	283	......	1,070	341	......	1,086	461
Newton.............	732	1,546	55	1,535	957	971	2,042	1,938
Nodaway............	2,411	2,213	59	2,485	2,303	941	3,043	3,353
Oregon..............	656	63	......	809	85	28	1,114	286
Osage...............	1,082	895	13	1,137	1,117	10	1,096	1,219
Ozark...............	231	427	....	314	409	132	344	634
Pemiscot............	745	8	1	749	85	......	683	120
Perry................	1,150	683	1	1,110	887	71	1,227	990
Pettis...............	2,833	2,098	3	2,908	416	306	3,477	3,067
Phelps...............	1,216	750	5	1,132	......	548	1,282	876
Pike.................	3,167	2,122	65	3,236	2,151	289	3,394	2,428
Platte...............	2,648	864	......	2,693	945	49	2,692	1,046
Polk.................	1,209	1,385	1	1,360	1,506	250	1,545	1,936
Pulaski..............	748	408	1	772	462	19	948	615
Putnam.............	809	1,478	26	725	1,513	424	984	1,835
Ralls................	1,687	511	......	1,800	603	14	1,756	714
Randolph...........	3,538	1,269	13	2,927	1,051	691	3,193	1,818
Ray.................	2,492	1,107	28	2,614	908	568	2,895	1,608
Reynolds............	622	115	......	747	39	......	790	198
Ripley...............	438	114	......	578	115	70	819	376
St. Charles..........	2,509	1,062	......	2,191	2,228	33	2,118	2,334
St. Clair............	1,190	931	......	963	765	1,053	1,687	1,631
St. Francois.........	1,524	554	24	1,750	778	60	1,875	1,001
Ste. Genevieve......	1,159	533	......	1,081	650	40	1,115	684
St. Louis............	25,385	22,916	79	2,719	3,223	4	2,513	3,547
St. Louis City.......	......	......	......	23,837	23,206	872	21,712	21,135
Saline...............	3,942	1,728	......	3,851	1,907	359	4,041	2,579

VOTE BY COUNTIES AT THE PRESIDENTIAL ELECTIONS OF 1876–80–84.—*Concluded.*

COUNTIES.	1876.			1880.			1884.	
	Tilden, Democrat.	Hayes, Republican.	Cooper, Greenbacker.	Hancock, Democrat.	Garfield, Republican.	Weaver, Greenbacker.	Cleveland, Democrat.	Blaine and Butler, Fusion.
Schuyler............	1,117	908	17	1,065	570	457	1,202	1,009
Scotland............	1,464	1,060	2	1,405	689	479	1,526	1,077
Scott................	1,163	306	.....	1,330	459	.....	1,331	515
Shannon............	419	96	.....	467	65	9	572	157
Shelby	1,672	957	14	1,770	350	847	1,910	1,128
Stoddard...........	1,403	406	2	1,541	590	92	1,718	761
Stone................	159	432	.....	140	435	136	282	671
Sullivan............	1,447	1,488	.....	1,717	1,693	187	1,768	1,882
Taney	351	368	.....	1,313	337	207	460	646
Texas................	1,144	563	1	1,250	477	285	1,652	970
Vernon.	1,874	774	26	2,338	940	360	3,781	2,007
Warren.............	818	1,263	7	662	1,343	203	596	1,349
Washington.........	1,607	759	.....	1,489	775	78	1,438	983
Wayne..............	1,114	395	.....	1,144	568	46	1,337	814
Webster.............	1,076	1,003	8	1,024	561	616	1,229	1,316
Worth...............	666	632	59	751	657	163	771	899
Wright..............	498	605	7	409	641	365	956	1,248
Total...........	203,077	145,029	3,498	208,609	153,567	35,045	235,988	202,929
Majority........	54,550			1,997			30,906	

Salaries of State Officers.—Governor, $5,000; lieutenant-governor, $5 per day; secretary of State, treasurer, auditor, superintendent of public schools, register of lands, and railroad commissioner, each, $3,000; superintendent of insurance department, $4,000: adjutant-general, $2,000; State law librarian, $900; supreme court judges, each $4,500; clerk of the supreme court, $3,000.

COUNTY ORGANIZATION.

Adair—Organized January 29, 1841. Named for Adair County, Ky., whence some of the first prominent settlers came. Kirksville, the county seat, was named for John Kirk, who settled the site.

Andrew—Organized January 29, 1841. Named in honor of Andrew Jackson Davis, a prominent lawyer of St. Louis.

Atchison—Organized February 14, 1845. Named in honor of Hon. David R. Atchison, then one of the United States senators.

The first county seat was Linden, so called from the number of linn or linden trees in the vicinity. The present county seat, Rock Port, was named because the Tarkio Creek at that point is rocky or stony.

Audrain—Organized December 17, 1836. Named in honor of Samuel Audrain, the first actual settler within its limits.

Barry—Organized January 5, 1835. Named in honor of Commodore Barry, of the American navy. Cassville, the county seat, was named for Hon. Lewis Cass.

Barton—Organized December 12, 1855. Named in honor of Hon. David Barton, one of the first two United States senators from Missouri.

Bates—Organized January 29, 1841. Named for Hon. Edward Bates, of St. Louis. Butler, the county seat, was named for Gen. William O. Butler, of Kentucky.

Benton—Organized January 3, 1835. Named for Hon. Thomas H. Benton, Missouri's great senator.

Bollinger—Organized March 1, 1851. Named in honor of Maj. George F. Bollinger, one of its first settlers, a prominent member of the Territorial Legislature, etc. The county seat, Marble Hill, was so named from the alleged natural character of the site. It was originally called Dallas.

Boone—Organized November 16, 1820. Named for Daniel Boone. The first county seat, Smithton, was named for Gen. T. A. Smith; the present, Columbia, a mile east of the former site of Smithton, was presumably called for "the queen of the world and the child of the skies."

Buchanan—Organized February 10, 1839. Named in honor of Hon. James Buchanan, of Pennsylvania. The first county seat was Sparta, near the center of the county; in 1846 the capital was removed to St. Joseph.

Butler—Organized February 27, 1849. Named for Gen. William O. Butler, of Kentucky, a prominent American officer in the war with Mexico, and Democratic candidate for vice-president in 1848.

Callaway—Organized November 25, 1820. Named in honor of Capt. James Callaway, a grandson of Daniel Boone, killed by the Indians in the southern part of Montgomery County, March

8, 1815. Fulton, the county seat, laid out in 1822, was named for Robert Fulton.

Camden—Originally created January 29, 1841, and called Kinderhook, for the country seat of President Van Buren. The name was changed to Camden, for a county in North Carolina, in 1843. The first county seat was Oregon; the second, Erie; the present, Linn Creek.

Caldwell—Organized December 26, 1836. Named by the author of the organizing act, Gen. Alex. W. Doniphan, for Col. John Caldwell, of Kentucky. The first county seat was Far West, but on the destruction and abandonment of that place during the Mormon War, it was removed to Kingston, named for Hon. Austin A. King, of Ray County.

Cape Girardeau—One of the original "districts." Organized October 1, 1812; reduced to its present limits March 5, 1849. Named for the town which was founded by Louis Lorimer in 1794. Jackson, the county seat, was incorporated in 1824, and named for "Old Hickory."

Carroll—Organized January 3, 1833. Named in honor of Charles Carroll, of Carrollton, one of the signers of the Declaration. The county seat, Carrollton, was laid out in 1837.

Carter—Organized March 10, 1859. Named for Zimri Carter, one of its earliest and most prominent citizens.

Cass—Organized September 14, 1835, and first called Van Buren, in honor of President Van Buren, whom Missourians delighted to honor at that day; but in 1849, after he had been the presidential candidate of the Free Soil party in the preceding canvass, the name was changed to Cass, in honor of Lewis Cass, of Michigan, who had been the Democratic candidate in 1848 and had been defeated by Gen. Taylor. The county seat, Harrisonville, was named for Hon. A. G. Harrison, of Callaway.

Cedar—Organized February 14, 1845, and named for its principal stream. The original county seat was called Lancaster. In 1847 the name was changed to Fremont, in honor of the "Pathfinder," but in 1856 Gen. Fremont became the Republican candidate for President, and the following winter the Democratic Legislature changed the name to Stockton, in honor of Commodore Richard Stockton, of the navy, who had arrested Fremont during the Mexican War, and sought to have him disgraced.

Chariton—Organized November 16, 1820. Named for the town of Chariton, which was laid out in 1818, and formerly stood near the mouth of the river of that name. Lewis and Clark were of the opinion that the original name of the Chariton was "Theriaton," but others asserted that the word is old French, and signifies a chariot or little wagon, a corruption of *charrette*, probably. The first county seat was Chariton, sometimes called Old Chariton, long extinct. The present capital, Keytesville, was laid out in 1832, and named by its founder, James Keyte, for himself.

Christian—Organized March 8, 1860. Named probably for a county in Kentucky.

Clark—Organized in 1838 (many authorities say in 1818 but the Clark County then organized was in Arkansas). Named in honor of Gov. William Clark, of the Lewis and Clark expedition, and first governor of the Territory of Missouri proper, serving from 1813 to 1820.

Clay—Organized January 2, 1822. Named for Henry Clay. Liberty, the county seat, was laid out in 1822.

Clinton—Organized January 15, 1833; reduced to its present limits in 1841. Named for Vice-President George Clinton, of New York. The county seat was first called Concord, then Springfield, and finally Plattsburg, for the residence of Gov. Clinton.

Cole—Organized November 16, 1820. Named for Capt. Stephen Cole, a noted pioneer of Missouri, who built Cole's Fort, at the present site of Boonville, and who died on "the plains," some time in the thirties, it is said.

Cooper—Organized December 17, 1818. Named for Capt. Sarshell Cooper, another prominent pioneer, who was killed by the Indians while seated at his own fireside in "Cooper's Fort," Howard County, on the night of April 14, 1814. Boonville, the county seat, was laid out in 1817, and named for Daniel Boone.

Crawford—Organized January 23, 1829. Named in honor of William H. Crawford, of Georgia, candidate for President in 1824. Until 1835 the county seat was at the mouth of Little Piney (now in Phelps County) at the dwelling house of James Harrison. The present county seat, Steelville, was located in 1835, and named for a prominent citizen.

Dade—Organized January 29, 1841. Named for Maj. Dade, of Seminole massacre fame. The name of the county seat, Greenfield, has no especial significance.

Dallas—Originally called Niangua, and organized in 1842; changed to Dallas December 10, 1844; and named in honor of Hon. George M. Dallas, of Pennsylvania, then Vice-President elect. Buffalo, the county seat, was named for the well-known city in New York by Joe Miles, an Irish bachelor, who first settled on the site. The word Niangua is a corruption of the original Indian name, Nehemgar.

Daviess—Organized December 29, 1836. Named in honor of Col. Jos. H. Daviess, of Kentucky, who fell at the battle of Tippecanoe, in 1811. Gallatin, the county seat, was laid out in 1837, and named for Albert Gallatin, the old Swiss financier, who was secretary of the treasury from 1801 to 1813.

De Kalb—Organized February 25, 1845, and named in honor of the Baron De Kalb, of the Revolution, who fell at the battle of Camden.

Dent—Organized February 10, 1851. Named in honor of Lewis Dent, a Tennesseean, who settled in the county in 1835, and was its first representative, elected in 1862. Salem, the county seat, was located in 1852. Perhaps when the founders christened it they had in mind the Hebrew word Salem, signifying peace.

Douglas—Organized October 19, 1857, and named for Stephen A. Douglas. The county seat has been alternately at Ava and Vera Cruz.

Dunklin—Organized February 14, 1845. Named in honor of Daniel Dunklin, governor of the State from 1832 to 1836, surveyor-general of the United States, etc. Kennett, the county seat, was named for Hon. Luther M. Kennett.

Franklin—Organized December 11, 1818. Named for Benjamin Franklin. The first county seat was at Newport, but in 1830 was removed to Union.

Gasconade—Organized November 25, 1820. Named for the river; reduced to its present limits (nearly) in 1835. Hermann was laid out in 1837, and became the county seat in 1845.

Gentry—Organized February 12, 1841. Named in honor of

Col. Richard Gentry, of Boone County, who fell at the head of the Missouri regiment in the battle against the Seminole Indians at Okeechobee, Fla., on Christmas Day, 1837. The county seat, Albany, was at first called Athens.

Greene—Organized January 2, 1833. Named for Gen. Nathaniel Greene, of the War of the Revolution. The county seat, Springfield, was named for the seat of justice of Robertson County, Tenn.

Grundy—Organized January 2, 1841. Named for Hon. Felix Grundy, of Tennessee, attorney-general of the United States from 1838 to 1840, etc. The county seat was located at Trenton in 1843.

Harrison—Organized February 14, 1845. Named in honor of Hon. Albert G. Harrison, of Callaway County, a representative in Congress from the State from 1834 to 1839, dying in the latter year. Bethany, the county seat, was laid out by Tennesseeans in 1845.

Henry—Originally called Rives, in honor of William C. Rives, of Virginia, then a Democratic politician of national reputation. Organized December 13, 1834. In 1840 Mr. Rives became a Whig, and in 1841 the name of the county was changed to Henry, in honor of Patrick Henry. Clinton, the county seat, was laid out in 1836, and named for George Clinton, of New York.

Hickory—Organized February 14, 1845, and named for the sobriquet of Andrew Jackson. The county seat, Hermitage, was named for "Old Hickory's" residence.

Holt—In 1839 the territory in the Platte Purchase north of Buchanan County was organized into the "Territory" of "Ne-at-a-wah," and attached to Buchanan. "Ne-at-a-wah" included the present counties of Andrew, Holt, Atchison and Nodaway. In 1841 this territory was subdivided and the county of "Nodaway" organized, but a few weeks later the Legislature changed the name to Holt, in honor of Hon. David Rice Holt, the representative from Platte County, who had died during the session, and who was buried at Jefferson City. Oregon, the county seat, was laid out in 1841, and at first called Finley.

Howard—Organized January 23, 1816. Named in honor of Col. Benjamin Howard, governor of the "Territory of Louisiana" from 1810 to 1812. The first county seat was at Old Franklin, on the Missouri, nearly opposite Boonville. Fayette (named for Gen. La Fayette) became the county seat in 1823.

Howell—Organized March 2, 1857. Named for James Howell, who settled in Howell's Valley in 1832.

Iron—Organized February 17, 1857, and named for its principal mineral. The origin of the name of its county seat, Ironton, is apparent.

Jackson—Organized December 15, 1826, and named for "the hero of New Orleans." Independence, the county seat, was laid out in 1827.

Jasper—Organized January 29, 1841. Named for Sergt. Jasper, a noted soldier of the Revolution, who planted the flag on Fort Moultrie amidst a shower of British cannon balls, and who fell at the assault on Savannah in 1779.

Jefferson—Organized December 8, 1818, and named for Thomas Jefferson. The first county seat was at Herculaneum. In 1835 it was removed to the present site, then called Monticello. There was already a county seat in the State (in Lewis County) bearing the name of Monticello, and in 1837 the designation of the capital of Jefferson was changed to Hillsboro.

Johnson—Organized December 13, 1834, and named for Col. Richard M. Johnson, of Kentucky, "the slayer of Tecumseh," who was afterward, from 1837 to 1841, Vice-President of the United States. The town of Warrensburg, the county seat, was laid out in 1835, and named for its founders, John and Martin D. Warren.

Knox—Organized February 14, 1845. Named in honor of Gen. Henry Knox, the Boston bookseller, who during the Revolution became Washington's chief of artillery, and who, the night before the battle of Trenton, we are told, "went about tugging at his guns like a Trojan and swearing like a pirate." He was the first secretary of war of the United States. Edina, the county seat, was laid out in 1839, and named by the surveyor, Hon. S. W. B. Carnegy, for the ancient name of the capital of Scotland.

Laclede—Organized February 24, 1849. Named for Pierre Laclede Liguest, often called Laclede, the founder of St. Louis.

The county seat, Lebanon, was named for a town in Tennessee.

La Fayette—Originally called Lillard, in honor of Hon. James C. Lillard, and organized November 16, 1820. In 1834 the name of the county was changed to La Fayette, in honor of the Marquis de La Fayette. The first county seat was at Mount Vernon, on the Missouri, but was removed to Lexington in 1824.

Lawrence—The first organization of a county called Lawrence, in 1818, was never perfected. The present county was created February 25, 1845, and named for the gallant Yankee sea captain, James Lawrence, who said, "Don't give up the ship." Mount Vernon, the county seat, was located the same year.

Lewis—Organized January 2, 1833. Named for Capt. Merriwether Lewis, of the Lewis and Clark expedition, who was governor of the Territory of Louisiana from 1807 to 1809, and who committed suicide in the latter year in a county in Tennessee now bearing his name, while on his way to Washington. Monticello ("Little Mountain"), the county seat, was laid out in 1834, and named for the country seat of Thomas Jefferson.

Lincoln—Organized December 14, 1818, and named for Gen. Benjamin Lincoln, of the Revolution. Troy (originally called Wood's Fort) became the county seat in 1819.

Linn—Organized January 7, 1837. Named in honor of Dr. Lewis F. Linn, of Ste. Genevieve, United States senator from 1833 to 1843, dying in office during the latter year. The origin of the name of the county seat, Linneus, is uncertain.

Livingston—Organized January 6, 1837. Named for Hon. Edward Livingston, of Louisiana, secretary of State from 1831 to 1833. The county seat, Chillicothe (an Indian name said to signify "the big town where we live"), was located in 1837.

McDonald—Organized March 3, 1849. Said to have been named for Sergt. McDonald, a South Carolina trooper of the Revolution. The first county seat was at Rutledge, but was subsequently removed to Pineville, which place was originally called Marysville.

Macon—Organized January 6, 1837. Named for Nathaniel Macon of North Carolina. The first county seat was called "Box

Ancle," afterward Bloomington. It was removed to Macon City in 1860.

Madison—Organized December 14, 1818, and named for President Madison. The first county seat was St. Michael, near the present capital, Fredericktown, which was located in 1821.

Maries—Organized March 2, 1855, and named for the two streams, Marie and Little Marie.

Marion—Organized December 23, 1826, and named for Gen. Francis Marion, "The Swamp Fox." Palmyra, which has always been the county seat, was laid off in 1819.

Mercer—Organized February 14, 1845. Named in honor of Gen. Hugh Mercer, of the Revolution, and the county seat, Princeton, was so called for the battle in which he lost his life.

Miller—Organized February 6, 1837. Named for John Miller, a colonel under Harrison in the War of 1812, governor of Missouri from 1826 to 1832, member of Congress from 1836 to 1842, etc.

Mississippi—Organized February 14, 1845, and named for the Father of Waters.

Moniteau—Organized February 14, 1845. Named for the stream which flows through the western part, whose name is a corruption of the Indian word *Manitou*, meaning the Deity. California, the county seat, was laid out in 1845, and originally called Boonsboro.

Monroe—Organized January 6, 1831, and named in honor of James Monroe. Paris, the county seat, was settled upon in 1831, and named for Paris, Ky.

Montgomery—Organized December 14, 1818, and named for Gen. Richard Montgomery, who fell at the storming of Quebec. The first county seat was at Pinckney, on the Missouri, afterward it was removed to Lewiston, near the center of the county, and finally to Danville, which was laid off in 1834.

Morgan—Organized January 5, 1833, and named for Gen. Daniel Morgan, who commanded the famous riflemen in the Revolution. The first county seat was at Millville, now extinct, but in 1834 it was removed to Versailles.

New Madrid—One of the original "districts." Organized

October 1, 1812. Named for the town (the county seat) which was, properly speaking, founded by Gen. Morgan, of New Jersey in 1788.

Newton—Organized December 31, 1838. Named for Sergt. Newton, the comrade of Jasper, the Revolutionary hero. The name given to the county seat, Neosho, is a corruption of the Osage Indian word, *Ne-o-zho*.

Nodaway—Organized February 14, 1845. Named for the stream flowing through it. The name is a corruption of *Ni-di-wah*, a Sac and Fox Indian word, meaning "hearsay." (It will be remembered that the original designation of Holt County was Nodaway.) The county seat, Maryville, was laid off in 1845, and named for the first resident lady, Mrs. Mary Graham.

Oregon—Organized February 14, 1845. Named for the territory then under discussion, in connection with which the phrase "54-40 or fight" was often heard.

Osage—Organized January 29, 1841, and named for the river which forms the greater portion of its western boundary. The Osage River was named by the French more than 100 years ago from the tribe of Indians upon its banks. The word is a corruption of *Oua-chage*, or *Ou-chage* (whence Wahsatch), and as applied to individual, means "the strong." Linn, the county seat, is named in honor of Senator Lewis F. Linn.

Ozark—Organized January 29, 1841. In 1843 its name was changed to Decatur, in honor of the famous fighting commodore, Stephen Decatur, but in 1845 its present title was restored. The first county seat was Rockbridge, near the north line; the present is Gainesville.

Pemiscot—Organized February 19, 1861. Named for the large bayou within its borders. The word signifies "liquid mud." Gayoso, the county seat, was named for a prominent Spanish official of the territorial days.

Perry—Organized November 16, 1820. Named in honor of Commodore Oliver H. Perry, the hero of Lake Erie. Perryville, the county seat, was located in 1821.

Pettis—Organized January 26, 1833. Named in honor of Hon. Spencer Pettis, of St. Louis, a member of Congress from

Missouri in 1828-31, and who was killed in a duel with Maj. Thomas Biddle, on Bloody Island, in the latter year. The first county seat was at St. Helena; in 1837 it was removed to Georgetown; in 1862 to Sedalia. The last named town was laid out in 1859, and named by its founder, Gen. George R. Smith, for his daughter Sarah, who was familiarly called "Sade" and "Sed." It was first called by Gen. Smith "Sedville," but he afterward gave it the more euphonious title which it now bears.

Phelps—Organized November 13, 1857. Named for Hon. John S. Phelps, of Greene County, member of Congress from 1844 to 1862; governor from 1877 to 1881, etc.

Pike—Organized December 14, 1818. Named in honor of Gen. Zebulon Pike, who explored the Upper Mississippi in 1805; visited Kansas, Colorado and New Mexico and other territory in the West in 1806, discovering the mountain which yet bears the name of Pike's Peak, and who was killed at the battle of York, Canada, in April, 1813. Bowling Green was laid out in 1819, and became the county seat in 1824, upon its removal from Louisiana.

Platte—Organized December 31, 1838, and named indirectly for the Platte River, which flows through it, and from which the Platte Purchase was named. Platte City, the county seat, was originally called Falls of Platte.

Polk—Organized March 13, 1835. Named in honor of James K. Polk, of Tennessee, who afterward, in 1844, became President. He had numerous admirers among the first settlers, who had known him in Tennessee before their removal to Missouri.

Pulaski—Organized December 15, 1818. Named in honor of Count Pulaski, who fell at Savannah during the Revolution.

Putnam—Organized February 28, 1845, and named for Gen. Israel Putnam. The first county seat was at Putnamville, afterward at Winchester, and finally at Harmony, whose present name is Unionville.

Ralls—Organized November 16, 1820. Named in honor of Daniel Ralls, a member of the Legislature at that time from Pike County. New London was laid out in 1819.

Randolph—Organized January 22, 1829. Named for John

Randolph, of Roanoke. Huntsville became the county seat in 1830, and named for Judge Ezra Hunt.

Ray—Organized November 16, 1820, and named for Hon. John Ray, a member of the Constitutional Convention from Howard County. The first county seat was at Bluffton, but in 1828 it was removed to Richmond.

Reynolds—Organized February 25, 1845. Named in honor of Hon. Thomas Reynolds, governor of Missouri from 1841 to 1844, in which latter year he committed suicide at the capital. His name was bestowed upon this county through the efforts of Hon. Pate Buford, his particular friend.

Ripley—Organized January 5, 1813, and named in honor of Gen. Ripley, of the War of 1812. Doniphan, the county seat, was named for Gen. A. W. Doniphan, Missouri's renowned hero of the Mexican War.

St. Charles—One of the original "districts." Organized October 1, 1812. Named for the town, which was named by the French.

St. Clair—Organized January 29, 1841. Named for Gen. Arthur St. Clair, of the Revolution. Osceola, named for the noted Seminole chief, became the county seat in 1842.

St. Francois—Organized December 19, 1821. Named for the river. Farmington, the present county seat, was not laid out until 1856.

Ste. Genevieve—One of the original "districts." Organized October 1, 1812. Named for the town, which was founded, practically, in 1763, although settled, probably, in 1735.

St. Louis—One of the original "districts." Organized October 1, 1812. Named for the town, which in turn was named for King Louis XV of France, having been founded by Pierre Laclede, in 1764. Clayton was made the county seat in 1875.

Saline—Organized November 25, 1820. County seats in their order have been Jefferson, Jonesboro, Arrow Rock and Marshall. The county was named for its salt springs.

Schuyler—Organized February 14, 1845, and named for Gen. Philip Schuyler of the Revolution. The first county seat was at Tippecanoe; Lancaster, the present capital, was laid out in 1845.

Scotland—Organized January 29, 1841. Named by Hon. S. W. B. Carnegy, now of Canton, in honor of the land of his ancestors. He surveyed and named the town of Edinburg in this county, and also the town of Edina, in Knox County. The first courts in Scotland were held at Sand Hill, but in 1843 the county seat was located at Memphis.

Scott—Organized December 28, 1821. Named for Hon. John Scott, the first congressman from Missouri. The first county seat was at Benton.

Shannon—Organized January 29, 1841. Named for Hon. George F. Shannon, a prominent lawyer and politician of the State, who dropped dead in the courthouse at Palmyra in August, 1836.

Shelby—Organized January 2, 1835. Named for Gen. Isaac Shelby, who fought at King's Mountain, in the Revolution, and was subsequently governor of Kentucky. The first county seat was at Oak Dale, but was located at Shelbyville in 1836.

Stoddard—Organized January 2, 1836. Named for Capt. Amos Stoddard, of Connecticut, who took possession of Missouri in the name of his government after the Louisiana Purchase.

Stone—Organized February 10, 1851, and named for the stony character of its soil. Galena, the county seat, was so named for the presence of that mineral in the vicinity.

Sullivan—Fully organized February 16, 1843, and named by Hon. E. C. Morelock for his native county in Tennessee. In the preliminary organization in 1843, the county was named Highland. The first courts were held at the house of A. C. Hill, on the present site of Milan, which became the county seat in 1845.

Taney—Organized January 6, 1837, and named for Chief Justice Roger B. Taney. Forsyth, the county seat, located in 1838, was named for Hon. John Forsyth, of Georgia, who was Secretary of State of the United States from 1834 to 1841.

Texas—Organized February 14, 1845, and named for the Lone Star State. Houston, the county seat, was named for Gen. Sam Houston, the "hero of San Jacinto."

Vernon—Organized as at present February 27, 1855. Named for Hon. Miles Vernon, a member of the State Senate from Laclede County, who fought under Gen. Jackson at New Orleans, and who presided over the Senate branch of the "Claib Jackson Legislature," which passed the "Ordinance of Secession, at Neosho, October 28, 1861. Nevada, the county seat, was originally called Nevada City, and named by Col. D. C. Hunter for a town in California.

Warren—Organized January 5, 1833, and named for Gen. Joseph Warren, who fell at Bunker Hill. Warrenton became the county seat in 1835.

Washington—Organized August 21, 1813, and named for the "Father of His Country." It is claimed that Potosi, the county seat, was first settled in 1765.

Wayne—Organized December 11, 1818, when it comprised the greater part of the southern one-third of the State. It was formerly called by the sobriquet of "the State of Wayne," and latterly "the Mother of Counties." It was named in honor of Gen. Anthony Wayne, of the Revolution, the famous "Mad Anthony" of history and legend. Greenville, the county seat, was laid out in 1818, and named for the scene of Gen. Wayne's treaty.

Webster—Organized March 3, 1855, and named for Daniel Webster. The county seat, Marshfield, was named for Webster's country seat.

Worth—Organized February 8, 1861, and named in honor of Gen. William Worth, one of the prominent American commanders in the Mexican War. Grant City was laid off in 1864, and named for Gen. Grant.

Wright—Organized January 29, 1841, and named in honor of Hon. Silas Wright, of New York, a leading Democratic statesman of that period. Hartville was named for the owner of the site.

There have been attempts at the creation of other counties from time to time. Dodge County, named for Gen. Henry Dodge, was organized in 1851, with a county seat at St. John, but in 1853 it was disorganized and its territory included within the limits of Putnam, of which county it had formed the western part. The organization of Donaldson, Merrimac, and perhaps two or three other counties, was never perfected.

POPULATION.

The annexed table shows the population of the State by the counties in existence at the several periods mentioned. The population of the Territory in 1810 was 20,845.

Counties.	1821.	1830.	1840.	1850.	1860.	1870.	1880.
Adair............				2,342	8,531	11,449	15,190
Andrew..........				9,433	11,850	15,137	16,318
Atchison.........				1,648	4,649	8,440	14,556
Audrain..........			1,949	3,506	8,075	12,307	19,732
Barry............			4,795	3,467	7,995	10,373	14,405
Barton...........					1,817	5,087	10,332
Bates............				3,669	7,215	15,960	25,381
Benton...........			4,205	5,015	9,072	11,322	12,396
Bollinger.........					7,371	8,162	11,130
Boone............	3,692	8,859	13,561	14,979	19,486	20,765	25,422
Buchanan........			6,237	12,975	23,861	35,109	49,792
Butler...........				1,616	2,891	4,298	6,011
Caldwell.........			1,458	2,316	5,034	11,390	13,646
Callaway........	1,797	6,102	11,765	13,827	17,049	19,202	23,670
Camden..........				2,338	4,975	6,108	7,266
Cape Girardeau...	7,852	7,430	9,359	13,912	15,547	17,558	20,998
Carroll...........			2,432	5,441	9,763	17,445	23,274
Carter...........					1,235	1,455	2,168
Cass.............			4,693	6,090	9,794	19,296	22,431
Cedar............				3,361	6,637	9,474	10,741
Chariton.........	1,426	1,776	4,746	7,514	12,562	19,135	25,224
Christian.........					5,491	6,707	9,628
Clark............			2,846	5,527	11,684	13,667	15,081
Clay.............		5,342	8,282	10,332	13,023	15,564	15,572
Clinton...........			2,724	3,786	7,748	14,063	16,073
Cole.............	1,028	3,006	9,286	6,696	9,697	10,292	15,515
Cooper...........	3,483	6,910	10,484	12,950	17,356	20,692	21,596
Crawford.........			1,709	3,561	5,823	7,982	10,756
Dade.............				4,246	7,072	8,683	12,557
Dallas............				3,648	5,892	8,383	9,263
Daviess..........			2,736	5,298	9,606	14,410	19,145
De Kalb.,........				2,075	5,224	9,858	13,334
Dent.............					5,654	6,357	10,646
Douglas..........					2,414	3,915	7,753
Dunklin..........				1,220	5,026	5,982	9,604
Franklin,.........	1,928	3,431	7,515	11,021	18,035	23,098	26,534
Gasconade.......	1,174	1,548	5,330	4,996	8,727	11,093	11,153
Gentry...........				4,248	11,980	11,607	17,176
Greene...........			5,372	12,785	13,186	21,549	28,801
Grundy..........				3,006	7,887	10,567	15,185
Harrison.........				2,447	10,626	14,635	20,304
Henry............			4,726	4,052	9,866	17,401	23,906
Hickory..........				2,329	4,705	6,452	7,387
Holt.............				3,957	6,550	11,652	15,509
Howard..........	7,821	10,314	13,108	13,969	15,946	17,233	18,428
Howell...........					3,169	4,218	8,814
Iron.............					5,842	6,278	8,183
Jackson..........		2,822	7,612	14,000	22,896	55,041	82,325
Jasper...........				4,223	6,883	14,928	32,019
Jefferson.........	1,838	2,586	4,296	6,928	10,344	15,380	18,736
Johnson..........			4,471	7,467	14,644	24,648	28,172

POPULATION OF MISSOURI BY COUNTIES.—*Continued.*

COUNTIES.	1821.	1830.	1840.	1850.	1860.	1870.	1880.
Knox............	......	......	......	2,894	8,727	10,974	13,047
Laclede..........	......	......	......	2,498	5,182	9,380	11,524
La Fayette.......	1,840	2,921	6,815	13.690	20,098	22,628	25,710
Lawrence........	......	......	......	4,859	8,846	13,067	17,583
Lewis............	......	......	6,040	6,578	12,286	15,114	15,925
Lincoln..........	1,674	4,060	7,449	9,421	14,210	15,960	17,426
Linn.............	......	......	2,345	4,058	9,112	15,900	20,016
Livingston.......	......	......	4,325	4,247	7,417	16,730	20,196
McDonald........	......	......	......	2,236	4,038	5,226	7,816
Macon............	......	......	6,034	6,565	14,346	23,230	26,222
Madison.........	......	2,371	3,395	6,003	5,664	5,849	8,876
Maries...........	......	......	......	......	4,901	5,916	7,304
Marion...........	1,907	4,839	9,623	12,230	18,838	23,780	24,837
Mercer...........	......	......	......	2,691	9,300	11,557	14,673
Miller............	......	......	2,282	3,834	6,812	6,616	9,805
Mississippi......	......	......	......	3,123	4,859	4,982	9,270
Moniteau........	......	......	......	6,004	10,124	11,375	14,346
Monroe..........	......	......	9,505	10,541	14,785	17,149	19,071
Montgomery.....	2,032	3,900	4,371	5,486	9,718	10,405	16,246
Morgan..........	......	......	4,407	4,650	8,202	8,434	10,132
New Madrid.....	2,445	2,351	4,554	5,541	5,654	6,357	7,694
Newton..........	......	......	3,790	4,268	9,319	12,821	18,947
Nodaway.........	......	......	......	2,118	5,252	14,751	29,544
Oregon...........	......	......	......	1,432	3,009	3,287	5,721
Osage............	......	......	......	6,704	7,879	10,793	11,824
Ozark............	......	......	......	2,294	2,447	3,363	5,618
Pemiscot.........	......	......	......	......	2,962	2,059	4,299
Perry............	1,599	3,371	5,760	7,215	9,128	9,877	11,895
Pettis............	......	......	2,930	5,150	9,392	18,706	27,271
Phelps...........	......	......	......	......	5,714	10,506	12,568
Pike..............	2,677	6,122	10,646	13,609	18,417	23,077	26,715
Platte............	......	......	8,913	16,845	18,350	17,352	17,366
Polk..............	......	......	8,449	6,186	9,995	12,445	15,734
Pulaski...........	......	......	6,529	3,998	3,835	4,714	7,250
Putnam..........	......	......	......	1,657	9,207	11,217	13,555
Ralls.............	1,684	4,346	5,670	6,151	8,592	10,510	11,838
Randolph........	......	2,942	7,198	9,439	11,407	15,908	22,751
Ray..............	1,789	2,658	6,053	10.353	14,092	18,700	20,190
Reynolds.........	......	......	......	1,849	3,173	3,756	5,722
Ripley............	......	......	2,856	2,830	3,747	3,175	5,377
St. Charles.......	4,058	4,822	7,911	11,454	16,523	21,304	23,065
St. Clair.........	......	......	......	3,556	6,812	5,747	14,125
St. Francois.....	......	2,386	3,211	4,964	4,249	9,742	13,822
Ste. Genevieve...	3,181	2,000	3,148	5,313	8,029	8,384	10,390
St. Louis........	8,190	14,909	35,975	104.978	190,524	351,189	382,406
Saline............	1,176	2,182	5,258	8,843	14,699	21,672	29,911
Schuyler.........	......	......	......	3,287	6,097	8,820	10,470
Scotland.........	......	......	......	3,782	8,873	10,670	12,508
Scott.............	......	......	2,136	5,974	3,182	5,247	7,317	8,587
Shannon..........	......	......	......	1,199	2,284	2,339	3,441
Shelby...........	......	......	3,056	4,253	7,301	10,119	14,024
Stoddard.........	......	......	3,153	4,277	7,877	8,535	13,431
Stone............	......	......	......	......	2,400	3,253	4,404
Sullivan.........	......	......	......	2,983	9,198	11,907	16,569
Taney...........	......	......	3,264	4,373	3,576	4,407	5,599
Texas............	......	......	......	2,313	6,067	9,618	12,206

POPULATION OF MISSOURI BY COUNTIES.—*Concluded.*

Counties.	1821.	1830.	1840.	1850.	1860.	1870.	1880.
Vernon............					4,850	11,247	19,369
Warren............			4,253	5,860	8,339	9,637	10,806
Washington......	3,741	6,779	7,213	8,811	9,728	11,719	12,896
Wayne............	1,614	3,254	3,403	5,518	5,629	6,068	9,096
Webster...........					7,099	10,434	12,175
Worth.............						5,004	8,203
Wright............				3,387	4,508	5,684	9,712
Total.........	70,647	140,304	383,702	682,043	1,182,012	1,721,295	2,168,380

CITIES AND TOWNS.

The following table shows the population of cities and towns in the State with a population of 4,000 and upward in 1880, as compared with 1870:

Towns.	1870.	1880.	Towns.	1870.	1880.
Carthage............	......	4,167	Moberly............	1,514	6,070
Chillicothe.........	3,978	4,078	St. Charles........	5,570	5,014
Hannibal............	10,125	11,074	St. Joseph.........	19,565	32,431
Jefferson City.....	4,420	5,271	St. Louis...........	310,864	350,518
Joplin...............	......	7,038	Sedalia.............	4,560	9,561
Kansas City........	32,260	55,785	Springfield.........	5,555	6,522
Louisiana..........	3,630	4,325	Warrensburg.......	2,945	4,040

UPPER LOUISIANA.

The following table shows the population of Upper Louisiana for the years given. In 1803–04 the number of slaves was 1,270; in 1810, whites, 13,834.

Districts.	Settlements.	Population in 1803-04 not including slaves.	Population in 1810 including slaves.
New Madrid....................	New Madrid............ Arkansas............... Hope Fields........... St. Francois.......... Little Prairie.........	1,350	4,165
Cape Girardeau...............	....	1,470	3,888
Ste. Genevieve................	Ste. Genevieve........ Southwestern Villages	2,350	4,620
St. Louis.......................	St. Louis.............. Carondelet............ St. Ferdinand........ Western Villages.....	2,280	5,667
St. Charles....................	St. Charles........... Portage des Sioux.... Femme Osage........	1,400	3,505
Troops in Territory (est.)......................................		50	200
Hunting and Trading Parties (est.)............................		200	300
Inhabitants Remote from Sheriff (est.)........................		75	300
		9,175	22,645

MISCELLANEOUS ITEMS.

The Great Fire at St. Louis.—In May, 1849, occurred the great fire at St. Louis; a brief account of it from Switzler's History of Missouri is here copied:

On the evening of the 19th of that month a fire broke out on the steamer "White Cloud," lying at the wharf between Vine and Cherry Streets, and set at defiance every effort to arrest its progress. The flames very soon communicated to four other boats lying contiguous. By the action of the fire, the "White Cloud" became loosened from her fastenings, and drifted out into the stream and among the other steamers in port. In a short time the spectacle of twenty-three boats on fire presented itself. The immense conflagration was a mile in length. The levee being covered with combustible materials, bales, barrels, boxes, etc., the fire reached the city and whole blocks were swept away. The area of the burnt district will be understood by the statement that Front Street, from Locust to Market, was entirely destroyed, with the exception of two or three houses on Commercial Street. Between Commercial and the levee, there was not one left. In this immense conflagration there were twenty-three steamboats, three barges and one canal boat destroyed, whose total values with their cargoes were estimated at $439,000. The whole value of property destroyed amounted to over $3,000,000.

The Murders at Gun City.—During the administration of Gov. Brown, a bloody infraction of the public peace occurred at Gun City, a small station on the Missouri, Kansas & Texas Railroad, in Cass County.

Judge J. C. Stevenson was one of the judges of the late county court of Cass County, that had made a fraudulent issue of bonds in the name of the county, thereby imposing heavy burdens upon the taxpayers. James C. Cline was county attorney, and was implicated in the swindle, and Thomas E. Detro was one of Cline's bondsmen. Both Stevenson and Cline had been indicted, and were under heavy bonds to answer for the offense with which they were charged. All of these men, together with Gen. Jo. Shelby, were on the eastern-bound train which reached Gun City on Wednesday, April 24, 1872. At this place logs, rails and rocks were found piled upon the track, and seventy or eighty masked and armed men compelled the engineer and fireman to leave the locomotive, and then commenced a terrible fusilade into and around the captured train. Loud cries were made for Cline, who stepped out on the platform and was instantly riddled with bullets. The murderers then rushed through the train calling for the "bond robbers." They shot Judge Stevenson down in the car, and afterward dragged him out on the grass. Mr. Detro they found in the mail car, and, after severely wounding him, threw him on the roadside, where he was allowed to bleed to death. The gang then called for Gen. Jo. Shelby, but his intrepidity saved him, as he coolly kept his seat, replying, "Here I am; if you want me come and get me."

Gov. Brown at once took measures to bring the murderers to justice, but they were never discovered. No further disturbance occurred, however.

Hannibal & St. Joseph Railroad Controversy.—By continued legislation, commencing with the act approved February 22, 1851, and ending with that of March 26, 1881, the State of Missouri granted liberal aid in the construction of railroads within her boundaries. The Hannibal & St. Joseph Railroad was among the enterprises thus assisted, and, for its construction, bonds of the State amounting to $3,000,000, bearing interest at 6 per cent per annum, payable semi-annually, were issued. One-half of these bonds were issued under the act of 1851, and the remainder under the act of 1855. The former were to run twenty years, and the latter thirty years. Some of these bonds have since been funded and renewed. Coupons for the interest of the entire $3,000,000 were executed and made payable in New York. The acts under which the bonds were issued contain various provisions designed to secure the State against loss and to make it certain that the railroad company would be bound to pay the principal and interest at maturity. It was especially made the duty of the railroad company to save the State from any and all loss on account of said bonds and coupons. The State treasurer was not to advance any money to meet either principal or interest. The State contracted with the railroad company for complete indemnity. Neither was she required to relinquish her statutory mortgage lien, except upon the payment into her treasury of a sum of money equal to the entire indebtedness incurred by the railroad company on account of the issue and loan of her bonds.

In June, 1881, the railroad company, through its attorney, George W. Easley, Esq., paid into the State treasury $3,000,000, and asked for a receipt in full of all dues to the State. The treasurer, Mr. Philip E. Chappell, refused to give such a receipt, but instead gave a receipt for the sum " on account." Although the debt was not due, the officers of the railroad wished to pay it at this time in order to save the interest. They first asked for the bonds of the road, but these the State refused to give up. They then demanded that the $3,000,000 be paid back, and this demand was also refused. The railroad company then brought suit in the United States Court for an equitable settlement of the matter in dispute. The $3,000,000 had been deposited in a bank by the State authorities, and was drawing interest at the rate of only one-fourth of one per cent. The railroad company asked that this money should be invested so as to yield a larger amount of interest, which interest should be allowed to its credit, in case anything should be found due from it to the State. Justice Miller, of the United States supreme court, who heard the case upon preliminary injunction in the spring of 1882, decided that the unpaid and unmatured coupons constituted a liability of the State, and a debt owing, though not due, and that until these were provided for, the State was not bound to assign her lien upon the road.

Another question which was raised, but not decided, was whether any, or if so what, account the State ought to render for the use of the money paid into the treasury by the complainants, June 20; and whether she could hold so large a sum of money, refusing to make any account of it, and yet insisting that the railroad company should make full payment of all the outstanding coupons.

Upon this subject Justice Miller, in the course of his opinion said; "I am of the opinion that the State, having accepted or got this money into her possession, is under a moral obligation (and I do not pretend to commit anybody as to how far its legal obligation goes) to so use that money as, so far as possible, to protect the parties who have paid it against the loss of the interest which it might accumulate, and which would go to extinguish the interest on the State's obligation."

February 25, 1881, Gov. Crittenden sent a special message to the Legislature in which he informed that body of the intention of the Hannibal & St. Joseph Railroad Comany to discharge the full amount of what it considered its present indebtedness to the State, and advised that arrangements be made for the profitable disposal of the sum as soon as paid. In response to this message the Legislature passed an act March 26, the second section of which is as follows:

SEC. 2. Whenever there is sufficient money in the sinking fund to redeem or purchase one or more of the bonds of the State of Missouri, such sum is hereby appropriated for such purpose, and the Fund Commissioners shall immediately call in for payment a like amount of the option bonds of the State, known as the "5-20 bonds," provided, that if there are no option bonds which can be called in for payment they may invest such money in the purchase of any of the bonds of the State, or bonds of the United States, the Hannibal & St. Joseph Railroad bonds excepted.

On the 1st of January, 1882, the regular semi-annual payment of interest on the railroad bonds became due, but the company refused to pay, claiming that it had already discharged the principal, and consequently was not liable for the interest. Thereupon, according to the provisions of the aiding act of 1885, Gov. Crittenden advertised the road for sale in default of the payment of interest. The company then brought suit before United States Circuit Judge McCrary at Keokuk, Iowa, to enjoin the State from selling the road, and for such other and further relief as the Court might see fit and proper to grant. August 2, 1882, Judge McCrary delivered his opinion and judgment as follows:

"First. That the payment by complainants into the treasury of the State of the sum of $3,000,000 on the 26th of June, 1881, did not satisfy the claim of the State in full, nor entitle complainants to an assignment of the State's statutory mortgage.

"Second. That the State was bound to invest the principal sum of $3,000,000 so paid by the complainants without unnecessary delay in the securities named in the act of March 26, 1881, or some of them, so as to save the State as large a sum as possible, which sum so saved would have constituted as between the State and complainants a credit *pro tanto* upon the unmatured coupons now in controversy.

"Third. That the rights and equity of the parties are to be determined upon the foregoing principles, and the State must stand charged with what would have been realized if the act of March, 1881, had been complied with. It only remains to consider what the rights of the parties are upon the principles here stated.

"In order to save the State from loss on account of the default of the railroad company, a further sum must be paid. In order to determine what that further sum is, an accounting must be had. The question to be settled by the accounting is, how much would the State have lost if the provisions of the act of March, 1881, had been complied with? * * * * I think a perfectly fair basis of settlement would be to hold the State liable for whatever could have been saved by the prompt execution of said act by taking up such 5–20 option bonds of the State as were subject to call when the money was paid to the State, and investing the remainder of the funds in the bonds of the United States at the market rates.

"Upon this basis a calculation can be made, and the exact sum still to be paid by the complainants in order to fully indemnify and protect the State can be ascertained. For the purpose of stating an account upon this basis, and of determining the sum to be paid by the complainants to the State, the cause will be referred to John K. Cravens, one of the masters of this court. In determining the time when the investment should have been made under the act of March, 1881, the master will allow a reasonable period for the time of the receipt of the said sum of $3,000,000 by the treasurer of the State—that is to say, such time as would have been required for that purpose had the officers charged with the duty of making said investment used reasonable diligence in its discharge.

"The Hannibal & St. Joseph Railroad is advertised for sale for the amount of the installment of interest due January 1, 1882, which installment amounts to less than the sum which the company must pay in order to discharge its liabilities to the State upon the theory of this opinion. The order will therefore be that an injunction be granted to enjoin the sale of the road upon the payment of the said installment of interest due January 1, 1882, and if such payment is made, the master will take it into account in making the computation above mentioned."

Manufacturing.—Missouri presents every facility for extensive and successful manufacturing; abundant timber of the best quality, exhaustless deposits of coal, iron, lead, zinc, marble and granite, unmeasured water power, distributed over the State, a home market among an industrious and wealth-accumulating people, and a system of navigable rivers and railway trunk line and branches, that permeate, not only the State, but reach out in direct lines from gulf to lake, and from ocean to ocean.

Of the manufacturing in Missouri over three-quarters of the whole is done in St. Louis, which produced, in 1880, $114,333,375 worth of manufactured articles, thus placing her as the sixth manufacturing city in the Union, being surpassed only by New York, Philadelphia, Chicago, Brooklyn and Boston.

The leading manufacturing counties of the State are St. Louis, Jackson, Buchanan, St. Charles, Marion, Franklin, Greene, Cape Girardeau, Platte, Boone, Lafayette, followed by Macon, Clay, Phelps, St. Francois, Washington and Lewis.

The subjoined table, arranged from the tenth United States census, will give the reader a comprehensive view of the present state of manufacturing in Missouri, and its variation during recent years:

Year.	No. Establishments.	Capital.	Average number of Hands Employed.			Total Amount Paid in Wages During the Year.	Value of Materials.	Value of Products.
			Males Above 16 years.	Females Above 15 years.	Children and Youths.			
1850	2,923	$ 8,576,607	14,880	928	....	$ 4,692,648	$ 12,798,351	$ 24,324,418
1860	3,157	20,084,220	18,628	1,053	....	6,669,916	23,849,941	41,782,781
1870	11,871	80,257,244	55,904	3,884	5,566	31,055,445	115,533,269	206,213,429
1880	8,592	72,507,844	54,200	5,474	4,821	24,309,716	110,798,892	165,386,205

The products of the principal lines of manufacturing interests, for the year 1880, are as follows: flouring and grist mills, $32,438,831; slaughtering and meat packing, $14,628,630; tobacco, $6,810,719; iron, steel, etc., $5,154,090; liquors, distilled and malt, $5,575,607; clothing, $4,409,376; lumber, $6,533,253; bagging and bags, $2,597,395; saddlery and harness, $3,976,175; oil, $851,000; foundry and machine shop products, $6,798,832; printing and publishing, $4,452,962; sugar and molasses, $4,475,740; boots and shoes, $1,982,993; furniture, $2,380,562; paints, $2,825,860; carriages and wagons, $2,483,738; marble and stone works, $1,003,544; bakery products, $3,250,192; brick and tile, $1,602,522; tinware, copper ware and sheet-iron ware, $1,687,320; sash, doors and blinds, $1,232,670; cooperage, $1,904,822; agricultural implements, $1,141,822; patent medicines, $1,197,090; soap and candles, $1,704,194; confectionery, $1,247,235; drugs and chemicals, $1,220,211; gold and silver reduced and refined, $4,158,606.

These, together with all other mechanical industries, aggregate $165,386,205.

Railroads.—Since 1852, when railroad building began in Missouri, between 4,000 and 5,000 miles of track have been laid. Additional roads are now in process of construction, and many others in contemplation. The State is well supplied with railroads which tread her surface in all directions, bringing her remotest districts into close connection with St. Louis, that great center of Western commerce. These roads have a capital stock aggregating more than $100,000,000, and a funded debt of about the same amount.

The lines of roads which are in operation in the State are as follows:

The Missouri Pacific, chartered May 10, 1850; the St. Louis, Iron Mountain & Southern Railroad, which is a consolidation of the Arkansas branch; the Cairo, Arkansas & Texas Railroad; the Cairo & Fulton Railroad; the Wabash Western Railway; the St. Louis & San Francisco Railway; the Chicago, Alton & St. Louis Railroad; the Hannibal & St. Joseph Railroad; the Missouri, Kansas & Texas Railroad; the Kansas City, St. Joseph & Council Bluffs Railroad; the Keokuk & Kansas City Railway Company; the St. Louis, Salem & Little Rock Railroad Company; the Missouri & Western; the St. Louis, Keokuk & Northwestern Railroad; the St. Louis, Hannibal & Keokuk Railroad; the Missouri, Iowa & Nebraska Railway; the Quincy, Missouri & Pacific

Railroad; the Chicago, Rock Island & Pacific Railway; the Burlington & Southwestern Railroad.

Steam Craft.—In 1880 there were 167 steam crafts owned in Missouri, including sixty passenger steamers, thirty-seven ferryboats, thirteen freight steamers, forty-six tow boats and eleven yachts. Their combined tonnage was 60,873.50; their total value, $2,098,800; their crews numbered 2,733 persons, whose wages amounted to $1,423,375, or an average of $281.13 to each person during the season; the number of passengers carried was 642,303; the freight in tons 2,556,815; coal used for fuel, 399,659 tons; wood used for fuel, 25,085 cords; gross earnings of all the steam crafts, $5,560,949.

Wealth.—The total valuation of Missouri's real estate and personal property, according to the census of 1880, was $532,795,801; of which her real estate was valued at $381,985,112, and her personal property at $150,810,689. At that time the bonded debt of the State was $55,446,001; the floating debt, $2,722,941; the gross debt, $58,168,942; the sinking fund, $681,558, and the net debt, $57,487,384.

INDEX

Adams, John Quincy 160; Washington 157
Alexander, A.M. 159
Allen, T. 159
Allsman, Andrew 126
Ampudia, Gen. 70
Anderson, Maj. 87(2); C.P. 90; George W. 158; Robert 87; Thomas L. 158
Arista, Gen. 70
Armstrong, D.H. 157
Asboth, Gen. 119,120
Asbury, Bishop 153
Ashley, H. 60,155,157
Asper, Joel F. 158
Atchison, David R. 68,77, 157,172
Atkinson, Brig. Gen. 62
Aubrey, M. 46
Audrain, Samuel 173
Augney, W.Z. 71
Austin, Moses 69; Stephen 69

Baber, Hiram H. 156
Backoff, Maj. 109-10
Barrett, J. Richard 158
Barry, Commodroe 173
Barton, David 59,60,157, 173; Joshua 155
Bates, Barton 157: Edward 59,156,173; Frederick 52,146,154; Moses D. 57
Bay, S.M. 156; W.V.N. 157, 158
Beauregard, Gen. 87
Bell, Maj. 94,97; John 84, 160
Benjamin, John F. 123,158
Benton, Thomas H. 60,75-6, 111,150,157,158,173
Biddle, Thomas 182
Bingham, George C. 127-8, 129,130,156
Bishop, William 156
Black, F.M. 159
Blackhawk, Chief 61,62,63
Blaine, James G. 161
Blair, Francis P. Jr. 158; Frank P. Jr. 99,108; James G. 158
Blandowski, C. 96
Bliss, Philemon 157
Blow, Henry T. 159
Blunt, James G.V. 130
Bogart, Sam 68
Boggs, Lilbourn W. 64,68, 155
Bogy, L.V. 157
Bollinger, Frederick 55n, 173; George F. 55n,173
Boone, D.G. 156; Daniel 50-1,61,173,175; Daniel M. 51; Nathan 51,59
Boothe, Emma 120
Bowen, John S. 93,94
Bower, Gustavus M. 157
Bowlin, James B. 157
Boyd, Sempromius T. 158
Bradford, Fanny B. 103-7
Breckenridge, Mr. 103; John C. 84,160
Broadhan, James O. 159
Brockmeyer, Henry C. 155
Brooke, Mr. 65
Brooks, John A. 145,161
Brown, B. Gratz 140,141, 155,157.189,190; Cyrus A. 96p; E.B. 127,130, 132; Joseph 154
Buckner, A.H. 158,159; Alexander 58,157;

Buckner cont's.
Aylett H. 158
Buell, J.T. 125
Buffington, William H. 156; Pate 183
Bull, John 157
Bullet, George 55n
Burkhartt, Nicholas S. 58
Burr, Aaron 52
Burrows, J.G. 159
Butler, Benjamin F. 87,161: William O. 173
Byrd, Stephen 55n,18

Cabanne, John P. 150
Cabell, Gen. 130
Caldwell, H.C. 123: John 174
Callaway, James 61,173
Cameron, Simon 86,91
Campbell. Robert A. 90,155
Cannon, Franklin 155
Carr, William C. 55n,150
Carroll, Charles 174
Cartabona, Silvio Franc 154
Caruthers, Samuel 158
Cass, Lewis 160,173,174
Caulk, Richard 55n
Cavener, George 55n
Center, Lt. 65
Chappell, Philip E. 156, 191
Chase, Salmon P. 78,86
Chouteau, August(e) 46, 55n,150; Pierre Jr. 59
Christie, William 156
Claiborne, William C.C. 51-2
Clardy, M.L. 159; Martin L. 159
Clark, George B. 156; George Rogers 48-9; J.B. Jr. 158; John 153: John B. 68,158,159; M.L. 71: Robert P. 58; William 53,56,150,154,175
Clay, Henry 59,160,175
Cleaver, Stephen 59
Cleveland, Grover 161
Cline, James C. 189-90
Clinton, George 175,177
Clopper, John Y. 123
Cockerill, Vard 125-6
Coffee, John 125-6,130
Cole, Nathan 158: Stephen 175; W.I. 61
Coleman, Norman J. 155
Conyers, Thomas 64
Cook, John D. 59; Nathaniel 59
Cooke, John D. 156; W.M. 159
Cooper, D.H. 126; Peter 161; Sarshell 61,175
Crabb. B. 127
Crabtree, Mr. 35
Craig, James 158
Crittenden, John J. 87; Thomas T. 155,156,158, 192
Crockett, David 70
Cruzat, Francisco 47,49, 50,154
Currier, Warren 157
Curtis, Gen. 120-1,133

D'Abadie, Gov. 154; Mr. 45,46
Dade, Maj. 176
Dallas, George M. 176
Dallmeyer, William Q. 156

Darby, John F. 157
Daviess, Joseph H. 176
Davis, Judge 52,145; Mr. 120: Andrew Jackson 172; Jefferson 85,87
Dawson, Robert D. 59
Debolt, Rezin A. 158
Decatur, Stephen 181
DeKalb, Baron 176
Delassus, Charles DeHault 50.51,52.154
Del'epinav, Gov. 154
Deleyba, Fernando 154
Deneyon, M. 45,46
Denver, J.W. 80
Desoto, Ferdinand 40-1
Detro, Thomas E. 189
Dickinson, Daniel S. 87
Didier, Peter 155
Dockery, Alex M. 159
Dodge, Granville M. 135; Henry 59
Doniphan, Alexander W. 68, 71-2.174,183
Dougherty, John 72
Douglas, Stephen A. 77, 78-9,81,84,87,160,176
Drake, Charles D. 137-40, 157
Draper, Daniel M. 156
Dryden, John D.S. 157

Easley, George W. 191
Easton, A.R. 71; Rufus 156
Edwards, John C. 71,72, 155.156,157
Ellis, Edmund J. 122
Emerson, Dr. 82
Emmons, Benjamin 55n,59
Ewing, Ephraim B. 155,157: Ephraim W. 156; H.C. 156; Patrick 63; Thomas 127-9,131

Fagg, Thomas J. 157
Farrar, Gen. 121; Bernard G. 55n
Ferguson, M. 108
Fillmore, Millard 160
Findlay, Jonathan S. 58
Finkelnburg, G.A. 158
Fischer, A.W. 71
Fisk, C.B. 132
Flaugherty, James 55n
Ford, N. 159; Nicholas 144,161
Forsyth, John 184
Foster, Emory 125-6
Franklin, B.J. 158; Benjamin 176; Cyrus 124
Freeman, Thomas W. 159
Fremont, John C. 111,112, 118-20.174
Frost, Daniel M. 93-101; R.G. 159
Fyan, R.W. 159

Gaines, Gen. 62-3
Gallatin, Albert 176
Gamble, Hamilton R. 90, 102-4,117,122,125,155, 156
Gardenshire, James B. 156
Garfield, James A. 161
Gates, Elijah 156
Geary, John W. 80
Gentry, Richard 62-3,64-5,177
George, Mr. 98
Geyer, H.S. 76,77,157
Glover, John M. 158-9; Peter C. 155,156;

Glover cont'd.
    Peter G. 156
Grant, Ulysses S. 120,161,
    185
Graves, Alexander 159
Gerrley, Horace 161
Greene, Nathaniel 177
Griffin, Judge 52,145
Grimsley, ----- 98
Grover, B.W. 90
Guitar, Col. 123,124,125

Hall, Willard P. 76,103,
    155,158; William A. 158
Hammond, Daniel 58; Samuel
    55n
Hancock, Winifield S. 161
Hardee, Gen. 111
Hardin, Charles H. 155
Harding, Chester 132-3
Harney, William S. 94,98-
    9,111
Harris, Thomas 159
Harrison, A.G. 174; Albert
    G. 157,177; William H.
    160; William Henry 52,
    145,154
Hatcher, Robert A. 158,159
Havens, Harrison E. 158
Hayes, R.B. 161
Hazeltine, R. 159
Heath, John G. 58
Hempstead, Edward 56,154
Henderson, J.B. 157; Thomas B. 71
Henry, John W. 157; Malcolm
    58; Patrick 48,177
Hickman, David M. 63
Hindman, Gen. 126
Hinkle, George B. 68;
    George W. 69
Hockaday, John A. 143,156
Holladay, Thomas 156
Holt, David Rice 177
Houts, Chirstopher G. 59
Howard, Benjamin 52-3,56,
    154,177
Howell, James 178
Hughes, James M. 157;
    John T. 125
Hunt, Ezra 183
Hunter, Gen. 119,120; D.C.
    125-6,185; Joseph 55n
Hutchings, John 59
Hutton, J.E. 159; John E.
    159
Hyde, Ira B. 158
Hyer, John 159

Ittner, Anthony 158

Jackman, S.D. 125-6
Jackson, Andrew 160,174,
    177,178; Claiborne F.
    74-6,89,91,99-103,111.
    155,160
Jamison, John 62-3
Jasper, Sergt. 178
Jefferson, Thomas 178
Jewett, D.F. 157
Johnson, Andrew 107; Charles P. 155; Horace P.
    156; Richard M. 178
Jones, John Rice 59

Kearney, Gen. 71-2
Kelsoe, John R. 158
Kennett, Luther M. 176
Keokuk, Chief 62
Kerlerec, Gov. 154
Keyte, James 175
King, Austin A. 68-9,155,
    158,174
Kirk, John 172

Kirtley, Sinclair 63
Knott, James P. 156

Laclede Liguest, Pierre
    45,46,48,178,183
Lafayette, Gen. 178,179
Lair, Wesley 123
Lamb, Alfred W. 158
Lamonthe, Cadillac, Gov.
    154
Lamotte, M. 24
Lasalle, Robert de 42-3
Lathrop, John H. 149
Laussat, M. 51
Lawrence, James 179
Leonard, Abiel 156
Lewis, L.M. 159; Meriwether 52,56,154,179
Leyba, Don Ferdinando 47-
    8,49
Lillard, James C. 179;
    William 58
Lincoln, Abraham 84,86-7,
    105,160.161
Linn, Lewis F. 157,179,
    181
Lipscomb, Col. 123
Loan, Benjamin F. 158
Lorimier, Louis 174
Lucas, J.B.C. 146; John
    B.C. 52; S.D. 68
Lyon, Nathaniel 91-101,
    107,111,112-6

McClurg, Joseph W. 140,
    141,155,158
McCormack, James R. 158
McCrary, Judge 192-4
McCulloch, F.H. 126; Robert 112,113-6,117,118,
    120,121
McCullough, Frisby H. 124
McDemon, J.R. 156
McDonald, Sergt. 179;
    Emmett 96
McFadin, Capt. 133
McFerron, Joseph 58
McGirk, Matthias 156
McGrath, Michael K. 155
McGready, Issac 55n
McKinstry, Gen. 119; J.
    117
McLaren, ----- 98
McNair, Alexander 59,60,
    150,154
McNeil, John 124,127,131,
    132
Macon, Nathaniel 179
Mansur, Charles H. 159
Marion, Francis 180
Marmaduke, John S. 108,
    126,127,143,144-5,155,
    161; M.M. 155
Marquette, Fr. Jacques
    41-2
Means, Benjamin 62
Medary, Samuel 81
Meigs, R.J. 52; Teturn J.
    146
Mercer, Hugh 180; Joseph
    W. 156
Merrill, Samuel 127
Miles, Joe 176
Miller, John 62.154,157,
    180; John G. 158
Mitchell, Col. 115
Monroe, William 156
Moore, William 26
Morehouse, A.P. 145,155
Morelock, E.C. 184
Morgan, Charles H. 158,
    159; Daniel 180
Morrison, A.W. 156
Mosely, William S. 156

Mulligan, Col. 117
Murphy, Capt. 71

Napton, William B. 75,
    156,157
Neeley, William 55n
Nelson, Capt. 57
Newcomb, C.A. 158
Newton, Seggt. 181
Noel, John W. 158; Thomas
    F. 158
Norton, Elijah H. 157,158

O'Conor, Charles 161
O'Reilly, Don Alexander
    47
Osceola, Chief 64

Parker, Isaac G. 158
Patten, Dante 68
Patton, Nathaniel 57
Perez, Manuel 50,154
Perier, Gov. 154
Pettibone, Rufus 156
Pettis, Spencer 155,157,
    181-2; William G. 155
Peyton, R.L.Y. 159
Phelps, John S. 155,158,
    182
Phillips, Samuel 55n
Pierce, Franklin 160
Piernas, Pedro 47,154
Pike, Zebulon M. 53,121,
    182
Pittis, William G. 59
Pleasanton, Alfred 132-3
Plummer, Capt. 114
Poindexter, J.A. 124-5
Polk, Gen. 112-3,120;
    James K. 160,182; T.
    157; Truston 155
Pollard, H.M. 159
Pontiac, Chief 46-7
Pope, Gen. 119
Porter, Gilchrist 158;
    Jo. C. 122-3,124,127
Post, T.M. 151
Pratt, Bernard 150
Pratte, Bernard 59
Prentiss, Mr. 120
Price, Sterling 72-3,
    89-90,99,100,103.107-8,
    112,113,117,121,127,155,
    157
Pulaski, Count Casimer
    182
Putnam, Israel 182

Quantrell, William Clarke
    128

Rains, Gen. 109
Ralls, Daniel 182; John
    73
Randolph, George W. 87;
    John 182-3
Ray, John 58,183; Robert
    D. 157
Rea, David 158,159
Read, Jacob 57
Rector, William 59;
    William V. 156
Reid, John W. 158
Renault, Phillipe Francois
    43
Reynolds, Thomas C. 103,
    111,155,160,183
Rice, T.M. 159; Thomas L.
    155
Riddick, Thomas F. 56,59
Riggs, Jonathan 62
Ripley, Gen. 183
Rives, William C. 177
Robardo, William A. 156

Rodman, Francis 155
Rollins, James S. 158
Rothwell, G.F. 159
Ryland, John F. 156

St. Ange, Mr. 46,47
St. Clair, Arthur 183
St. John, John P. 161
Sanborn, J.B. 132
Sandford, John F.A. 82
Santa Anna, Pres. 70
Sauvelle, Gov. 154
Sawyer, S.L. 159
Schofield, Gen. 122,128-130,131
Schurlds, Henry 156.
Schurz, Carl 140,141,157
Schuyler, Philip 183
Scott, Andrew 55n; John 55n,57,59,60,157.184; John G. 158; William 156; Winfield 71,86,88. 160
Seibert, J.M. 156
Seward, William H. 86,105-7
Seymour, Horatio 161
Shaffer, Co. 123
Shelby, Col. 131,132
Sherwood, T.A. 157; Thomas A. 157
Siegel, Gen. 99,109,113,115-7,119,120
Simonds, Nathanieo 155
Sims, Leonard H. 158
Smith, A.J. 131,132; George 155; George R. 182; Hiram 69
Snead, Thomas L. 99,159
Standwatie, Chief 130
Stanton, Edwin M. 86
Sterling, Capt. 46
Stevens, Alexander H. 85
Stevenson, J.C. 189-90
Steward, Edwin O. 155,158
Stewart, Robert M. 89,155
Stockton, Richard 174
Stoddard, Amos 52,154,184
Stone, William H. 158; William J. 159
Stover, John H. 158
Stringfellow, B.F. 156
Sturgis, Maj. 115; S.D. 112

Talbott, James 59
Taney, Judge 83; Roger B. 184
Taylor, Zachariah 65,70,71,160,174
Tecumseh, Chief 178
Thompson, Alonzo 156; G.W. 125; George 156
Tilden, Samuel J. 161
Todd, George 133
Totten, Capt. 108
Travis, John 153
Trias, Gen. 73
Trudeau, Zenon 154

Van Buren, Martin 160,174
Vanderberg, Judge 52,145
Van Dorn, Gen. 121
Van Horn, R.T. 158,159
Vanswearingen, Capt. 65
Vernon, Miles 184-5
Vest, George G. 157,159

Wade, William H. 159
Wagner, David 157
Walker, James L. 159; Jesse 153; John 155; John W. 35; R. 74; Robert J. 80

Ward, John 151
Warner, William 159
Warren, John 178; Joseph 185; Martin D. 178
Wash, Robert 156
Washington, George 44-5, 48,185
Weaver, James B. 161
Webster, Daniel 85
Weightman, R.H. 71
Welch, Aikman 156
Welles, Gideon 86
Wells, Carty 74; Erastus 158; Robert W. 74,156
White, Maj. 119-20; Hugh L. 160
Wilkinson, James 51-2, 146,154
Williams, Capt. 94; Abraham J. 154
Willock, David 72
Wilson, Robert 90,157
Wingate, Robert F. 156
Wood, Jesse T. 62
Woodson, Co. 127; Silas 155; Silas H. 158
Worth, William 185
Wright, Silas 185

Zagonyi, Maj. 119-20

www.ingramcontent.com/pod-product-compliance
Lightning Source LLC
Chambersburg PA
CBHW031417290426
44110CB00011B/418